Programming PIC Microcontrollers with XC8

Armstrong Subero

Apress®

Programming PIC Microcontrollers with XC8

Armstrong Subero
Moruga, Trinidad and Tobago

ISBN-13 (pbk): 978-1-4842-3272-9 ISBN-13 (electronic): 978-1-4842-3273-6
https://doi.org/10.1007/978-1-4842-3273-6

Library of Congress Control Number: 2017962909

Cover image designed by Freepik

Managing Director: Welmoed Spahr
Editorial Director: Todd Green
Acquisitions Editor: Natalie Pao
Development Editor: James Markham
Technical Reviewer: Logan West
Coordinating Editor: Jessica Vakili
Copy Editor: Kezia Endsley
Compositor: SPi Global
Indexer: SPi Global
Artist: SPi Global

Distributed to the book trade worldwide by Springer Science+Business Media New York, 233 Spring Street, 6th Floor, New York, NY 10013. Phone 1-800-SPRINGER, fax (201) 348-4505, e-mail orders-ny@springer-sbm.com, or visit www.springeronline.com. Apress Media, LLC is a California LLC and the sole member (owner) is Springer Science + Business Media Finance Inc (SSBM Finance Inc). SSBM Finance Inc is a **Delaware** corporation.

For information on translations, please e-mail rights@apress.com, or visit http://www.apress.com/rights-permissions.

Apress titles may be purchased in bulk for academic, corporate, or promotional use. eBook versions and licenses are also available for most titles. For more information, reference our Print and eBook Bulk Sales web page at http://www.apress.com/bulk-sales.

Any source code or other supplementary material referenced by the author in this book is available to readers on GitHub via the book's product page, located at www.apress.com/978-1-4842-3272-9. For more detailed information, please visit http://www.apress.com/source-code.

Printed on acid-free paper

Table of Contents

About the Author

Armstrong Subero has been tinkering with electronics for as long as he can remember. The thrill of creating something from the ground up and watching it work is something that he never tires of. His entire life changed when he discovered microcontrollers. They were so powerful and simple and complex all at the same time. When he finished school, he taught himself programming and, for a while, worked part-time from a home office. He landed his first job as a systems technologist completely self-taught and a lot of it was due to his in-depth knowledge and passion for the microcontroller technology. Armstrong has used many microcontroller families during the course of his work, but he has an affinity for PIC® microcontrollers. Armstrong currently works for the Ministry of National Security in his country. He designs robots and writes books, blogs, and software on `trinirobotics.com` and `angelstemlabs.org` in his free time.

Introduction

With the onset of the Internet of Things (IoT) revolution, embedded systems development is becoming very popular in the maker community and the professional space as well. IoT is a trillion-dollar business. PIC® microcontrollers are one of the technologies that can be used to develop IoT devices. This is due to the low cost, wide availability, and low power consumption of these devices. Additionally, due to the wide range of PIC® microcontrollers available, there are PIC® microcontrollers that can match your designs, from 8 pins to over 144 pins. They covers 8-, 16-, and 32-bit architectures.

People argue that 8-bit architecture is irrelevant in the complex embedded systems of today. However, 8-bit microcontrollers are here to stay, even if it is for the simple purpose of learning about microcontroller architecture. The relatively simple and beautifully engineered architecture of 8-bit PIC® microcontrollers makes them invaluable for learning the inner workings of microcontrollers. It is a lot easier to learn all the registers of these simple 8-bit devices and follow the path of program execution than with more complex ones. After learning about PIC® microcontrollers, I found it easy to move on to the more popular 16-bit and then 32-bit devices. In this book, I hope to share the tips and tricks I learned along the way.

Why Did I Write This Book?

When I first started programming PIC® microcontrollers, I imagined that a lot of information would be available on the Internet on which people could base their designs. Little did I know at the time that programming these useful devices would take a lot of work, dedication, and finding code that actually worked. In addition, when I did find code, it was usually for ancient PIC® microcontrollers that are NRND or have a lack of modern peripherals and capabilities. When I finally did find a suitable language in the name of HI-TECH C for the PIC® microcontroller series, I found out that XC8 would be released to take its place. Despite being compatible with HI-TECH C, I realized upon using the compiler that a lot of the code did not work out of the box and a lot of my libraries had to be rewritten. This was a time-consuming process and the lack of information on the language was frustrating, leaving me to think that XC8 was not everything I expected it to be.

A lot has changed since then. Now I love XC8 and all the features it provides and I'm thankful that Microchip provides it free of cost. A lot of people might wonder why I chose XC8 to program PIC® microcontrollers when other simpler options in BASIC and C exist with a lot of libraries available. To them I say that even if those languages are easier to use, there are some versions where the libraries are not open and thus cannot be examined. In cases where software must receive government approval, closed libraries are not an option. Also, the knowledge gained from writing your own libraries is invaluable. Microchip technology provides the MPLAB® Code Configurator (MCC) that can generate code to use the onboard peripherals of a lot of PIC® microcontrollers and, even more recently, for Click boards using the ubiquitous mikroBUS for communication. The other reason is that by learning to use the compiler provided by the manufacturer, you avoid the problem of a chip with a killer new feature not being supported by the manufacturer of a third-party compiler. For the sake of understanding exactly what is happening, I make minimal use of the MCC in this book despite its ease of use.

Who Is This Book For?

For this book, you will need some basic electronic devices and some electronic equipment and knowledge of how to use them. I expect that the reader has knowledge of the C programming language. Knowledge of variables, loops, and basic data structures will suffice. I also assume you have knowledge of basic digital electronics. I also make the presumption that you have used another simpler platform, such as Arduino, since the focus of this book is on the specifics of the PIC® microcontroller. A complete newcomer can follow along, but this book is heavy on code, schematics, and images and focuses less on the theoretical aspects of using microcontrollers.

What You Will Need for This Book?

You will need a few components to get all the examples up and running. All of these are covered in Chapter 1. I know of individuals who build microcontroller circuits in simulation. I recommend building the actual circuits to gain hands-on experience that will help you in the industry. Unlike other programming disciplines, embedded systems development allows you to build things that can be used in our physical world, not just push pixels around the screen. I have also found it more enjoyable to prototype circuits, as you also learn valuable skills in circuit design and troubleshooting that you will have for a lifetime. Although for many people using a development board is simpler, for those wanting a true "hands-on" approach to learning, prototyping on breadboards is a valuable skill.

What Will You Learn in This Book?

This book consists of 15 chapters that will help you get on your way to programming PIC® microcontrollers in XC8.

- Chapter 1 looks at setting up shop, including the hardware and software necessary to get the most out of this book.

- Chapter 2 covers the basics of the C programming language.

- Chapter 3 reviews the basics of electronics.

- Chapter 4 presents the basics of PIC® microcontrollers and looks at the PIC16F1717.

- Chapter 5 covers the basics of connecting your PIC® microcontroller to your computer.

- Chapter 6 presents the basics of I/O, including PPS, interfacing LEDs, push buttons, and seven segment displays.

- Chapter 7 demonstrates using actuators, DC motors, servos, and stepper motors.

- Chapter 8 examines the use of interrupts, timers, counters, and PWM.

- Chapter 9 presents the use of serial communication protocols, including USART with GPS and GSM, SPI, and I2C.

- Chapter 10 looks at using displays including the SSD1306 and Nextion touch screen displays.

- Chapter 11 consists of understanding the ADC and DAC.

- Chapter 12 covers using the onboard peripherals of the CLC, NCO, Comparator, and FVR.

- Chapter 13 takes us into the wireless connectivity with Wi-Fi and Bluetooth.

- Chapter 14 demonstrates the use of the low-power features of the microcontroller, minimizing power consumption and the WDT.

- Chapter 15 is a project-based chapter where we build two projects.

Upon finishing this book, I hope that you will have the foundation you need to take on the world of embedded systems design and build useful gadgets, IoT devices, and beyond. This is the book I wish I had when I was getting started with PIC® microcontrollers.

CHAPTER 1

Preparing for Development

It would be nice to be able to jump right into building projects and using our microcontroller. However, before we do so, we need to properly set up our environment for working. This chapter is catered to people who have used microcontroller platforms such as Arduino, PICAXE, or Basic Stamp-based platforms and want to build barebones microcontroller systems. Beginners should have no trouble following along though. If you have experience breadboarding circuits or using ICSP tools or have previously used PIC® microcontrollers, you may skip this chapter. However, I *strongly* recommend that you read this chapter, as it provides a lot of insight as to what you need as well as getting everything prepared.

Gathering Your Hardware

This is the first chapter on your journey to embedded systems design with PIC® microcontrollers and XC8. The first thing we will do is gather the necessary components you will need to follow along with this book. Long gone are the days where a couple thousands of dollars would be needed to begin microcontroller development. For relatively little money, you can experiment with microcontroller development. This is especially true of PIC® microcontrollers, where for a few pennies, you can purchase one of these ubiquitous beasts.

1

© Armstrong Subero 2018
A. Subero, *Programming PIC Microcontrollers with XC8*,
https://doi.org/10.1007/978-1-4842-3273-6_1

People familiar with programming place emphasis on writing programs, while people with a background in electronics place emphasis on building the circuits for the controllers. I have found that both are equally important and, as you follow along with this book, remember that not everything can be solved using software. If you correctly learn how the hardware operates, you could potentially write very little code that combines hardware in unique ways to get the desired result.

Let's jump into it and look at the things you will need.

Microcontroller

Although the book generally assumes that you have some experience with microcontrollers, this section reviews the basic microcontroller technology. Read this section thoroughly if you're a first-time user of microcontrollers. The information you learn in this section will not only be applicable to PIC® microcontrollers, but also to other microcontrollers you may use.

General-purpose computers such as the smartphones, tablets, laptops, and desktops are designed to perform a variety of tasks. A laptop or tablet can be used to read books, watch movies, and even write programs and web applications. This is because they were designed for that purpose, thanks to the integration of the microprocessors into these units that allow them to perform these many different tasks.

The microprocessor, however, is not an island. It is dependent on supporting circuitry in order to work properly. These include RAM chips, SSD, and other peripherals. While it is revolutionary, the strength of the microprocessor is also its shortcoming. Although it can perform general tasks, it may not be the best solution for performing a single task.

Let's take the example of an electric toothbrush. If we want to design a basic electric toothbrush, then some basic considerations must go into its function. The toothbrush must turn on a motor when the user pushes a button and alert the user if they have been brushing their teeth too long. In such an instance, a minimum of processing power is needed to adequately perform this task. Yes, it is possible to program a board that contains a 4GHz 64-bit processor with 16GB of RAM running the latest OS to do this task, but that would be akin to using a lawnmower to shave your legs. It would be better for many reasons to use a microcontroller.

So what exactly is a microcontroller? A *microcontroller* is a self-contained unit that has a microprocessor with RAM, ROM, I/O, and a host of other peripherals onboard. Thus a microcontroller contains all the processing power necessary to perform the specific task at hand and that task alone. Back to the toothbrush example, it would be more feasible to use a 4-bit microcontroller with a few bytes of RAM and ROM to check the switch, turn on the motor, keep track of how long the user has been brushing, and sound an alarm if that time exceeds some preset value.

Microcontrollers are used for applications that have specific requirements such as low-cost, low-power consumption and systems that require real-time performance. It is thanks to these features that a world where computers are becoming increasingly ubiquitous is now possible.

At the time of writing, there are 4-, 8-, 16-, and 32-bit microcontrollers. Anyone looking to start a new design should realistically choose an 8-bit or a 32-bit microcontroller. Large volume, low-cost, and lowest power consumption 8-bit devices generally tend to have an edge. Whereas for higher performance applications, 32-bit devices are the obvious choice. It is very important that you do not get attached to one particular microcontroller. There are people who insist that they can do anything with 8-bits, whereas others only use 32-bit parts. You must realize that microcontrollers are simply tools applied to the particular task, so it stands to reason that some tasks are better suited to 8-bit microcontrollers and others to 32-bit ones.

The microcontroller we use in this book is the 8-bit PIC16F1717 (see Figure 1-1). The PIC® microcontroller was chosen because it has a relatively simple architecture. Once you understand 8-bit PIC® microcontrollers, it's easy to understand more complex micros. I chose this particular PIC® microcontroller because it is a modern device and has a lot of onboard peripherals. It also has a relatively large amount of RAM and program memory and, most importantly, a lot of onboard peripherals. There are members of its family with the same features that have a smaller pin count.

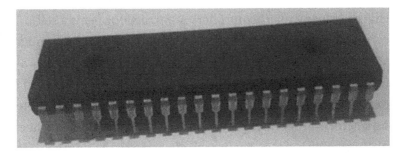

Figure 1-1. *PIC16F1717 in DIP package*

A benefit of this particular microcontroller is that, in addition to being modern, it is produced in a DIP package, which makes it very easy for prototyping on a breadboard. Therefore, you use it to test your design and use an SMD version in the final version of your product.

Programmer

A microcontroller is a blank slate without a program. Microcontrollers and other stored program devices rely on a programmer to load the program to the chip. I have found that using a microchip makes it easiest to understand how to program devices. Many device vendors have extremely expensive tools that are hard to find, even on their own web site! In order to program PIC® microcontrollers, you need a PICkit™ 3 or an MPLAB® ICD 3.

I personally have used both and highly recommend that you buy an ICD 3. The reason is that the ICD 3 is much faster and saves you a lot of time in programming and debugging, especially if you plan on moving up to the larger devices. However, you should only buy the ICD 3 if you are certain that you will be working with PIC® microcontrollers for a long time, as at the time of writing, it costs over $200. The PICkit™ 3 may be used if you are evaluating the PIC microcontroller series, as it is available for $50.00. Generally, get the PICkit™ 3 if you are evaluating PIC® microcontrollers and the ICD 3 if you intend to work with these devices for a while.

Figure 1-2 shows the PICkit™ 3 and Figure 1-3 shows the ICD 3.

Figure 1-2. *PICkit 3*

Figure 1-3. *ICD 3*

The ICD 3 uses an RJ-11 type adapter. I recommend that you get this programmer as well as an adapter to allow for easy breadboaring from RJ-11 to ICSP.

Gathering the Software

The hardware is necessary for building the circuits. However, we are not fiddling with 555 timers here! We need software to make everything work. All the software needed to program PIC microcontrollers can be found on the Microchip Technology web site.

MPLAB® X IDE

I have heard people complain about the old IDE microchip thousands of times. Let me assure you that MPLAB® X is nothing like MPLAB® IDE (see Figure 1-4). It is a lot better. Microchip technology has come a long way. I have used a lot of vendor tools and Microchip offers the most effective plug-and-play functionality I have come across. Some rather pricey compilers don't offer much more over the ones provided for PIC® microcontrollers. In fact, Microchip even offers an IDE that is cloud based! This cloud-based MPLAB® Xpress IDE is best suited for new users or if you want to program the microcontroller on a machine that you need special permissions for. A good example of this is would-be students or a corporate environment where going through the IT department would be a lengthy process.

If you purchased an Xpress evaluation board and are still not sure if you want to use the PIC® microcontroller, then you may use the cloud-based IDE to get up and running quickly. However, if you decided on using PIC® microcontrollers then the on-premises software for microcontroller development is a lot better. The primary reason is that if something goes wrong, you can be assured that it is not a connection problem. The other reason is that as your code grows and your skills develop, you will need all the features of MPLAB® X, which has the power of NetBeans behind it. Stick with the on-premises software.

I know there are going to be those among you who prefer to use a command-line interface and text editor. In fact, I also enjoy that method of doing things, when there is no IDE available. I like the KISS principle—let's not make things more complicated than they need to be. This book takes a pragmatic approach. IDEs are simple to use. Thus we use them.

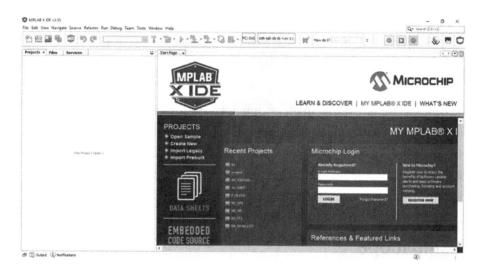

Figure 1-4. *MPLAB X IDE*

XC Compilers

A lot of people don't value compilers. Many vendors boast about how easy it is to get started with their chips and pack mouthwatering goodies into every bite of silicon. However, they make the compilers so expensive that they aren't worth it in the end. Microchip offers the XC compilers to get started with PIC® microcontrollers. The best part is it's free of charge. In this book, I focus on XC8. However, be rest assured that once you get over the learning curve of how this compiler operates, you will be thankful that you chose to use PIC® microcontrollers. This is because it is easy to transition from 8- to 16- and 32-bit microcontrollers without having to learn a totally different environment. The XC8 compiler is available for download on the Microchip technology web site.

Setting Up Shop

In this book, I interface the microcontroller to a lot of modules and design a lot of circuits. However, if you want to do likewise, it is very important that you acquire at least a minimum of equipment to be able to get the most of this book. Recommended equipment is covered in the following sections.

Multimeter

The multimeter is a staple of electronics. Therefore I highly recommend you invest in at least *two* multimeters. The reason you need at least two is because you need to measure voltage and current at the same time. For this book, any multimeter that has the ability to measure DC voltage, current, and resistance should suffice.

Oscilloscope

No electronics workbench, lab, or shop is complete without an oscilloscope. This device is undoubtedly one on the most important test instruments you'll have, particularly when you're working with microcontroller-based circuits. Even if you do not want a full scope, I recommend you get the Velleman pocket oscilloscope. It is reasonably priced and works rather well for basic work.

Power Supply

Make sure to get a good bench power supply. The 1.2v-15v range and at least a 5 amp rating will suffice.

Shopping for Supplies

When starting with microcontrollers and electronics in general, people often wonder where they can buy supplies and items. In general, you can buy most of these items from Amazon, eBay, Digi-Key, Mouser Electronics, or and AliExpress. I recommend you buy passives from sites like AliExpress and eBay, as you are likely to get better deals on these in the Chinese market. However microcontrollers, active devices in general, and programmers should always be bought from reputable suppliers, as they may not be genuine or may not function as required. In fact, there are instances where companies bought chips (namely ATmega328p) from the Chinese market and it turned out that these chips were total imitations and did not work.

To sum it all up: be vigilant when purchasing electronic components and equipment. If it's too good to be true, *then stay away. Do not buy it.*

In general you need to set up a basic electronic shop. You need various resistors, capacitors, and a few semiconductors and of course your basic side cutters, pliers, and screwdrivers.

Table 1-1 lists the components you need to purchase to get the most out of this book.

Table 1-1. *Recommended Hardware for This Book*

Item	Quantity	Vendors	Product Numbers
ICD 3/PICkit 3	1	Digi-Key Electronics	PG164130-ND (PICkit™ 3) DV164035-ND (ICD 3)
		Mouser Electronics	579-PG164130 (PICkit™ 3) 579-DV164035 (ICD 3)
PIC 16F1717	1	Digi-Key Electronics	PIC16F1717-I/P-ND
		Mouser Electronics	579-PIC16F1717-I/P
ESP8266 Wi-Fi Module	1	Digi-Key Electronics	1188-1154-ND
		Mouser Electronics	909-MOD-WIFI-ESP8266
Logic Level Converter Module	2	Digi-Key Electronics	1568-1209-ND
		Mouser Electronics	474-BOB-12009
2n2222 or Similar (2N3904)	2	Digi-Key Electronics	2N3904FS-ND
		Mouser Electronics	610-2N3904
LM34 Temperature Sensor	1	Digi-Key Electronics	LM34DZ/NOPB-ND
		Mouser Electronics	926-LM34DZ/NOPB
Nextion NX3224T024_11 Touch LCD	1	ITEAD Studio	IM150416002
		Amazon ASIN	B015DMP45K

(*continued*)

Table 1-1. (*continued*)

Item	Quantity	Vendors	Product Numbers
SSD1306 OLED (I2C)	1	Amazon ASIN	B01G6SAWNY
		AliExpress (Various Sellers)	
24LC16B EEPROM	1	Digi-Key Electronics	24LC16B-I/P-ND
		Arrow Electronics	24LC16B-E/P
HD44780 Character LCD	1	Digi-Key Electronics	1528-1502-ND
		Adafruit Industries	181
MCP4131 Digital Potentiometer	1	Digi-Key Electronics	MCP4131-104E/P-ND
		Arrow Electronics	MCP4131-103E/P
SIM800L GSM Module	1	Amazon ASIN	B01A8DQ53E
		AliExpress (Various Sellers)	
UBLOX Neo-6M GPS Module	1	Amazon ASIN	B071GGZDDR
		AliExpress (Various Sellers)	
EMIC 2 TTS Module	1	Parallax Inc.	30016
		SparkFun Electronics	DEV-11711

(*continued*)

Table 1-1. (*continued*)

Item	Quantity	Vendors	Product Numbers
Serial LCD Module	1	Parallax Inc.	27977
		Digi-Key Electronics	27977-ND
RGB LED	1	Digi-Key Electronics	754-1492-ND
		Mouser Electronics	604-WP154A4SUREQBFZW
SN754410NE	1	Digi-Key Electronics	296-9911-5-ND
		Mouser Electronics	595-SN754410NE
ULN2003	1	Digi-Key Electronics	497-2344-5-ND
		Mouser Electronics	511-ULN2003A
Servo Motor	1	Jameco Electronics	1528-1075-ND
		Mouser Electronics	485-154
5v Stepper Motor	1	Jameco Electronics	237825
Brushed DC Motor	1	Digi-Key Electronics	1528-1150-ND
		Mouser Electronics	485-711
Seven Segment Displays	2	Digi-Key Electronics	754-1467-5-ND
		Mouser Electronics	630-HDSP-513E
Pushbuttons	5	Digi-Key Electronics	P8011S-ND
		Mouser Electronics	667-EVQ-PAC07K
LEDs	10	Digi-Key Electronics	C503B-RCN-CW0Z0AA1-ND
		Mouser Electronics	941-C503BAANCY0B025
1N4001 Diode	2	Digi-Key Electronics	641-1310-3-ND
		Mouser Electronics	821-1N4001

(*continued*)

Table 1-1. (*continued*)

Item	Quantity	Vendors	Product Numbers
10 uF Capacitors	2	Digi-Key Electronics	493-4771-1-ND
		Mouser Electronics	647-UCA2G100MPD1TD
1k Resistors	10	Digi-Key Electronics	CF14JT1K00CT-ND
		Mouser Electronics	71-PTF561K0000BZEK
10k Resistors	10	Digi-Key Electronics	CF14JT10K0CT-ND
		Mouser Electronics	279-YR1B10KCC

In addition, you need an HC-05 Bluetooth module, which can be found on various sellers on AliExpress and Amazon. Make sure to have a bench to dedicate solely to electronics work and you will also need to buy some storage containers for all your components. Unlike using platforms, where everything is on a board that you can simply pack away in a kit, setting up your chip on a breadboard requires time. Therefore, having a dedicated workbench will save you a lot of time.

Conclusion

That brings us to the end of the first chapter. In this chapter, we covered gathering the required hardware and software to get started with PIC® microcontroller development. This chapter laid the ground work required to continue your fascinating journey. While you are waiting for your items to arrive, you may take a look at the next chapter, which focuses on getting you acquainted with the C programming language.

CHAPTER 2

The C Programming Language

C

C. The language we all love to hate. We've seen C++, Java, C#, Go, Python, and a host of other languages come and go. Yet C remains. C was, is, and will be. Assembly used to be the language of choice for programming 8-bit microcontrollers. However, the newer PIC® microcontrollers have a C-optimized architecture and a lot of memory. Assembly does have its place and it is still sometimes needed to optimize code. C programs typically occupy more code space than an equivalent Assembly one. In this book, I make an effort to maintain KISS principles; therefore, we use the simpler solution, which is C. So let's look at some basic C.

This chapter can be skipped if you are a C programming guru, for anyone else though, it's best you read this chapter.

C Programming

The C programming language was designed at a time when computing power was at a fraction of what it is today. Forget gigabytes of memory, there were kilobytes. Forget gigahertz of computing speed, we are talking megahertz here. Its sounds familiar, doesn't it? Kilobytes of

© Armstrong Subero 2018
A. Subero, *Programming PIC Microcontrollers with XC8*,
https://doi.org/10.1007/978-1-4842-3273-6_2

memory and a speed measured in megahertz. In fact, it sounds like a PIC® microcontroller, does it not? That's essentially why C is ideal for programming microcontrollers.

C Program Structure

C programs have a structure they must follow. Listing 2-1 is a typical C program.

Listing 2-1. Typical C Program

```
/* This is a comment that usually contains information such as
the name of the author, date and program name and details */

// This is where files are included and preprocessor directives
take place

#include <stdio.h> // This is an example of a header file

// This is the main function, all C programs have a main
function and
// This is where program execution begins

int main(void)
{ // opening parentheses very important
printf("Hello World!"); // some code is executed

return 0; // no code is executed after a return statement
} // closing parentheses
```

As you see, the typical C program has a comment block, include files, and a main function. As we examine further programs, you will notice that this template is maintained.

Comments

Comments are used in your program to describe lines of code. Comments are very useful because they help you remember what your code does. Comments can be used as needed, as they are completely ignored by the compiler. The C language uses comments that can be written using forward slashes and asterisks (see Listing 2-2).

Listing 2-2. Comments Using Forward Slashes and Asterisks

```
/* This is a comment
that can be used
to span multiple lines */
```

Comments can also be written with two forward slashes and these occupy one line (see Listing 2-3).

Listing 2-3. Comments Using Two Forward Slashes

```
// This comment occupies one line
```

Variables and Constants

A variable in C is a name used to refer to some location in memory and allows the programmer to assign a value to that location. Variables can be changed during the execution of a program unless they are explicitly declared as constants. Variables must be declared before they are used in a program (see Listing 2-4).

Listing 2-4. Declaring a Variable

```
// This is a variable being declared
int A;
```

After being declared, a variable can be initialized, that is to say, it can have an initial value assigned to it (see Listing 2-5).

Listing 2-5. Initializing a Variable

```
// This is a variable having a value assigned
A = 10;
```

Variables can also be declared and initialized at the same time (see Listing 2-6).

Listing 2-6. Declaring and Initializing a Variable

```
// This is a variable being declared and initialized at the
same time.
int A = 10;
```

In the C language, variables may be of different types. For example, the variables used to store letters are different from the one used to store numbers. Table 2-1 shows some of the common variable types available in the C language.

Table 2-1. *Common variables*

Variable	Definition	Example
char	This variable type is used to store single characters.	`1 char A = 'A'`
int	This variable type stores integers.	`1 int A = 1;`
float	A float is used to store decimal numbers and usually has up to 23 significant figures.	`1 float A = 6.1234567890...23`
double	These are used to store decimal numbers and usually have up to 52 significant figures.	`1 double A = 01234567890123456789...52`
Constants	Constants can be thought of as special variables where the value cannot be changed. Constants are declared using the `const` keyword.	`1 const int A = 10;`

Arrays, Pointers, and Structures

Arrays

In C, an array is a type of data structure that can store several items, known as elements, of the same array. Arrays are very useful in C and embedded programming. The use of an array is fundamental when working with PIC® microcontrollers. An array can be declared with or without a specified size.

Example:

```
int temperatures[5] = {29, 25, 26, 25, 28};
```

The same sequence can be written as follows:

```
int temperatures[] = {29, 25, 26, 25, 28};
```

Elements of an array are accessed with the first element having an index of 0. These elements are accessed as follows:

```c
int monday = temperature[0]; // monday will have value 29
```

You may also assign a value to a single element of an array using the following:

```c
temperatures[2] = 27; // element 2 now has the value of 27
```

Pointers

The pointer. Many people have difficulty grasping the simple proposition. Pointers are powerful. Although I sparingly use pointers in this book, they are one of the most important C concepts.

Most people are confused as to what a pointer is and its purpose. A pointer is just another variable. Think of pointers like an int, char, or float. We know that an int stores numbers, char stores individual characters, and float stores decimal numbers. However, don't let the asterisk and ampersand scare you.

A pointer simply is a variable that stores the memory address of another variable. It is quite simple to understand. Listing 2-7 shows an example of how to declare a pointer and common assignment.

Listing 2-7. Declaring a Pointer

```c
// an integer declaration
int num;

// a pointer to an integer
int *num_pointer;

// the pointer now has memory address of the integer 'num'
num_pointer = &num;
```

See how simple pointers are to use? If you still have difficulty understanding them, then do some further research. There are entire books dedicated to the use of pointers.

Structures

You can get by with most simple C programming just by using arrays. However, when you want to store several data types, you must use a structure.

The struct keyword is used to declare structures. Listing 2-8 shows how you declare a structure.

Listing 2-8. Declaring a Structure

```
struct Speed{
byte slow;
byte normal;
byte fast;
};
```

To use a struct, you declare a type of the struct (see Listing 2-9).

Listing 2-9. Declaring a Type of Structure

```
// Declare MotorSpeed of type speed
struct Speed Motorspeed;
```

You then access a member of a structure with a dot (.) as the member access operator as follows:

```
MotorSpeed.slow = 10;
```

structs are very useful when programming microcontrollers.

Operators

Mathematics and logic are what a CPU thrives on. In C, there are many symbols that allow the microcontroller to perform logical and mathematical functions. I briefly go over them in Listings 2-10 through Listing 2-12.

Listing 2-10. Examples of Arithmetic Operators

```
// Addition operation adds operands
X + Y;

// Subtraction operation subtracts operands
X - Y;

// Multiplication multiples operands
X * Y;

// Division divides operands
X / Y;

// Modulus finds remainder after division
X % Y;

// Increment increases value by one
X++;

// Decrement decreases value by one
Y--;
```

Listing 2-11. Examples of Relational Operators

```
// Checks for equality
X == Y;
```

```
// Checks that values are not equal
X != Y;
```

```
// Determines if first operand is greater than the second
X > Y;
```

```
// Determines if first operand is less than the second
X < Y;
```

```
// Checks if the left operand is greater than or equal to the
right one
X >= Y;
```

```
// Checks of the left operand is less than or equal to the
right one
X <= Y;
```

Listing 2-12. Examples of Logical Operators

```
// Logical AND operator
X && Y;
```

```
// Logical OR operator
X || Y;
```

```
// Logical NOT operator
!(X)
```

Controlling Program Flow

if Statement

The if statement is used to make decisions within a program
(see Listing 2-13).

Listing 2-13. Example of an if Statement

```
if (speed == 200)
{
turnLightOn();
}
```

else Statement

The else statement allows the programmer to perform another action and is a complement to the if statement (see Listing 2-14).

Listing 2-14. Example of an else Statement

```
if(speed == 200)
{
turnLightOn();
}

else
{
keepLightOff();
}
```

else if Statement

Sometimes we need to test for more than two conditions of the program and that is when we use an else if statement (see Listing 2-15).

Listing 2-15. Example of an else if Statement

```
if(speed == 200)
{
turnRedLightOn();
}
```

```c
else if (speed == 150)
{
turnYellowLightOn();
}

else
{

}
```

switch statement

The switch statement is used when we need to compare a variable against different values (see Listing 2-16). It is used in situations where excessive if and else if statements would have been used. You must remember to include break statements within the cases; otherwise, the flow would fall to subsequent cases until a break statement. The default case is used when none of the other cases is true.

Listing 2-16. Example of a switch Statement

```c
switch (speed)
{
case 100:
beepOneTime();
break;

case 150:
beepTwoTimes();
break;

case 200:

case 250:
turnOffEngine();
break;
```

```
break:
keepEngineRunning();
}
```

for Loop

The for loop is used when you need to execute a sequence of statements a number of times (see Listing 2-17).

Listing 2-17. Example of a for Loop

```
for(int x = 0; x<= 10; x++)
{
spi_send(0x01);

delay_ms(1000);
}
```

while Loop

The while loop repeats a group of statements while the condition specified is true (see Listing 2-18). while loops are very important in embedded systems and are typically used to create an infinite loop since there is usually no operating system to keep the program running. All the programs in this book utilize an infinite while loop.

Listing 2-18. Example of a while Loop

```
while(1)
{
readSensor();
checkBattery();
updateDisplay();
}
```

do Loop

The do loop works just like the while loop, except that it checks the conditions of the loop after execution and it will execute at least once. See Listing 2-19.

Listing 2-19. Example of do Loop

```
do
{
temp = readTemperature();
} while(temp < 40);
```

break Statement

The break statement is used to terminate a loop and, when it's used, the statement immediately following the loop is executed (see Listing 2-20).

Listing 2-20. Example of a break Statement

```
if (temperature > 35)
{
break;
}
```

continue Statement

The continue statement causes a skip in the rest of the current iteration of the loop to take place (see Listing 2-21).

Listing 2-21. Example of a continue Statement

```
for (i = 0; i < 1023; i++)
{
if (i > 100 && i < 400)
```

```
{
continue;
}

spi_send(0x02);
}
```

goto Statement

The goto statement is looked upon with shame. However, there are instances when an unconditional jump is useful. Although using the goto statement often leads to spaghetti code, it is useful to understand how it operates.

The goto statement simply transfers the program flow to a point in the program that has a label (see Listing 2-22). The one time it may be necessary to use a goto loop is when there are deeply nested for loops or if statements.

Listing 2-22. Example of a goto Statement

```
myLabel:
turnOnSomething();

goto myLabel;
```

Preprocessor Directives

Before we discuss preprocessor directives, let's take some time to think a little about IDEs and compilers. The IDE (Integrated Development Environment) is basically a program just like your text editor, browser, or video game. The difference is that the IDE program has a special purpose. It contains everything you need to develop the program that will run on your microcontroller. That means it consists of various parts, such as a code editor where you type your code, a debugger that helps you look for errors in your code, and a lot of other things that simplify the whole process of development.

One such part in the IDE is the *compiler*. A compiler converts your code (in this case written in C) into instructions that the microcontroller will understand. When this code is compiled, it is converted into something called an *object* file. After this step, basically a component called the *linker* takes these object files and converts them into the final file that will be executed by your microcontroller. There may be other steps in this process of generating the final *hex file* (program to be written to the microcontroller), but this is all you need to know.

Now we can understand what a preprocessor directive is. The preprocessor is another part of the IDE that uses directives, which cause the C program to be edited prior to compilation.

These preprocessor directives begin with a hash tag symbol. In XC8, you will encounter preprocessor directives a lot, especially with libraries that are designed to target more than one chip.

#define

The `#define` directive is the first we will look at. The `#define` statement in C defines macros. This statement is used a lot in embedded programming and is very useful. Instead of having to keep typing some constant, it is easier to use the `#define` directive. This is also useful in instances where constants may need to be changed.

For example, if we are writing a driver for an LCD that comes in two compatible variants—128x64 and 128x32—then instead of having to constantly write those numbers, since the dimensions of the LCD would remain the same, it is easier to write it as shown in Listing 2-23.

Listing 2-23. Define Macros Using #define

```
#define LCD_HEIGHT 128
#define LCD_WIDTH 64
```

A little warning though: Remember to omit the semicolon after the macro as it will generate compiler errors. Another important use of the #define directive is in the creation of function-like macros. These are macros that can be used to create a small "function" and are useful for the creation of small functions that may appear many times in your code. See Listing 2-24.

Listing 2-24. Example of #define Statement

```
#define MAX(x, y) ((X) > (Y) ? (X) : (Y))
```

The most important use of such functions I have found in practice is that they do not require a specific type and can use any generic type. In the example in Listing 2-24, it doesn't matter if the parameters are int, float, or double, the maximum would still be returned. Learning to use the #define directive as it is very important. Sometimes you may see this referred to as a *lambda function*.

#if, #ifdef, #ifndef, #elif, and #else

These preprocessor directives are used for conditional compilation in the program. These directives are important. These directives are commonly used for debugging and to develop libraries that target multiple chips. They are straightforward. Listing 2-25 shows how the directives are used.

Listing 2-25. Examples of Preprocessor Directives in Use

```
#ifdef PIC16F1717
#define SPEED 200
#elif defined (__PIC24F__)
```

```
#define SPEED 300
#else
#define SPEED 100
#endif
```

Note that the conditional directives must end with an #endif statement.

#pragma

This is a C directive that in general-purpose programming is used for machine- or operating system-specific directives. This directive is most commonly encountered to set the configuration bits of the PIC® microcontroller (see Listing 2-26).

Listing 2-26. Example of #pragma

```
#pragma config PLLDIV = 2
```

Assembly vs. C

There are people who think Assembly is better for 8-bit microcontroller design. This may have been the case several years ago, but now that microcontrollers have a C optimized architecture, the need to have handwritten Assembly is less important now than it was before. The only case in which you may use Assembly is if you need to generate efficient code in the free version of the XC8 compiler, you have a chip in a legacy design that can only use Assembly, or of course you want to learn the architecture of the microcontroller on a deeper level. However, in this book I omit the use of Assembly.

Conclusion

This chapter contained a basic overview of the C programming language. With just the concepts presented here, you can do a lot, as we covered the most important keywords for our purposes. However, simply knowing the keywords to a language does not help you master it. It takes practice. If you are not proficient in the C language, I encourage you to find books and Internet resources to help you in your journey with the C programming language. If you are completely new to programming in general, I recommend you learn the basics. The book I personally recommend is *Beginning C, 5th Edition* by Ivor Horton, available from Apress®. There are also many free resources on the web that teach complete beginner programming concepts.

CHAPTER 3

Basic Electronics for Embedded Systems

Electronics

The difference between embedded systems designers and software engineers or IT technicians is the in-depth knowledge of the hardware that embedded designers possess. Embedded designers must have knowledge of electronics to effectively design embedded systems. We must remember, above everything else, that computers are simply complex electronic devices and microcontrollers are simply miniature computers. Resistors, capacitors, diodes, and transistors are some of the building blocks of computer hardware. In order to understand these more complex devices, it is important to understand the basic electronic components from which these devices are built.

Resistors

A *resistor* is used in electronics to impose resistance into circuits. Resistors are rated by the amount of ohms, which is essentially a measure of the amount of resistance they provide.

33

© Armstrong Subero 2018
A. Subero, *Programming PIC Microcontrollers with XC8*,
https://doi.org/10.1007/978-1-4842-3273-6_3

Resistors are used to reduce the flow of current in a circuit and to reduce the voltage. They are also used to divide voltages and pull up I/O lines.

Resistors come in a variety of packages, including an axial package, radial package, surface mount package, and a type of Single Inline Package (SIL) called a resistor array. Resistors are passive components and are one of the simplest types of devices you'll encounter.

Resistors have wattage ratings that must not be exceeded. Typically, ratings range from 1/8 watt to 2 watts. 1/4-watt resistors are the most common ones used in embedded systems design. The commonly found surface mount variety typically have a rating of 1/16 and 1/10 watts. However, it is best to consult the datasheet for the resistor you are planning to use.

A datasheet is a document that tells you a little bit about the technical specifications of a product. For example, a resistor's datasheet includes electrical characteristics such as tolerance and operating curve, as well as the dimensions of the part. This information is very useful when you are designing a printed circuit board or PCB. For the microcontroller, a datasheet includes the block diagram (as you'll see in a later chapter) as well as a lot of other useful information. Datasheets are your friends and you should always keep them handy. You can get the datasheets from the manufacturer's web site. Some component suppliers, such as Digi-Key and Mouser, also list the datasheets on their product pages.

Resistance is measured in ohms, as shown in Figure 3-1.

Figure 3-1. Ohm symbol

Most resistors have four bands. The first two bands are the most significant digits. The third bands tells you of the power of 10 you have to multiply by and the final band is the tolerance of the resistor. Usually the tolerance can be ignored; however, for some applications the tolerance must be within a very narrow range.

Surface mount resistors typically either use the E24 or E96 type markings. The E24 has three numbers. The first two numbers are the significant digits and the third is the index of base 10 to multiply by. For example, a resistor marked 104 would be 10x10^4, which is 100 kiloohms. Figure 3-2 shows the resistor schematic symbol and Figure 3-3 shows an actual resistor.

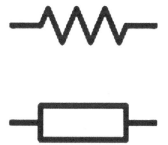

Figure 3-2. *Resistor schematic symbol*

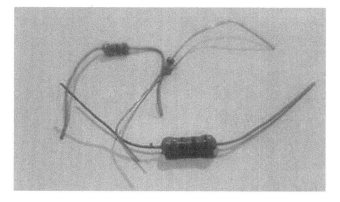

Figure 3-3. *Resistor*

Potentiometer

A *potentiometer* is an electronic component used to vary the amount of resistance in a circuit. The potentiometer is also known as a "pot" and contains three terminals. A pot is nothing more than a voltage divider that the user can adjust. A rheostat is another device you may encounter, and it is simply an adjustable resistor. The two-axis joystick commonly found in game controllers and volume adjust buttons are common real-world applications of potentiometers. Figure 3-4 shows the potentiometer schematic symbol and Figure 3-5 shows an actual potentiometer.

Figure 3-4. *Potentiometer schematic symbol*

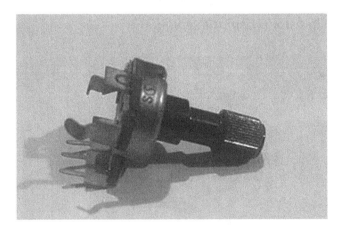

Figure 3-5. *Potentiometer*

Digital Potentiometer

A digital potentiometer or *digipot* is a digital version of a potentiometer. Electronically speaking, it performs the same functions as a potentiometer. The advantage of the digipot is that microcontrollers can adjust their resistance using some digital interface protocol, such as SPI or I2C, using software.

Since they can be controlled via software unlike their mechanical counterparts, it is possible to adjust the value in ways other than a linear fashion (typically in a logarithmic fashion). This gives digipots additional applications such as scaling and trimming of analog signals. The digipot has a different appearance than a regular potentiometer and they are packaged to look just like any other IC. The MCP 4131 digipot that we'll be using in our projects is shown in Figure 3-6. Figure 3-7 shows the digipot schematic symbol.

Figure 3-6. *MCP 4131*

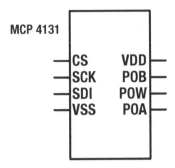

Figure 3-7. Digipot schematic symbol

Photoresistor

A *photoresistor*, also known as a light dependent resistor (LDR) or photocell, is a type of resistor where the resistance changes with light intensity. Figure 3-8 shows the photoresistor schematic symbol and Figure 3-9 shows an actual photoresistor.

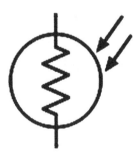

Figure 3-8. Photoresistor schematic symbol

Figure 3-9. *Photoresistor*

Capacitor

Capacitors are used to store electrical energy in an electronic circuit (see Figure 3-12). Capacitors come in axial, radial, and SMT packages. They consist of two metal plates separated by an insulator, called the *dielectric*. This dielectric material is made of many materials, including paper, ceramic, plastic, and even air. Capacitance is measured in Farads (F), although microfarads and picofarads are the commonly used units of measurement in everyday usage.

The type of dielectric influences the properties of the capacitor and determines if the capacitor is polarized or non-polarized. Figure 3-10 shows the polarized cap schematic symbols and Figure 3-11 shows the non-polarized cap schematic symbols.

The most commonly encountered capacitor is the electrolytic capacitor. This is because they store a relatively large capacitance relative to their size. They are polarized and care must be taken not to connect them backward. They come in two varieties—Tantalum and Aluminum. Aluminum capacitors are easily recognizable since they usually come in cylindrical tin cans. Tantalum capacitors have a higher capacitance to weight ratio than aluminum capacitors and are usually more expensive.

Ceramic capacitors are another commonly encountered type of capacitor in embedded system design. Unlike electrolytic capacitors, they have the advantage of not being polarized. However, they have a lower capacitance.

The most prominent use of capacitors in the embedded space is in filtering the output of power supplies. Many microcontrollers require filtering capacitors on their power pins. Decoupling capacitors act as a temporary voltage source for microcontrollers and are very important in suppressing high-frequency noise on the power supply. When used in this way, decoupling capacitors are also known as bypass capacitors since they bypass the power supply. It is important to consult the datasheet to determine the value of bypass capacitors you should use.

There are many occasions where many intermittent problems in your circuits can be traced to having a noisy power supply. A power supply is *noisy* when there are ripples on the power rail. These ripples are essentially fluctuations in the supply voltage. If you look at your DC output from a power supply with an oscilloscope, you will notice these ripples. If they are too large, they can cause a lot of problems in your circuit and may lead to undesired operations and, in some cases, damages to the IC and other sensitive electronics.

Figure 3-10. *Polarized cap schematic symbols*

Figure 3-11. *Non-polarized cap schematic symbols*

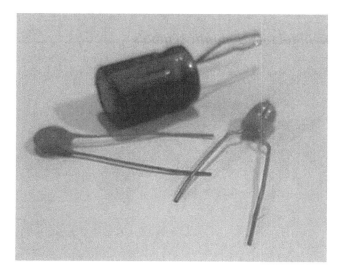

Figure 3-12. *Some capacitors*

Inductor

Inductors are used to resist changes in electric current flowing through it (see Figure 3-14). The most common use of inductors is in filters as an inductor passes low frequency signals and resists high frequency ones.

The Henry (H) is used to measure inductance. The nanohenry, microhenry, and millihenry are the most commonly encountered units. Figure 3-13 shows the inductor schematic symbols.

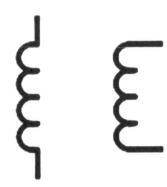

Figure 3-13. *Inductor schematic symbols*

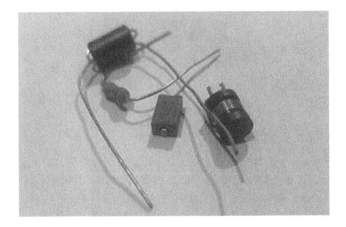

Figure 3-14. *Inductor*

Transformers

A *transformer* is a device used to step up or step down voltages in electronic devices.

Transformers require an alternating current to operate. Figure 3-15 shows the transformer schematic symbols and Figure 3-16 shows an actual transformer.

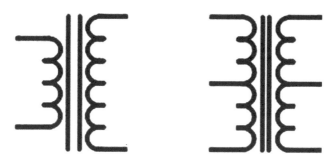

Figure 3-15. *Transformer schematic symbols*

Figure 3-16. *Transformer*

Diode

A *diode* is a device used to allow current to flow in a particular direction. When the diode is forward biased, current can flow. When the diode is reverse biased, current cannot flow. If a certain voltage is applied in the reverse direction, the diode will break down and allow current to flow in the opposite direction. Diodes are extremely important in embedded

43

devices, as they are imperative to suppressing voltage spikes that can be present when driving inductive loads. Figure 3-17 shows the diode schematic symbol.

Figure 3-17. *Diode schematic symbol*

Zener Diode

Zener diodes are devices that operate in the breakdown voltage region and are used for voltage stabilization, voltage regulation, and as a voltage reference. Figure 3-18 shows the Zener diode schematic symbol. In Figure 3-19, you see the Zener diode (glass body) under a regular diode (black body). You must be aware that regular diodes may also have glass bodies.

Figure 3-18. *Zener diode schematic symbol*

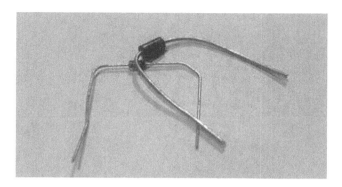

Figure 3-19. *Zener and regular diode*

Light Emitting Diode

A Light Emitting Diode (LED) is a type of diode that emits light when a voltage is applied to it. Diodes come in a variety of colors and sizes. The types encountered are infrared, red, orange, yellow, green, blue, violet, purple, pink, ultraviolet, and white. There are also bi-color LEDs and RGB LEDs. There are surface-mount LEDs and of course standard 3mm and 5mm LEDs that are used in most projects. Seven segment, sixteen segment, and dot-matrix LEDs are also used in a variety of projects. Figure 3-20 shows the LED schematic symbols and Figure 3-21 shows an LED.

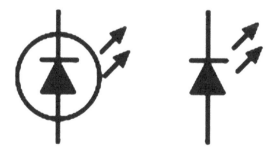

Figure 3-20. *LED schematic symbols*

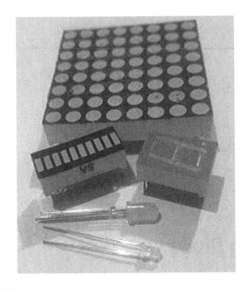

Figure 3-21. *LEDs*

Laser Diode

The laser diode (see Figure 3-22) is another type of diode common in embedded systems. They are low cost and weigh very little, making them very useful for a variety of projects.

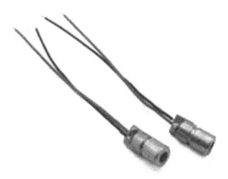

Figure 3-22. *Laser diode*

Transistors

Transistors are arguably the most revolutionary devices ever invented. Modern devices would not be possible without the transistor. Transistors are mainly used for switching and rectification in electronic circuits. Transistors come in a variety of types, which will be briefly discussed in the following sections.

Bipolar Junction Transistors

The Bipolar Junction Transistor (BJT) comes in two varieties and may be either NPN- or PNP-based. These names come from the designation of the semiconductor material of which it is constructed. A semiconductor with extra electrons is of the N-type variety and one with fewer electrons is of the P-type variety. If that semiconductor is stacked in the order of N-type, P-type, N-type, then you get the NPN variety. Similarly, if it is stacked P-type, N-type, P-type, then the PNP variety is created.

As mentioned, they come in two varieties—NPN based and PNP based. These two types of transistors can be differentiated by the direction of the arrow on the emitter pin in schematic drawings. The PNP type transistor has the arrow pointing inward, while the NPN variety has the arrow pointing outward (see Figure 3-23).

Transistors are three pin devices—the collector (C), the base (B), and the emitter (E). The transistor is used extensively for signal amplifying and electronic switching. When used for amplification, the transistors convert a low power signal into one of higher power. The name given to the type of transistor amplifier is determined by the pin into which the signal to be amplified enters and exits.

The most common type of amplifier is the common-emitter type amplifier. In this mode, the emitter is tied to the ground, the signal entry point is the base, and the exit point is the collector. This type of amplifier is commonly used to amplify audio signals since it performs voltage amplification.

The common-collector is the other type of amplifier configuration of the transistor. In this mode, the collector is connected to the ground and the signal enters the base and exits the emitter. This type of amplifier is used for voltage buffering and current amplification.

The final type of amplifier we will look at is the common-base configuration, which is rarely used in practice. The base is connected to the ground with the emitter as the input and the collector as the output. It has applications as a current buffer. Figure 3-23 shows the transistor schematic symbols and Figure 3-24 shows some common NPN transistors.

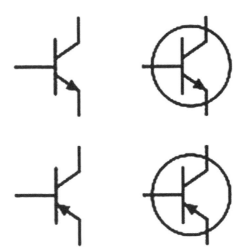

Figure 3-23. *Transistor schematic symbols*

Figure 3-24. *Commonly used NPN transistors*

Darlington Transistor

A *Darlington transistor* consists of two transistors connected in such a manner that the current output of the first transistor is further amplified by the second one. The Darlington pair uses two PNP or two NPN transistors and a complementary Darlington uses one NPN and one PNP transistor.

They act as a single transistor with a high current gain. This property is important in embedded applications, as in microcontroller based circuits, they can use a small amount of current from the microcontroller to run a larger load. This gives them many uses, such as display drivers and control of motors and solenoids.

Another Darlington Transistor that you may have to use is the Photodarlington transistor. This transistor consists of two transistors just like a regular Darlington. However, they differ in that the first transistor acts as a photodetector and its emitter is coupled with the base of the second transistor. Figure 3-25 shows the Darlington transistor schematic symbols.

The Photodarlington has a high gain but is slower than ordinary phototransistors.

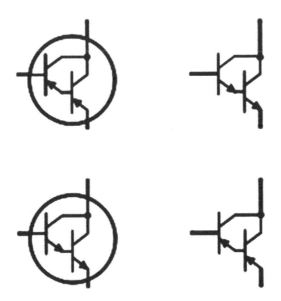

Figure 3-25. Darlington transistor schematic symbols

The ULN2003, which will be used to drive small stepper motors in this book, consists of an array of Darlington transistors. Figure 3-26 shows the ULN2003 schematic symbol.

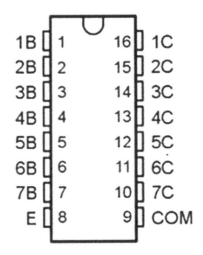

Figure 3-26. ULN2003 schematic symbol

Field Effect Transistor

Field Effect Transistors or FETs can be either N-channel or P-channel based and operate in a similar way to bipolar transistors.

Metal Oxide Semiconductor Field Effect Transistor (MOSFET)

The transistor was the pioneer of modern digital electronics. However, as time progressed, the Metal Oxide Semiconductor Field Effect Transistor (MOSFET) has taken over a lot of applications of the transistor and is used for amplification and switching and in modern integrated circuits.

The MOSFET consists of three pins—Gate (G), Source (S), and Drain (D)—which are the equivalent of the base, emitter, and collector, respectively, of the transistor. There is also a fourth pin called the body or substrate, but it's usually internally connected.

MOSFETs come in the N-channel and P-channel varieties. MOSFETs have a major advantage over BJTs, as they require less voltage to turn on. Thus, while transistors are current-based devices, MOSFETs are voltage-based.

MOSFETs must be handled carefully, as they are easily damaged by static electricity. Figure 3-27 shows the MOSFET schematic symbol.

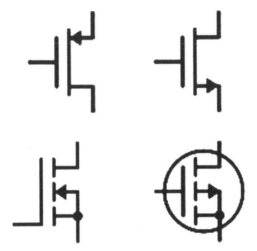

Figure 3-27. *MOSFET schematic symbol*

Junction Field Effect Transistor

The Junction Field Effect Transistor (JFET) is used for switching, amplification, and as a voltage controlled resistor. JFETs are not commonly used in normal circuit design, but do find use in specialty analog circuits. BJTs or MOSFETs can do most of what is required.

The JFET also finds use as a voltage controlled switch and as a chopper. Figure 3-28 shows the JFET schematic symbol.

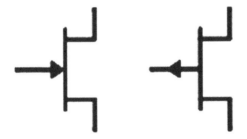

Figure 3-28. *JFET schematic symbol*

Operational Amplifier

The operational amplifier or *op-amp* is one of the fundamental building blocks of analog electronics. I would even go so far as to say that an op-amp is to analog electronics what a transistor is to digital ones. After you learn about microcontroller technology, I recommend you take an in-depth look at op-amps. With knowledge of op-amps and microcontrollers, you can design very powerful embedded systems. Figure 3-29 shows the op-amp schematic symbol.

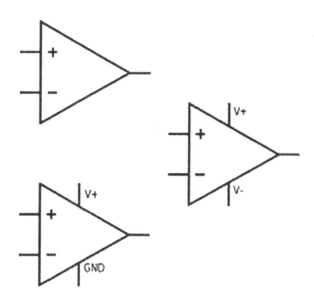

Figure 3-29. *Op-amp schematic symbol*

As the name implies, the op-amp is used for DC signal amplification. It is also used to filter and condition signals as well as for integration, differentiation, subtraction, and addition.

When looking at op-amp schematic symbols, in addition to the power supply pins (which are usually omitted), you will see two terminals, one with the minus sign and the other with the positive sign. The input with the positive sign is known as the non-inverting input and the one with the minus sign is called the inverting input. There is a third pin at the vertex of the triangular shaped op-amp symbol, known as the output port, and this pin can allow voltage or current to flow into the device, called *sinking*, or to supply current from the device, called *sourcing*.

Some common applications of op-amps in embedded systems design is as a buffer for the output of voltage divider voltage references, instrumentation amplifiers for differential pairs, active low-pass and high-pass filters, photodiode amplification, and more. In fact, an entire book can be written on op-amps and their applications!

There are hundreds of op-amps to choose from and I recommend you prototype with the TL081CP, KIA324, MCP6001, and MCP6002. These op-amps are great for rapid prototyping. Once you have a working system, you can determine the best amplifier for your needs.

Digital Electronics

Logic gates are the building blocks of digital circuits. When you combine several transistors, you get logic gates. I leave it up to you to read about the intricacies of digital electronics with regard to specific aspects of sequential and combinational circuits. Some basic gates are described in the following sections.

The AND Gate

The AND gate is one of the foundational building blocks of digital logic. The AND gate works by treating two logical inputs and outputs as a logical high only if both inputs are high. If only one of the inputs is high, then the output will be a logical low. Figure 3-30 shows the AND gate schematic symbol.

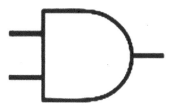

Figure 3-30. *AND gate schematic symbol*

The OR Gate

The OR gate works by outputting a logical high if either of its inputs are a logical high. If both inputs are a logical high, then the output is also a logical high. The only time the OR gate outputs a logical low is if both inputs are a logical low. Figure 3-31 shows the OR gate schematic symbol.

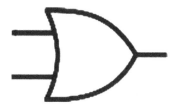

Figure 3-31. *OR gate schematic symbol*

The NOT Gate

The NOT gate, also known as an inversion gate, produces the exact opposite of its input. If the input is a logical high, then the output will be a logical low, and if the input is a logical low, then the output will be a logical high. Figure 3-32 shows the NOT gate schematic symbol.

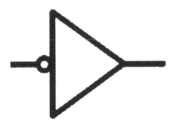

Figure 3-32. *NOT gate schematic symbol*

The NAND Gate

The NOT AND (NAND) gate is a logical gate that combines a NOT gate and an AND gate. The only distinguishing feature between the NAND gate and AND gate is the little circle on the end that symbolizes inversion. The NAND gate only gives a logical low if both its inputs are logical highs. Figure 3-33 shows the NAND gate schematic symbol.

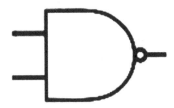

Figure 3-33. *NAND gate schematic symbol*

The NOR Gate

The NOT OR (NOR) gate is a logic gate that combines a NOT gate and an OR gate. The NOR gate, like the NAND gate, simply inverts the output of an OR gate and has the same distinguishing feature. Figure 3-34 shows the NOR gate schematic symbol.

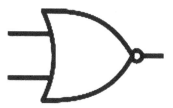

Figure 3-34. *NOR gate schematic symbol*

The Buffer Gate

The buffer gate is simply two NOT gates combined. The buffer gate might seem useless, but in actuality it has a lot of applications with logic-level conversion, discussed in the next section. Figure 3-35 shows the buffer gate schematic symbol.

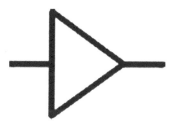

Figure 3-35. *The buffer gate schematic symbol*

The XOR Gate

The eXclusive OR (XOR) gate is a logic gate that gives a logic low when both inputs are true or when both inputs are false. It gives a logical high when both inputs are logically the opposite. Figure 3-36 shows the XOR gate schematic symbol.

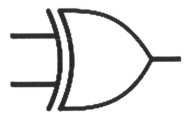

Figure 3-36. *XOR gate schematic symbol*

Logic-Level Conversion

An important concept to understand in the realm of digital electronics, especially when pertaining to interfacing microcontrollers, is the logic-level conversion. Before we discuss ways to convert between logic levels, we must first understand the concept of a logic level.

As you know in digital systems, data is represented in binary format, with a 0 representing off or low and a 1 representing on or high. While this knowledge may be sufficient for programming in general, when you use physical hardware, you must understand that low is 0 volts and high is the voltage that the system will recognize as a high signal when compared to the ground.

Early microcontroller systems used 5 volts as the standard, because this is the voltage with which the microcontroller and any external modules operate. Recently, however, the trend has been toward using 3.3v and even 1.8v as the voltage to power these systems. This presents a problem because a lot of existing modules, like LCDs for example, were made to use 5 volts, whereas newer microcontrollers typically use 3.3v. The problem also arises if you have a newer module that uses 3.3v logic and your systems runs on 5v logic.

In order to solve this problem, logic-level conversion is in order. Systems typically have some tolerance with their logic level. What this means is that if you have a 5v system, it will recognize a 3.3v signal as a logic high. However, you cannot drive a 3.3v logic-level system with 5 volts, as this will damage the module.

To avoid this, there are common ways to covert a 5v logic-level system to be interfaced with a 3.3 volt logic-level system, discussed next.

Run the Entire System on 3.3v

Although it's not necessarily a logic-level conversion technique, running your system on 3.3v will eliminate any additional components being purchased, thus reducing your bill of materials (BOM) costs. In addition, running the entire system on 3.3v will lower overall power consumption. For these reasons, it is recommended that once it is possible, you lower the overall operating voltage of your system.

The PIC16F1717 and newer microcontrollers are capable of being run at 3.3v or 5v. In this book, I use 5v as much as possible, simply because a lot of modules and sensors cater to being used by a 5v system (although this is slowly changing). If you are an Arduino user, you may have built up your electronics arsenal with 5v components. Another advantage of 5v is that they are much less susceptible to being disturbed by noise than 3.3v ones, because you need more noise to disturb the operation of the 5v circuit. However, feel free to run your system at 3.3v in your end application.

Use a Voltage Divider

Using a voltage divider is another way to interface between logic-level signals (see Figure 3-37). As mentioned, if your 3.3v device is transmitting at 3.3v then you can directly connect this line to the 5v device input. However, on the transmitting end of the 5v device, it may be necessary to use a voltage divider to convert the higher logic level to a lower one.

A good resistor combination for this type of circuit is a 1k and 2k pair. The output would be close to 3.3v. The downside of this system is that it is best suited for very slow signals. If you are on a tight budget, then this is the method I recommend.

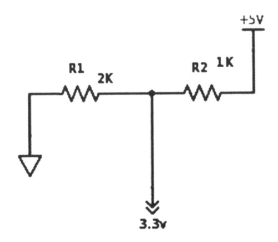

Figure 3-37. *Voltage divider method*

Use a Bi-Directional Logic Level Shifter

When you are interfacing between logic levels and a very high speed conversion needs to be done, it is simple to use a dedicated bi-directional logic-level shifter to convert between signal levels. For prototyping purposes, I recommend the ubiquitous logic-level converter modules, as they are designed for breadboarding and work well (see Figure 3-38). For moving to a PCB, I recommend the 74LVC245, because they are simple to use and work really well.

Figure 3-38. *Common logic-level converter*

Conclusion

This chapter looked at basic electronic components commonly found in embedded systems. We covered various components as well as basic logic gates and methods of logic-level conversion. This chapter is essential to understanding how to connect devices and sensors to your microcontroller. It was a very basic introduction; however, if you understand the content here, you should be able to construct your own circuits. If you need further information, there are books available that give a more detailed description of the components. There is also an app called Logic Gates for Android devices that allows users to experiment with logic gates.

CHAPTER 4

PIC® Microcontrollers

PIC® Microcontrollers Overview

Microchip manufactures 8-, 16-, and 32-bit microcontrollers. In this chapter, we discuss the 8-bit families. 8-bit PIC® microcontrollers belong to different groups as microchip classifies them. They groups are baseline, mid-range, enhanced mid-range, and high-performance. We look at each of them in this chapter.

Baseline PIC® Microcontrollers

These are at the bottom of the 8-bit Microchip food chain. Baseline PIC® microcontrollers consists of family members from PIC10, PIC12, and PIC16. These devices are typically used in applications that need a low pin count, extremely low power requirements, and contain small programs. Some members of this family include an onboard oscillator. There are members of this family that have as few as six pins!

The PIC16F57 is one member of the baseline family that has found widespread use. The BASIC stamp I uses the PIC16C56 and the BASIC stamp II uses the PIC16F57 as its microcontrollers.

© Armstrong Subero 2018
A. Subero, *Programming PIC Microcontrollers with XC8*,
https://doi.org/10.1007/978-1-4842-3273-6_4

Mid-Range PIC® Microcontrollers

The mid-range family of PIC® microcontrollers have members in the PIC10, PIC12, and PIC16 families. These devices are used when you need more features, such as onboard communication peripherals and possibly core independent peripherals.

Devices such as the PIC16F877, 16F84A, and 16F887 were and still are very popular with microcontroller enthusiasts and there is a lot of code available for using these devices. However, unless you are supporting a legacy design, it is advisable to use the enhanced mid-range microcontrollers, which have a lot of useful features.

Enhanced Mid-Range PIC® Microcontrollers

The enhanced mid-range core includes members of the PIC12 and PIC16 families. This core was developed by Microchip to be compatible with the mid-range devices while offering several improvements, including more program memory, more on-chip peripherals, and of course the C optimized architecture.

In this book, we focus on the enhanced mid-range family of microcontrollers. The chip we are using—the PIC16F1717—has a lot of useful goodies onboard, including analog peripherals.

High-Performance PIC® Microcontrollers

These are the highest performing members of the PIC® 8-bit family and are members of the 18F family. They feature large Flash program memory, extended instruction set, and of course integrated protocol communications such as USB, CAN, and Ethernet. They are intended for high performance 8-bit devices and have hardware multipliers.

If you need to use USB, I recommend that you use the PIC18F4553 for your USB based projects. Though there are newer versions of the PIC18 family, this chip has a lot of existing code related to its use for USB applications, as it is identical to the PIC18F4550. The exception is that the PIC18F4553 contains a larger resolution analog-to-digital converter. However, I would generally say that if you require USB, a member of the PIC24 or PIC32 family provides a lot more powerful features.

PIC® 16F1717 Block Diagram

Now that you have learned about the different types of PIC® microcontroller families and groups, let's look at the architecture of the PIC16F1717 (see Figure 4-1).

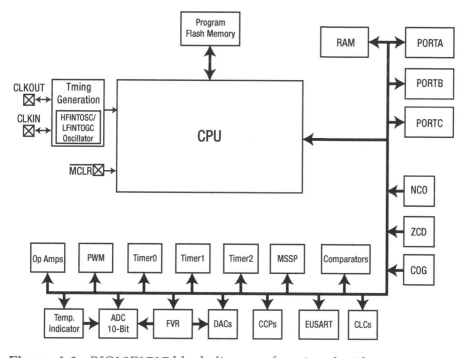

Figure 4-1. *PIC16F1717 block diagram (reprinted with permission)*

Looking at the block diagram shown in Figure 4-1, we see that the PIC16F1717 is very complex. It consists of a lot of peripherals, which we will discuss in the next few sections.

Program Flash Memory

The program Flash memory is memory that stores our program and is made from Flash memory technology. Older chips required UV light to erase their memory. However, with the advent of Flash-based technology, microcontrollers are extremely low cost and can be reprogrammed in seconds. Flash is also a non-volatile form of memory and features a long data retention. The PIC16F1717 Flash memory has a data retention of about 40 years!

The 8-bit PIC® microcontrollers' Flash memory size usually consists of several kilobytes and, in the PIC16F1717, it is 14KB of program memory. This can store quite a lot of instructions, as you will see in this book. Microcontroller systems generally never use more than a couple of megabytes of program memory.

Random Access Memory

Random Access Memory (RAM), as you know, stores program instructions to increase the speed of program execution. There are two main types of RAM—Static RAM (SRAM) and Dynamic RAM (DRAM). There are other types of RAM, such as FRAM and EERAM; however, they will not be discussed here.

In your general-purpose computer, you find DRAM in the gigabyte range being used for memory. However, in microcontrollers, you find SRAM being used for main memory. General-purpose CPUs do contain SRAM; however, it is usually found on the processor and used for cache memory. The major differences are that SRAM retains its data if power is applied, whereas DRAM needs constant refreshing. SRAM is also faster than DRAM.

The PIC16F1717 contains 1024 bytes of SRAM. Now, before you complain about the tiny amount of RAM on this controller, let me tell you this is quite a lot. Microcontroller programs typically never require more than a few kilobytes of RAM.

Timing Generation

If you look at the block diagram in Figure 4-1, you see a block entitled "Timing Generation". This block contains the HFINTOSC and LFINTOSC, which are the high-frequency internal oscillator and low-frequency internal oscillator, respectively. Also, not mentioned here, is the MFINTOSC (medium frequency internal oscillator). The LFINTOSC operates at 31kHz and is not calibrated. The MFINTOSC operates at 500kHz and is factory calibrated. The HFINTOSC derives its speed from the MFINTOSC and runs at a speed of up to 16MHz.

The maximum speed of the PIC16F1717 is 32MHz, which can be obtained by using the Phase Locked Loop (PLL). PLLs are used to generate some multiple of the input frequency. The one onboard the PIC16F1717 is a 4x PLL, which means it will give an output frequency four times the input frequency.

PLLs have a period of time before they match the frequency and phase that is expected from them and when this is done the PLL is said to be locked. The PLL on the PIC16F1717 has a lock time of 2ms.

It is important to note that the HFINTOSC and MFINTOSC, although calibrated, fall within a margin of 2% of the stipulated frequency. Thus, if you need extremely accurate timing, an external oscillator would be required. However, in this book the internal oscillator would suffice.

!MCLR

The !MCLR pin is used to reset the PIC® microcontroller. When designing circuits, do not leave this pin floating. This pin must be connected to VDD if not in use. The circuit used for the !MCLR is shown below.

Ports

If you look at the microcontroller block diagram, you'll notice several ports marked as PORTA to PORTE. On a microcontroller, there are several pins sticking out of it. Pins are used to interface the microcontroller to the outside world. However, inside the microcontroller these pins are controlled by registers within the microcontroller which are represented by ports.

Onboard Peripherals

The PIC® microcontroller consists of several digital peripherals. These peripherals are either digital or analog in nature. Microchip recently introduced a lot of core independent peripherals. Core independent peripherals require no intervention from the CPU to maintain operation. Let's look at these peripherals.

Analog to Digital Converter

The Analog to Digital Converter (ADC) is used to convert analog signals to digital ones. The ADC converter onboard the PIC16F1717 has a resolution of 10 bits. What this means is that it can take a signal and break it into 1023 "steps," with the value of a step being the input voltage divided by the number of steps.

For example, if we use a 4.096v voltage reference, then we have a resolution of 4mV per bit. For accurate ADC reading, it is advised to have a clean power supply and a stable voltage reference.

Digital to Analog Converter

The Digital to Analog Converter (DAC) does the exact opposite of the ADC. The DAC converts an analog signal to a digital one. The DAC is typically used to generate sound and waveforms. The PIC16F1717 has two DACs. DAC1 has a resolution of 8 bits and DAC2 has a resolution of 5 bits.

Capture/Compare/Pulse Width Modulation Module

The capture/compare/PWM (CCP module) is an important module on the PIC® microcontroller.

Capture mode is used to measure a particular number of falling or rising edges of a timer and essentially allows the timing of an event. Compare mode allows the comparing of the value of the timer to a preset comparison value. Pulse Width Modulation (PWM) mode generates a square wave of varying frequency and duty cycle, which can be determined by the user.

Pulse Width Modulation Module

In practice, I have found that one tends to use PWM more often because of its use in applications such as lighting and motor control. Even Microchip has realized the importance of PWM and provides a dedicated PWM module in addition to the regular CCP modules. The PWM module on the PIC16F1717 has a resolution of 10 bits.

Timers

Though you may see the word "Timerx" in the block diagram of the microcontroller, the timers on board the PIC16F1717 can also function as counters and perform timer/counter functions. Timers are used for time measurement, pulse generation, and counting pulses, and are also very accurate time delays. Hence, although you may see these modules simply referred to as "timers," bear in mind that they really perform Timer/Counter functions.

The PIC16F1717 has four 8-bit timers and one 16-bit timer. Timers 0, 2, 4, and 6 are 8-bit and timer 1 is 16-bit.

Comparators

The comparator on the PIC16F1717 compares two voltages and gives a digital output to indicate which is larger. The comparator has a minimum hysteresis of 20mV and a maximum of 75mV. It also has a response time of under 100ns.

Fixed Voltage Reference

The Fixed Voltage Reference (FVR) is used to provide a stable reference voltage to the comparator, DAC, or ADC. By doing this, the cost of paying for an external voltage reference is eliminated.

Temperature Indicator

There is a temperature indicator onboard the PIC16F1717 that has a range from -40 to 85 degrees Celsius. This temperature indicator is useful when you do not have space on the board for a temperature sensor or you want to reduce system cost.

EUSART

The Enhanced Universal Synchronous Asynchronous Receiver Transmitter (EUSART) module is used for serial communications and a lot of external modules require this interface to communicate with the microcontroller.

CLC

The Configurable Logic Cell (CLC) is a module on the microcontroller that provides a bit of onboard sequential and combinational logic functions.

MSSP

The Master Synchronous Serial Port (MSSP) module provides two modes of operation to be configured for use—either for Serial Peripheral Interface Function (SPI) or Inter-Integrated Circuit (I2C) functions.

NCO

The Numerically Controlled Oscillator (NCO) is used to provide a very precise and fine resolution frequency at a duty cycle. The NCO on the PIC 16F1717 uses the overflow of a 20-bit accumulator to achieve this function.

ZCD

The Zero Cross Detection module detects the point when there is no voltage present on the AC waveform. The ZCD module can be used to detect the fundamental frequency of a waveform and for sending digital data over AC circuits, such as what is done in X10 systems. The zero cross detect on the PIC16F1717 has a response time of 1uS.

COG

The Complementary Output Generator (COG) module takes one PWM signal and converts it into two complementary signals.

Operational Amplifiers

Operational Amplifiers (OPA) or Op Amps are the building block of analog systems. The PIC16F1717 includes onboard Op Amps. They have a gain bandwidth product of 2MHz and a slew rate of of 3V per uS, assuming a VDD of 3.0V.

High Endurance Flash Block

The High Endurance Flash (HEF) cell is designed to be a replacement for EEPROM, which is present on some microcontrollers. While the regular flash on the PIC16F1717 can withstand only 10,000 erase and write cycles, the HEF can withstand 100,000 erase and write cycles. The HEF has a size of 128 bytes.

The Enhanced Mid-Range CPU Core

Now that you have a basic understanding of the onboard peripherals of the microcontroller, let's take a look at the 8-bit CPU core (see Figure 4-2).

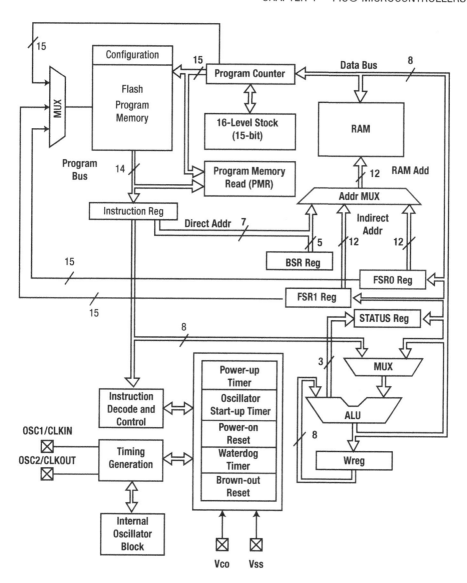

Figure 4-2. *PIC16F1717 core diagram (reprinted with permission)*

Let's look at what some of these blocks in the core are responsible for. We will not discuss every detail of the architecture; however, the components that can be configured in software are discussed in the following sections.

Power-Up Timer

The power-up timer is responsible for providing a short delay to allow time for the power supply to reach to the required value. After the time has passed, the program can begin to execute. The reason for this is that it is a precaution to prevent adverse effects on program execution. The power-up timer takes between 40 and 140ms to do this.

Oscillator Start-Up Timer

The oscillator start-up timer (OST) provides a delay (in addition to the one offered by the power-up timer) to allow the clock to become stable before program execution begins. The OST counts for a period of 1024 cycles and is independent of the frequency of the microcontroller.

Power-On Reset

While the power-up timer and oscillator start-up timer are working, the power-on reset timer holds the device in reset until the power and clock stabilize.

Watchdog Timer

The watchdog timer (WDT) automatically resets the processor after a given period as defined by the user. This is extremely important in order to allow an application to escape from an endless loop. To keep the program running, the WDT must be cleared or else the program will not run as intended. It is therefore important to turn off the WDT when configuring the microcontroller.

Brown-Out Reset

The brown-out reset is used to detect a brown-out condition within the microcontroller. A brown-out condition is one in which there is a drop in voltage of the power supply. The brown-out reset circuitry holds the microcontroller in reset until the power supply returns to an acceptable level. The brown-out reset has a response time of between 1 to 35uS on the PIC16F1717 before it activates.

Conclusion

In this chapter, we briefly examined the PIC® microcontroller, which is the main topic of this book. Learn the information presented in this chapter and learn it well. The chapter covered some of the most important peripherals onboard the microcontroller as well as provided a general overview of some of the features of the core.

CHAPTER 5

Connecting and Creating

Let's Get Started

In this chapter, we look at the process of connecting a PIC® microcontroller to an In-Circuit Serial Programmer, or ICSP. Some people also call them In-Circuit Debuggers, since they also have debugging capabilities. We look at the process of creating and running a new project in MPLAB X as well as creating source files. Beginners and first-time users of bare-bones microcontrollers should pay special attention to this chapter because, unlike the Arduino and other development boards, there is a need to connect the microcontroller to a programmer to load your program onto the chip. The process is not as "plug and play" as using a development board. So, let's get started!

A Look at Programmers

As was explained in Chapter 1, there are different programmers you can use to program your PIC® microcontroller. The two most popular right now are the PICkit™ 3 and the MPLAB® ICD 3. (There is also an ICD 4; however, at the time of writing it does not support all of the PIC® chips and is not as popular as the aforementioned programmers.) Regardless of if you purchased an ICD 3 or a PICkit™ 3, the process of connecting the programmer to your microcontroller is the same.

77

© Armstrong Subero 2018
A. Subero, *Programming PIC Microcontrollers with XC8*,
https://doi.org/10.1007/978-1-4842-3273-6_5

We will not take an in-depth look at the mechanics of how these programmers work, because in this book, all we will look at is using them as programmers and will not explore their debugging capabilities. We will simply treat the programmers as "black boxes" that allow you to load your program onto the chip. Figure 5-1 shows a closeup of the PICkit™ 3.

Figure 5-1. *Closeup of PICkit™3*

If you look in the foreground of Figure 5-1, you will see an arrow. This arrow is the position where you place the wire that is connected to the !MCLR pin of your microcontroller. Moving across to the left, the subsequent pins that will be connected are the Vdd pin, Vss pin, PGD (data) pin, and the PGC (clock) pin. There is also an LVP (low voltage programming) pin; however, we can safely ignore it for now.

If you are using the ICD 3, I *strongly* recommend that you buy an adapter that coverts the RJ-11 type connector on the programmer to an ICSP-type interface. As a beginner, this will make connecting the programmer to your various chips and development boards very easy, as you will be able to simply stick a wire into the connector and connect it to your chip. Figure 5-2 shows an example of how one of these RJ-11 to ICSP connectors looks. I also recommend you repeat these steps or connect the chip to the programmer with the programmer *disconnected* from your computer to avoid any mishaps.

Figure 5-2. *RJ-11 to ICSP adapter*

Once you have set up your programmer, the next step is to connect the programmer to the physical chip. There are a lot of ways to do this. However, the simplest way is simply to connect a male to male jumper wire from the hole on the connector to the target device. Figure 5-3 shows how to connect the male jumper wire to the ISCP connector. After this process is done, you can connect the jumper wires to the PIC16F1717, as shown in Figure 5-4.

Figure 5-3. *Connecting jumper wires to ICSP connector*

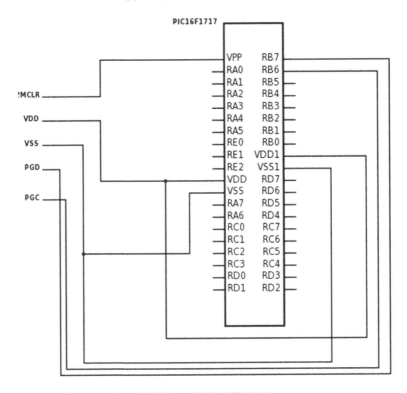

Figure 5-4. *Connecting ICSP to PIC16F1717*

A Look at Programming

After you have connected your programmer to your chip, you can plug in the USB cable from your programmer to your computer. If no magic smoke is released, and you have your programmer connected to the microcontroller, the next step is to write your program and download it to the microcontroller.

First, open MPLAB® X. You will be presented with the window shown in Figure 5-5.

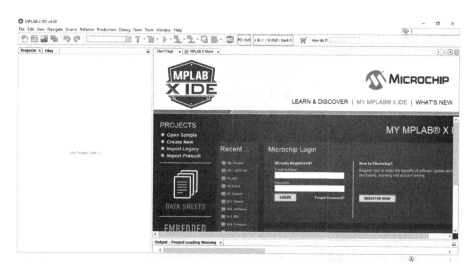

Figure 5-5. *MPLAB® X home screen*

Choose File ➤ New Project, as is indicated in the upper-left corner of the IDE shown in Figure 5-6.

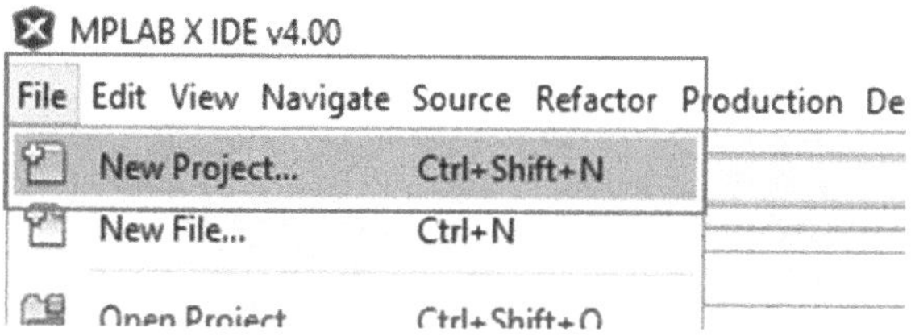

Figure 5-6. *Creating a new project*

81

Next, choose Microchip Embedded followed by Standalone Project, as shown in Figure 5-7.

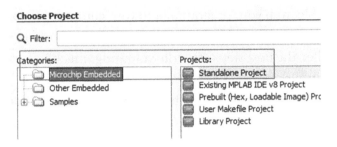

Figure 5-7. *Selecting a standalone project*

Next, select your device family followed by your device. In this case, it will be PIC16F1717. Type this into the Device box, as shown in Figure 5-8.

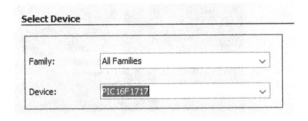

Figure 5-8. *Choosing your device*

Click Next and then Next again. Select the programmer you will be using from the Hardware Tools option. In this case, you select either the PICkit 3 or the ICD 3, as shown in Figure 5-9.

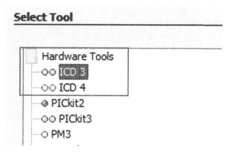

Figure 5-9. *Selecting your hardware tool*

Select your compiler. We will be using the XC8 compiler in this example, so ensure that this option is selected, as shown in Figure 5-10.

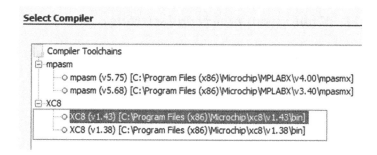

Figure 5-10. *Choosing the XC8 compiler*

Select a name for your project and choose a path. Then click the Finish button. This is depicted in Figure 5-11. Congratulations! You have created a new project!

Select Project Name and Folder

Project Name:	My_Project|
Project Location:	C:\Users\armst\Desktop\New Folder	Browse...
Project Folder:	C:\Users\armst\Desktop\New Folder\My_Project.X

☐ Overwrite existing project.

☐ Also delete sources.

☑ Set as main project

☐ Use project location as the project folder

Figure 5-11. *Naming your project and selecting a path*

You should see your new project created, as shown in Figure 5-12.

Figure 5-12. *Newly created project*

Now you are ready to write your program. In order to do this, you need to create header files and source files. Let's look at how you create a source file.

Click the Source Files folder. Then right-click it and choose New. Create a new main.c file, as shown in Figure 5-13.

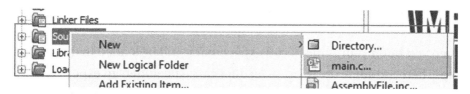

Figure 5-13. *Creating a new main file*

The process for creating a header file is the same. The difference is instead of clicking the Source Files folder, you click the Header Files folder and create a header file instead of a source file.

Your file will be created. We won't run a program now.

Look the top of the IDE and you'll see the two icons we'll be using. The icon with the hammer and broom is the Clean and Build option and the green arrow is used to run the main project (see Figure 5-14). We use the Clean and Build button to verify that our program is free of errors. When you click the Run Main Project icon, the program will be loaded onto the microcontroller.

Figure 5-14. *Clean and Build and Run Icons*

85

If you try to run the current project and download it to your microcontroller, nothing will happen. This is because we haven't given the microcontroller any instructions. In the next chapter, we look at writing a program to make the microcontroller do something.

Traps for Beginners

When you build your project, you expect that it will be loaded to the chip. There are some traps, however, that cause beginners to experience problems. The first trap is that the PICkit® 3 or ICD 3 does *not* provide power to your microcontroller by default and I recommend you keep it that way. Therefore, you need to power the target circuit from its own power source. The reason for this is when we start using inductive or high-current loads such as DC motors and servos, for example, we may draw more current than the programmer can provide.

The other trap you need to look out for is the length of your wires from the programmer to the chip. *Keep these wires as short as possible,* which will ensure that you do not experience any errors when trying to run your project.

The final trap you need to be careful about is having a noisy power supply. I recommend you use a dedicated power supply, as it will have the least amount of noise. Even with a good power supply, I recommend you still use some smoothing capacitors on the supply rails. Countless avoidable problems can be traced to having a noisy power supply.

Remember that programming a chip is a complex process and a lot of things happen in the background. Therefore, anything can go wrong. It is very important that you pay attention to the output window. It will save you many hours of frustration.

Remember also to triple check your connections. Sometimes you'll accidently connect things the way they ought not be connected. PIC® microcontrollers are resilient and easy-to-use devices, but there are some rules you must pay attention to.

Additional Information

Should you need more information about how the actual programming of the PIC microcontroller is carried out, I recommend you look at app note DS30277. Microchip also provides a lot of information on their web site about using PIC microcontrollers in general at `www.microchip.com`. There are lots of additional resources on the manufacturer's web site.

Conclusion

This chapter looked at the process of connecting our microcontroller to our programmer. We also looked at the processes of creating a new project source file as well as how you would go about building and running a project.

CHAPTER 6

Input and Output

Let's Begin I/O

In the last chapter, we looked at the peripherals available to users of PIC®
microcontrollers. One of the things we saw on the block diagram were
the ports. As was described, the ports are registers that provide access
to the pins of the microcontroller. The ports on the PIC16F1717 can be
used for input or output and can provide access to the many peripherals
onboard the microcontroller. In this chapter, we discuss input and output,
also written as I/O. We use I/O to interface to LEDs, switches, and seven
segment displays.

   Before we look at the code to make this happen, there are some
registers that you must understand, including knowing how to configure
them in order to effectively use I/O on the microcontroller.

TRIS Register

The first register we examine is the TRIState (TRIS) register. The TRIS
register gets its name from the fact that it can be in three states. It can be
configured for output high, output low, or input. The TRIS register is used
to make a port either an input or an output. To make a port an output,
we write a 0 to the corresponding TRIS register of that port. To make it an
input, we write a 1.

© Armstrong Subero 2018
A. Subero, *Programming PIC Microcontrollers with XC8*,
https://doi.org/10.1007/978-1-4842-3273-6_6

For example, to set PORTB as an output port, we do the following:

```
TRISB = 0;
```

Similarly, if we wanted to make that same port an input port, we do the following:

```
TRISB = 1;
```

It is important to efficiently manage the precious I/O since PIC® microcontrollers do not contain an infinite number of pins. The DIP version of the PIC16F1717 used for prototyping contains 40 pins. The reason I stated this obvious point is to reiterate the fact that I/O must be properly designated. Thus, it is sometimes necessary to assign one pin on a particular port to serve either an input or output function. For example, to set one individual bit (in this case, BIT 0 on PORTB) as an output, we do the following:

```
TRISBbits.TRISB0 = 0;
```

Similarly, if we wanted to set one bit as an input, we write:

```
TRISBbits.TRISB1 = 1;
```

As you can see from these assignments, Microchip makes it very easy to access individual I/O on PIC® microcontrollers and configure their associated registers. There is no need to mess with esoteric pointer functions or deal with mind-boggling bitwise logic. In fact, accessing individual pins for I/O operations on PIC® microcontrollers is easiest on a Microcontroller.

It is imperative to remember that data will not move from the port register to the pins on the microcontroller unless you give the appropriate TRIS register some value.

Now let's look at some other important registers.

PORT Register

We have referred to the ports of the PIC® microcontrollers on several occasions. On the PIC16F1717, there are a total of five ports ranging from A to E. These ports are 8-bit wide and therefore generally these ports have from bits 0 to 7. The exception to this on the PIC16F1717 is PORTE, which is a 4-bit wide input port and 3-bit wide output port.

The port register essentially reads the voltage levels of the pins on the device.

Output Latch Registers

The Output Latch Registers (LAT) are an important and overlooked type of register related to I/O. Prior to the enhancements made by Microchip to the PIC16F family, only the 18F family contained LAT registers. The LAT registers are an improvement on the PORT registers for writing data to output. The LAT register improves on problems associated with the PORT register for writing data to the pins. Note that *it is advisable to output data to ports using the LATx register and to read data using the PORTx register.*

This is because, as previously stated, the LAT register improves on any problems that may occur while simply using the PORT register for outputting data. The reason you use the PORT register for reading data from the input pins is because the PORT register reads the actual voltage level on the pin, whereas a read of the LAT register simply reads the same without regard for the voltage level of the associated pin.

Analog Select Registers

The analog select registers (ANSEL) are used to enable or disable analog input functions on a particular pin. When using a particular I/O pin for output, it is not necessary to adjust the ANSEL register corresponding to that bit. However, if you want to use a particular I/O pin as an analog input pin, you must set the corresponding ANSEL register.

Weak Pull-Up

The ports on the PIC16F1717 have internal pull-up resistors. These are important as they reduce component count by eliminating the need for an external resistor. The weak pull-up can be used as seen in Listing 6-1.

Listing 6-1. Example of Weak Pull-Up

```
// First we must enable weak pull-ups globally

OPTION_REGbits.nWPUEN = 0;

// Then we configure it for the individual pin, in this PINB0 5
WPUBbits.WPUB0 = 1;
```

Once this is completed, we can connect a switch to the microcontroller without the need for an external pull-up resistor.

There are also options for other registers associated with the PORT, including those for input level control, open-drain, and slew rare control.

Making an LED Blink

Finally, we get to the good parts! We look at making an LED blink, which is essentially the "hello world" of embedded programming. In order to do this, we first need connect the LED to the pin we intend to use. For this example, we connect the LED to PIN RD1.

Do not forget to connect a resistor to the LED or else you risk damaging it.

Let's review the steps for creating a project in MPLAB X IDE.

1. Open the IDE. You will be presented with the start page.

2. Click the Create New icon.

3. Select Microchip Embedded followed by Standalone Project.

4. Select your device family and device.

5. Select your programmer. In my case, I use the ICD 3; however, you may use the PICkit™ 3 or another programmer of your choice.

6. Select your compiler. In this case, it's the XC8.

7. Give your project a name and location.

8. After your project is created, right-click it and select New followed by the file of your choice.

If you forget how to create a new project, Chapter 5 provides a step-by-step guide to the process.

Now you can write some code. Based on what you have learned, you can use the following steps to set up the microcontroller for I/0. Let's review what we must do to make this happen:

1. Configure the TRIS register to output on a particular port pin.

2. Turn off the ANSEL register associated with that particular pin.

3. Set the LAT register for that pin.

It would be nice to do this alone, but first there are some things we must do. As important as software is, the hardware is very important when designing with microcontrollers. Sometimes a program will compile and will not run as expected.

First, you connect the LED via a 1K resistor to PIND1, as shown in Figure 6-1.

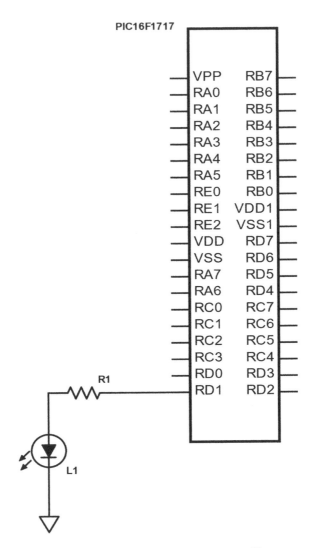

Figure 6-1. *LED connected to PIC® microcontroller*

Even though the hardware is connected, you simply cannot write the main program and get the code to work. You must first create a file to set the configuration bits of the microcontroller. Type the code first, then we will discuss what it does. Create a header file called 16F1717_Internal.h and enter the code shown in Listing 6-2.

Listing 6-2. PIC16F1717 Standard Header File

```
/*
* File: 16F1717_Internal.h
* Author: Armstrong Subero
* PIC: 16F1717 w/X OSC @ 16MHz, 5v
* Program: Header file to setup PIC16F1717
* Compiler: XC8 (v1.35, MPLAX X v3.10)
* Program Version 2.0
**Separated file into Header and C source file
**Changed comments and layout
*
* Program Description: This program header allows setup of
configuration
* bits and provides routines for setting up internal
* oscillator and includes all devices and MCU modules
*
* Created on January 9th, 2016, 2:50 PM
******************************************************************
***************/

/*****************************************************************
*****************
*Includes and defines
******************************************************************
**************/
```

```
// PIC16F1717 Configuration Bit Settings

// CONFIG1
#pragma config FOSC = INTOSC     // Oscillator Selection Bits
                                 (INTOSC oscillator:I/O
                                 function on CLKIN pin)
#pragma config WDTE = OFF        // Watchdog Timer Enable(WDT
                                 disabled)
#pragma config PWRTE = OFF       // Power-up Timer Enable(PWRT
                                 disabled)
#pragma config MCLRE = OFF       // MCLR Pin Function Select
                                 (MCLR/VPP pin function is
                                 MCLR)
#pragma config CP = OFF          // Flash Program Memory Code
                                 Protection (Program\memory
                                 code protection is disabled)
#pragma config BOREN = OFF       // Brown-out Reset Enable
                                 (Brown-out Reset disabled)
#pragma config CLKOUTEN = OFF    // Clock Out Enable (CLKOUT
                                 function is disabled.
                                 I/O or oscillator function
                                 on the CLKOUT pin)
#pragma config IESO = ON         // Internal/External Switchover
                                 Mode (Internal/External
                                 Switchover Mode is enabled)
#pragma config FCMEN = OFF       // Fail-Safe Clock Monitor
                                 Enable (Fail-Safe Clock
                                 Monitor is enabled)
```

```
// CONFIG2
#pragma config WRT = OFF        // Flash Memory Self-Write
                                   Protection (Write protection off)
#pragma config PPS1WAY = ON     // Peripheral Pin Select one-
                                   way control (The PP\SLOCK bit
                                   cannot be cleared once it is
                                   set by software)
#pragma config ZCDDIS = ON      // Zero-cross detect disable
                                   (Zero-cross detect circuit is
                                   disabled at POR and can be
                                   enabled with ZCDSEN bit.)
#pragma config PLLEN = OFF      // Phase Lock Loop enable (4x PLL
                                   is enabled when software sets
                                   the SPLLEN bit)
pragma config STVREN = ON       // Stack Overflow/Underflow Reset
                                   Enable (Stack\Overflow or
                                   Underflow will cause a Reset)
#pragma config BORV = LO        // Brown-out Reset Voltage Selection
                                   (Brown-out\Reset Voltage (Vbor),
                                   low trip point selected.)
#pragma config LPBOR = OFF      // Low-Power Brown Out Reset
                                   (Low-Power BOR is disabled)
#pragma config LVP = OFF        // Low-Voltage Programming Enable
                                   (High-voltage\on MCLR/VPP must
                                   be used for programming)

//XC8 Standard Include
#include <xc.h>
#include <stdio.h>
#include <stdlib.h>
```

```
//Other Includes
#include <stdint.h>
#include <stdbool.h>
#include <stddef.h>
#include <math.h>

//For delay routines
#define _XTAL_FREQ 16000000

//MCU Modules Includes

//Internal oscillator setup
void internal_32();
void internal_16(); //16 MHz
void internal_8();
void internal_4();
void internal_2();
void internal_1();
void internal_31(); //31 kHz
```

In this book, I use heavily commented code, thus line-by-line explanation are not included. I do, however, explain the most important aspects of the code.

This file configures the PIC® microcontroller with options such as clocks, power-up timers, brown-out resets, and watchdog timers, to name a few. These options are known as the configuration bits of the microcontroller. If the configuration bits are not set, the microcontroller will not run. You can identify the configuration bits by the prefix #pragma config. If you look below this block, you will see several standard include files. The one unique to the XC8 compiler is <xc.h> and is required for every program to be written using the XC8 compiler.

Below this section you will see a define statement: #define _XTAL_FREQ 16000000. This statement defines the speed at which the microcontroller runs, which is 16MHz. In order to ensure consistency, in this book we maintain this frequency throughout.

Moving down, you will notice some custom function declarations. These declarations allow the user to quickly and effectively change the speed of the microcontroller as needed.

Next, we look at the file that contains the body of the functions. Create another file called PIC16F1717_Internal.c and enter the code shown in Listing 6-3.

Listing 6-3. PIC16F1717 Standard Source File

```
/*
* File: 16F1717_Internal.c
* Author: Armstrong Subero
* PIC: 16F1717 w/Int OSC @ 16MHz, 5v
* Program: Library file to configure PIC16F1717
* Compiler: XC8 (v1.35, MPLAX X v3.10)
* Program Version: 1.2
**Added additional comments
*
* Program Description: This Library allows you to setup a
PIC16F1717
*
* Created on January 9th, 2016, 6:45 PM
*/

/****************************************************************
****************
*Includes and defines
****************************************************************
**************/
#include "16F1717_Internal.h"
```

```
/*************************************************************
****************
* Function: internal_32()
*
* Returns: Nothing
*
* Description: Sets internal oscillator to 32MHz
*
* Usage: internal_32()
*************************************************************
**************/
//Set to 32MHz
void internal_32(){
//Clock determined by FOSC in configuration bits
SCS0 = 0;
SCS1 = 0;

//Frequency select bits
IRCF0 = 0;
IRCF1 = 1;
IRCF2 = 1;
IRCF3 = 1;

//SET PLLx4 ON
SPLLEN = 1;
}

/*************************************************************
****************
* Function: internal_16()
*
* Returns: Nothing
*
```

```
* Description: Sets internal oscillator to 16MHz
*
* Usage: internal_16()
**************************************************************
**************/
//Set to 16MHz
void internal_16(){
//Clock determined by FOSC in configuration bits
SCS0 = 0;
SCS1 = 0;

//Frequency select bits
IRCF0 = 1;
IRCF1 = 1;
IRCF2 = 1;
IRCF3 = 1;

//SET PLLx4 OFF
SPLLEN = 0;
}

/************************************************************
****************
* Function: internal_8()
*
* Returns: Nothing
*
* Description: Sets internal oscillator to 8MHz
*
* Usage: internal_8()
**************************************************************
**************/
```

```
//Set to 8MHz
void internal_8(){
//Clock determined by FOSC in configuration bits
SCS0 = 0;
SCS1 = 0;

//Frequency select bits
IRCF0 = 0;
IRCF1 = 1;
IRCF2 = 1;
IRCF3 = 1;

//SET PLLx4 OFF
SPLLEN = 0;
}

/****************************************************************
****************
* Function: internal_4()
*
* Returns: Nothing
*
* Description: Sets internal oscillator to 4MHz
*
* Usage: internal_4()
****************************************************************
**************/
//Set to 4MHz
void internal_4(){
//Clock determined by FOSC in configuration bits
SCS0 = 0;
SCS1 = 0;
```

```c
//Frequency select bits
IRCF0 = 1;
IRCF1 = 0;
IRCF2 = 1;
IRCF3 = 1;

//SET PLLx4 OFF
SPLLEN = 0;
}

/****************************************************************
****************
* Function: internal_2()
*
* Returns: Nothing
*
* Description: Sets internal oscillator to 2MHz
*
* Usage: internal_2()
****************************************************************
**************/
//Set to 2MHz
void internal_2(){
//Clock determined by FOSC in configuration bits
SCS0 = 0;
SCS1 = 0;

//Frequency select bits
IRCF0 = 0;
IRCF1 = 0;
IRCF2 = 1;
IRCF3 = 1;
```

```
//SET PLLx4 OFF
SPLLEN = 0;
}

/****************************************************************
****************
* Function: internal_1()
*
* Returns: Nothing
*
* Description: Sets internal oscillator to 1MHz
*
* Usage: internal_1()
****************************************************************
**************/
//Set to 1MHz
void internal_1(){
//Clock determined by FOSC in configuration bits
SCS0 = 0;
SCS1 = 0;

//Frequency select bits
IRCF0 = 1;
IRCF1 = 1;
IRCF2 = 0;
IRCF3 = 1;

//SET PLLx4 OFF
SPLLEN = 0;
}
```

```
/****************************************************************
****************
* Function: internal_31()
*
* Returns: Nothing
*
* Description: Sets internal oscillator to 31kHz
*
* Usage: internal_31()
*****************************************************************
**************/
//Set to 31kHz(LFINTOSC)
void internal_31(){
//Clock determined by FOSC in configuration bits
SCS0 = 0;
SCS1 = 0;

//Frequency select bits
IRCF0 = 0;
IRCF1 = 0;
IRCF2 = 0;
IRCF3 = 0;

//SET PLLx4 OFF
SPLLEN = 0;
}
```

This file implements the functions necessary to set the speed of the PIC® microcontroller clock.

Now comes the good part—actually making the LED light. All C programs, as you know, must contain a main function. Traditionally, the file containing this function is called main as well. Thus, create a new file called main.c and input the code, as shown in Listing 6-4.

Listing 6-4. PIC16F1717 Output Source File

```
/*
* File: Main.c
* Author: Armstrong Subero
* PIC: 16F1717 w/Int OSC @ 16MHz, 5v
* Program: 00_Output
* Compiler: XC8 (v1.38, MPLAX X v3.40)
* Program Version: 1.0
*
*
* Program Description: This Program Allows PIC16F1717 to Turn
on an LED
*
* Hardware Description: An LED is connected via a 10k resistor
to PIN D1
*
* Created November 4th, 2016, 1:00 PM
*/

/************************************************************
****************
*Includes and defines
************************************************************
**************/

#include "16F1717_Internal.h"

/************************************************************
****************
* Function: void initMain()
*
* Returns: Nothing
*
```

```
* Description: Contains initializations for main
*
* Usage: initMain()
***************************************************************
**************/

void initMain(){
// Run at 16 MHz
internal_16();

// Set PIN D1 as output
TRISDbits.TRISD1 = 0;
}

/*************************************************************
***************
* Function: Main
*
* Returns: Nothing
*
* Description: Program entry point
***************************************************************
**************/

void main(void) {
initMain();

while(1){
// Set PIND1 High
LATDbits.LATD1 = 1;
}

return;

}
```

Compile the program and run it. The LED should light up! If the LED does not light up, ensure that you tested your connections properly. A lot of problems can be solved by simply ensuring everything is wired correctly.

Great, the LED lights up. However, we want the LED to blink. To do this, you must use the built-in delay macro in XC8. There are options to delay for clock cycles, milliseconds, or microseconds. To make the LED blink, we will use the millisecond option. This code is shown in Listing 6-5.

Listing 6-5. PIC16F1717 Flash Source File

```
/*
* File: Main.c
* Author: Armstrong Subero
* PIC: 16F1717 w/Int OSC @ 16MHz, 5v
* Program: 01_Flash
* Compiler: XC8 (v1.38, MPLAX X v3.40)
* Program Version: 1.0
*
9    *
* Program Description: This Program Allows PIC16F1717 to blink
an LED at
* 50% duty cycle
*
* Hardware Description: An LED is connected via a 10k resistor
to PIN D1
*
* Created November 4th, 2016, 1:08 PM
*/
```

```
/*************************************************************
****************
*Includes and defines
*************************************************************
**************/

#include "16F1717_Internal.h"


/*************************************************************
****************
* Function: void initMain()
*
* Returns: Nothing
*
* Description: Contains initializations for main
*
* Usage: initMain()
*************************************************************
**************/

void initMain(){
// Run at 16 MHz
internal_16();

// Set PIN D1 as output
TRISDbits.TRISD1 = 0;
}

/*************************************************************
****************
* Function: Main
*
* Returns: Nothing
*
```

```
* Description: Program entry point
*************************************************************
**************/

void main(void) {
initMain();

while(1){
// Toggle LED
LATDbits.LATD1 = ~LATDbits.LATD1;

// delay 500 ms
__delay_ms(500);
}

return;

}
```

The __delay_ms macro allows you to delay a particular period of time. We use the bitwise NOT operator to toggle the LED.

Using a Pushbutton

Now that we examined the output, let's look at the input. As mentioned earlier, the TRIS register must be set to allow the I/O pin to act as an input. We also use the internal pull-up to avoid the use of an external resistor.

As we did with output, there is also a process to make the pin an input pin. Here are the steps for configuring a pin as an input using the internal weak pull-up resistors on the chip:

1. Configure the TRIS register for that pin as an input.

2. Turn off the ANSEL for that particular pin.

3. Enable weak pull-ups globally.

4. Enable the weak pull-ups for that particular pin.

The schematic in Figure 6-2 shows how we connect the switch and LED. The LED remains connected to RD1 and we now connect the switch to RB0.

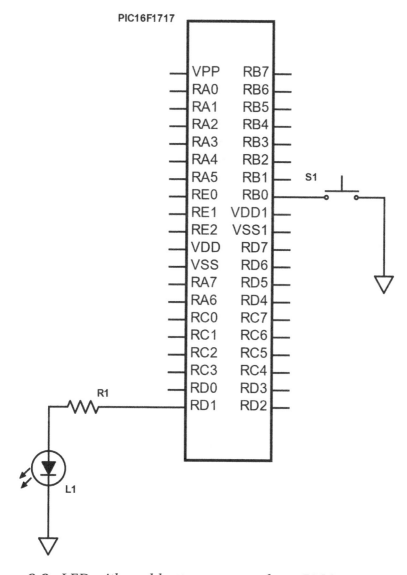

Figure 6-2. *LED with pushbutton connected to a PIC®*
microcontroller

Listing 6-6 shows the main code. The header files and configuration bits are the same as in the last example.

Listing 6-6. PIC16F1717 Pushbutton with Internal Weak Pull-Up

```
/*
* File: Main.c
* Author: Armstrong Subero
* PIC: 16F1717 w/Int OSC @ 16MHz, 5v
* Program: 02_Internal_Pullups
* Compiler: XC8 (v1.38, MPLAX X v3.40)
* Program Version: 1.0
*
*
* Program Description: This Program Allows PIC16F1717 to turn
on an LED based
* on a Pushbutton
*
* Hardware Description: An LED is connected via a 1k resistor
to PIN D1 and a
* switch is connected to PIN B0
*
* Created November 4th, 2016, 1:08 PM
*/

/***********************************************************
****************
*Includes and defines
************************************************************
**************/

#include "16F1717_Internal.h"
```

```
/*****************************************************************
****************
* Function: void initMain()
*
* Returns: Nothing
*
* Description: Contains initializations for main
*
* Usage: initMain()
*****************************************************************
**************/

void initMain(){
// Run at 16 MHz
internal_16();

// Set PIN D1 as output
TRISDbits.TRISD1 = 0;

// Turn off LED
LATDbits.LATD1 = 0;

// Set PIN B0 as input
TRISBbits.TRISB0 = 1;

// Configure ANSELB0
ANSELBbits.ANSB0 = 0;

// Enable weak-pullups global
OPTION_REGbits.nWPUEN = 0;

// Enable weak-pullup on PINB0
WPUBbits.WPUB0 = 1;
}
```

```
/*************************************************************
****************
* Function: Main
*
* Returns: Nothing
*
* Description: Program entry point
*************************************************************
**************/

void main(void) {
initMain();

while(1){
// Toggle LED on pushbutton
LATDbits.LATD1 = ~PORTBbits.RB0;
}

return;

}
```

There may be times when it is necessary to debounce your switch. Debouncing is when you allow the microcontroller to only recognize the switch as being pressed once even when it's pressed multiple times. Some very poor-quality switches can make multiple contacts on one button push. This in turn causes the microcontroller to register several occurrences of the switch being pushed.

There are several options for debouncing, including hardware and software methods. However, I have found that in practice, high-quality mechanical pushbuttons being used for prototyping applications do not necessarily need debouncing, especially for applications as trivial as ours. However, if you are designing a commercial product, it is highly recommended that you add debouncing to your switches. Should you need to debounce your switch, you can do so using the software and the simple method shown in Listing 6-7. Simply replace the code after the // Toggle LED on pushbutton comment in Listing 6-6 with this code.

Listing 6-7. Button Debounce Snippet

```
// Check if switch pressed
if (RB0 == 0)
{
// short delay
__delay_ms(100);

// if switch still pressed
if (RB0 == 0)
{
// turn led on
LATDbits.LATD1 = 1;
}
}

else{
// keep LED off
LATDbits.LATD1 = 0;
}
```

We use the method of inputting a short delay after the initial button press is detected, then we recheck the switch before any further action is performed. If the switch is still closed, we turn on the LED. Note also that the actual delay time before the recheck may vary according to the switch. Hence, you should test the delay time to ensure that it is compatible with your particular pushbutton.

There may also be a time when you don't want to use the internal weak pull-up. In this case, you can omit all parts of the code related to setting up the weak pull-up resistors. Here is how you do that. You add a pull-up resistor externally, which is connected as shown in the schematic in Figure 6-3.

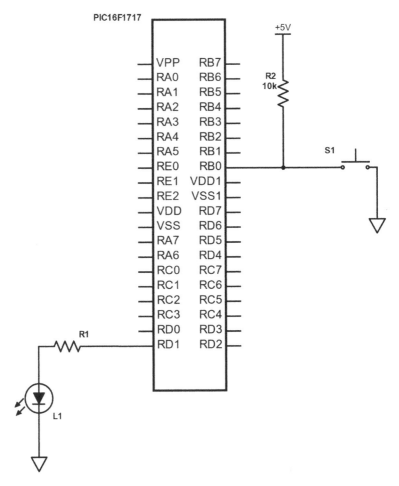

Figure 6-3. *Connecting the switch with external pull-up*

The only thing that changes in the hardware configuration is the addition of a pull-up resistor. The standard value of the pull-up resistor is 10k.

As for the software, we will remove the parts of the code that set up the internal pull-ups for use (see Listing 6-8).

Listing 6-8. PIC16F1717 Pushbutton Without Internal Pull-Up

```
/*
* File: Main.c
* Author: Armstrong Subero
* PIC: 16F1717 w/Int OSC @ 16MHz, 5v
* Program: 03_Pushbutton
* Compiler: XC8 (v1.38, MPLAX X v3.40)
* Program Version: 1.0
*
*
* Program Description: This Program Allows PIC16F1717 to turn
on an LED
* based on a Pushbutton
*
* Hardware Description: An LED is connected via a 10k resistor
to PIN D1 and a
* switch is connected to PIN B0
*
* Created November 4th, 2016, 1:08 PM
*/

/***********************************************************
****************
*Includes and defines
***********************************************************
**************/

#include "16F1717_Internal.h"
```

```
/****************************************************************
****************
* Function: void initMain()
*
* Returns: Nothing
*
* Description: Contains initializations for main
*
* Usage: initMain()
****************************************************************
**************/

void initMain(){
// Run at 16 MHz
internal_16();

// Set PIN D1 as output
TRISDbits.TRISD1 = 0;

// Turn off LED
LATDbits.LATD1 = 0;

// Set PIN B0 as input
TRISBbits.TRISB0 = 1;

// Configure ANSELB0
ANSELBbits.ANSB0 = 0;

}


/****************************************************************
****************
* Function: Main
*
* Returns: Nothing
```

```
*
* Description: Program entry point
***************************************************************
***************/

void main(void) {
initMain();

while(1){
// Toggle LED on PUSH Button
LATDbits.LATD1 = ~PORTBbits.RB0;
}

return;

}
```

Seven Segment Displays

LCDs and OLED displays are undoubtedly the most popular choices for
relaying output to users of embedded systems. Adding a display will add
cost to your system. There will be times when you'll want to give the users
output and mere LED output won't suffice. In such cases, you can use a
seven segment display to give the users a little more information.

Seven segment displays are basically packages that traditionally
contain seven LEDs. If you count the decimal point segment available on
most seven segment displays, it is eight in reality. Each one of the LEDs in
this package is referred to as a segment. Hence the name seven segment
display; see Figure 6-4.

These LEDs can output hexadecimal digits in the form of the digits
0-F. These displays also come in two varieties, which can either be
common anode or common cathode. In this book, we use the common
cathode variety. Figure 6-4 shows how the digits of a common-cathode
seven segment LED are arranged.

119

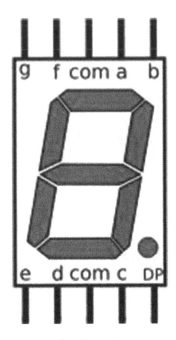

Figure 6-4. *A seven segment display pinout*

As you see, each pin is associated with a letter A-G, and there is also a pin for the decimal point marked as DP. There are two pins marked COM. This is short for "common" and will connect to the ground.

To display numbers on the display, the segments associated with that pin are turned on. For example, in order to display the number 8, all of the segments on the LED would be on. These pins would then be connected to a particular port on the microcontroller. The numbers would then be sent to the microcontroller port that the seven segment display is connected to.

Since the seven segment display is, after all, a group of LEDs in one package, you need to connect resistors to each segment of the displays to ensure that you do not damage them.

Note that if you are using the common anode variety, the hexadecimal numbers sent to the port will be slightly different. This is because in the common anode variety, all the LEDs are connected to power instead of ground.

Now that you have a fair idea about how these displays operate, let's look at the schematic for connecting the seven segment display to the microcontroller (see Figure 6-5). The pins are connected to PORTD, with A being connected to RD0, B being connected to RD1, and so forth, until all the pins are connected with the exception of the decimal point pin. The common is connected to ground.

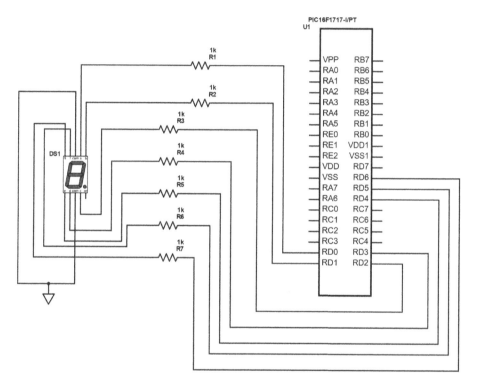

Figure 6-5. *PIC16F1717 with seven segment connected*

Now we write the code required for using a seven segment display, as shown in Listing 6-9.

Listing 6-9. PIC16F1717 Seven Segment Display

```
/*
* File: Main.c
* Author: Armstrong Subero
* PIC: 16F1717 w/Int OSC @ 16MHz, 5v
* Program: IO1_Seven_Segment
* Compiler: XC8 (v1.38, MPLAX X v3.40)
* Program Version: 1.0
*
* Program Description: This Program Allows PIC16F1717 to drive
a single
* seven segment display, it displays the hexadecimal
* digits O-F on the seven segment display.
*
* Hardware Description: An seven segment display of the cathode
variety is
* connected to port D of the microcontroller via 1k
* resistors.
*
* Created February 16th, 2017, 6:31 PM
*/

/*************************************************************
****************
*Includes and defines
*************************************************************
**************/

#include "16F1717_Internal.h"

unsigned char Display(unsigned char digit);
```

```
/*************************************************************
****************
* Function: void initMain()
*
* Returns: Nothing
*
* Description: Contains initializations for main
*
* Usage: initMain()
*************************************************************
**************/

void initMain(){
// Run at 16 MHz
internal_16();

// Set PORTD as output
TRISD = 0;
ANSELD = 0;
}

/*************************************************************
****************
* Function: Main
*
* Returns: Nothing
*
* Description: Program entry point
*************************************************************
**************/
```

```
void main(void) {

// loop variable
int i;

initMain();

// Keep displaying digits 0-F
// and update it every second
while(1){
for (i = 0; i <= 15; i++){
// Now the hex values for the array are derived based on the
type of seven
// segment display. In our case we use the common cathode
version.
// For example to display the number '7', this means that we
must have segments
// a,b and c enabled. This would be "0000111" in binary with a
'1' signifying
// the particular segment. This would equate to 0x07 in hex. So
when
//'0x07' is written to the PORTD.
// based on the iteration of the array by the for loop, we
display each letter
// to PORTD.

LATD = Display(i);
__delay_ms(1000);
}

}

return;

}
```

```
/**********************************************************
****************

* Function: unsigned char Display(unsigned char digit)
*

* Returns: unsigned char numbers
*

* Description: Function that takes a number and returns its
index in an array
* corresponding to the hexadecimal digit
**********************************************************
**************/

unsigned char Display(unsigned char digit)
{
// variable representing numbers
unsigned char numbers;

// an array of the digits 0-F
unsigned char DIGITS[] = {0x3F, 0x06, 0x5B, 0x4F, 0x66, 0x6D,
0x7D, 0x07, 0x7F, 0x6F, 0x77, 0x7C, 0x39, 0x5E, 0x79, 0x71};

// assign index given by user to variable
numbers = DIGITS[digit];

// return it
return numbers;
}
```

Seven Segment Display Multiplexing

There are times when you'll want to want to use more than one seven segment display in your application. One seven segment display typically uses a full port of your microcontroller (see Figure 6-6). Driving two seven segment displays would use about 16 pins of your microcontroller! This is almost half of the pins on the PIC16F1717. To avoid this, you can either use a higher pin count microcontroller, which costs more and adds to the total cost of your system, or you can use multiplexing.

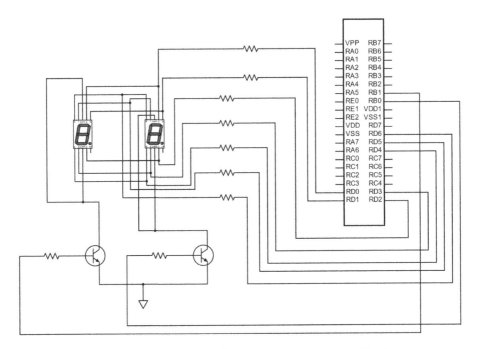

Figure 6-6. *PIC16F1717 multiplexed seven segment display*

Display multiplexing is the process of using displays in such a way that the entire display is not on at the same time. What this means for seven segment displays is that only one digit is on at a time. However, the microcontroller switches between updating these two displays so quickly that users cannot detect it. In order to multiplex these displays, we use transistors to turn the displays on and off.

The major advantage of multiplexing is that it uses less I/O on the microcontroller. Let's look at how we can multiplex seven segment displays on the PIC16F1717 (see Listing 6-10).

Listing 6-10. PIC16F1717 Dual Seven Segment Display

```
/*
* File: Main.c
* Author: Armstrong Subero
* PIC: 16F1717 w/Int OSC @ 16MHz, 5v
* Program: IO2_Seven_Segment_Mul
* Compiler: XC8 (v1.38, MPLAX X v3.40)
* Program Version: 1.0
*
* Program Description: This Program Allows PIC16F1717 to drive dual
* multiplexed seven segment displays, it displays the
* numbers from 0 to 99 on the displays depending on
* which of two pushbuttons is pressed.
*
* Hardware Description: Dual seven segment displays of the
cathode variety is
* connected to port D of the microcontroller via 1k
* resistors. There are two transistors connected in
* common emitter configuration on pins RB0 and RB1
* respectively. There are also two pushbuttons connected
* to pins RC4 and RC5.
*
* Created February 16th, 2017, 9:55 PM
*/

/*************************************************************
****************
*Includes and defines
*************************************************************
**************/
```

```
#include "16F1717_Internal.h"
```

unsigned char Display(**unsigned char** digit);

```
// digit one enable
#define DIGITONE LATB0

// digit two enable
#define DIGITTWO LATB1

/****************************************************************
****************
* Function: void initMain()
*
* Returns: Nothing
*
* Description: Contains initializations for main
*
* Usage: initMain()
****************************************************************
**************/

void initMain(){
// Run at 16 MHz
internal_16();

// Set PORTD as output
// Analog disabled
TRISD = 0;
ANSELD = 0;

// Set PORTB as output
// Analog disabled
TRISB = 0;
ANSELB = 0;
```

```
// Set RC4 and RC5 as input
TRISCbits.TRISC4 = 1;
TRISCbits.TRISC5 = 1;

// Turn of analog on C
ANSELC = 0;

// Enable weak-pullups global
OPTION_REGbits.nWPUEN = 0;

// Enable weak-pullup on RC4 and RC5
WPUCbits.WPUC4 = 1;
WPUCbits.WPUC5 = 1;
}

/****************************************************************
****************
* Function: Main
*
* Returns: Nothing
*
* Description: Program entry point
****************************************************************
**************/

void main(void) {

// count variable
int count = 0;

// most significant digit
int MSD;

// least significant digit
int LSD;

initMain();
```

```
// Keep displaying digits 0-F
// and update it ever second
while(1){

// If RC4 pressed increment count
if(RC4 == 0){
__delay_ms(100);

if (RC4 == 0){
count++;
}
}

// IF RC5 pressed decrement count
if (RC5 == 0)
{
__delay_ms(100);

if(RC5 == 0){
count--;
}
}

// Get MSD and LSD
MSD = count/10;
LSD = count%10;

// Display MSD
LATD = Display(MSD);
DIGITTWO = 1;
__delay_ms(20);
DIGITTWO = 0;
```

```c
// Display LSD
LATD = Display(LSD);
DIGITONE = 1;
__delay_ms(20);
DIGITONE = 0;

// If value invalid set to 0
if (count > 99 || count < 0){
count = 0;
}

__delay_ms(1);
}

return;

}

/*************************************************************
*****************
* Function: unsigned char Display(unsigned char digit)
*
* Returns: unsigned char numbers
*
* Description: Function that takes a number and returns its
index in an array
* corresponding to the hexadecimal digit
*************************************************************
***************/

unsigned char Display(unsigned char digit)
{
// variable representing numbers
unsigned char numbers;
```

```
// an array of the digits 0-F
unsigned char DIGITS[] = {0x3F, 0x06, 0x5B, 0x4F, 0x66, 0x6D,
0x7D, 0x07, 0x7F, 0x6F, 0x77, 0x7C, 0x39, 0x5E, 0x79, 0x71};

// assign index given by user to variable
numbers = DIGITS[digit];

// return it
return numbers;
}
```

This program displays the Most Significant Digit (MSD) by dividing the current count by 10. The Least Significant Digit (LSD) is found by finding the modulo of the count and 10. Two pushbuttons are used to increment and decrement the count. If the user tries to enter a count of more than 99 or less than 0, the counter resets to 0. The program runs in a 1ms loop and slight jitter can be seen on the seven segment displays.

Project: Countdown Timer

Although we haven't covered much, we can still build a useful project. We will use the knowledge we have gained so far to make a basic countdown timer. The idea is to build a timer that can count down from a value of up to 99 seconds based on what is set by the user. We will use one button for incrementing the time, one for decrementing time, and another button to begin the countdown. The schematic for this circuit is shown in Figure 6-7 and the code is shown in Listing 6-11.

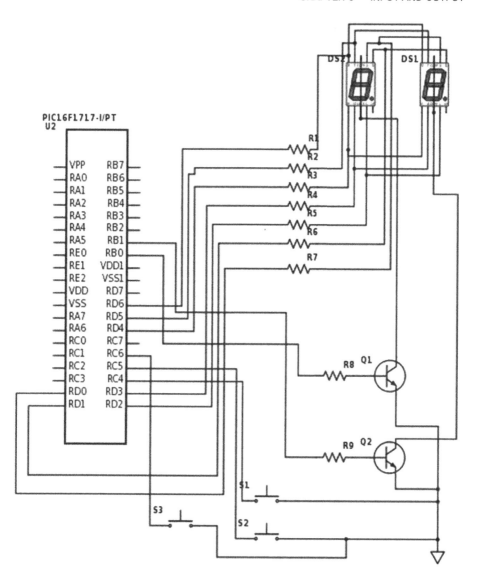

Figure 6-7. *PIC16F1717 countdown timer project schematic*

Listing 6-11. PIC16F1717 Countdown Timer Project Code

```
/*
* File: Main.c
* Author: Armstrong Subero
* PIC: 16F1717 w/Int OSC @ 16MHz, 5v
* Program: P01_Countdown_Timer
* Compiler: XC8 (v1.38, MPLAX X v3.40)
* Program Version: 1.0
*
* Program Description: This Program Allows PIC16F1717 to
countdown from a
* time of up to 99 seconds which is determined by the
* user.
*
* Hardware Description: Dual seven segment displays of the
cathode variety is
* connected to port D of the microcontroller via 1k
* resistors. There are two transistors connected in
* common emitter configuration on pins RB0 and RB1
* respectively. There are also two pushbuttons connected
* to pins RC4 and RC5 used for decrementing and
* incrementing. There is also a button connected to
* RC6 used to begin the countdown.
*
* Created February 16th, 2017, 11:16 PM
*/

/************************************************************
****************
*Includes and defines
*************************************************************
**************/
```

```c
#include "16F1717_Internal.h"

unsigned char display(unsigned char digit);
void countDown(unsigned char number);
void showNumber(unsigned char number);

// display port
#define DISPLAYPORT LATD

// digit one enable
#define DIGITONE LATB0

// digit two enable
#define DIGITTWO LATB1

/*************************************************************
****************
* Function: void initMain()
*
* Returns: Nothing
*
* Description: Contains initializations for main
*
* Usage: initMain()
*************************************************************
**************/

void initMain(){
// Run at 16 MHz
internal_16();

// Set PORTD as output
// Analog disabled
TRISD = 0;
ANSELD = 0;
```

```
// Set PORTB as output
// Analog disabled
TRISB = 0;
ANSELB = 0;

// Set RC4, RC5 and RC6 as input
TRISCbits.TRISC4 = 1;
TRISCbits.TRISC5 = 1;
TRISCbits.TRISC6 = 1;

// Turn of analog on C
ANSELC = 0;

// Enable weak-pullups global
OPTION_REGbits.nWPUEN = 0;

// Enable weak-pullup on RC4, RC5 and RC6
WPUCbits.WPUC4 = 1;
WPUCbits.WPUC5 = 1;
WPUCbits.WPUC6 = 1;
}

/***********************************************************
****************
* Function: Main
*
* Returns: Nothing
*
* Description: Program entry point
***********************************************************
**************/

void main(void) {
```

```
// count variable
unsigned char count = 0;

initMain();

while(1){

// If RC4 pressed increment count
if(RC4 == 0){
__delay_ms(100);

if (RC4 == 0){
count++;
}
}

// If RC5 pressed decrement count
if (RC5 == 0)
{
__delay_ms(100);

if(RC5 == 0){
count--;
}
}

// If RC6 pressed begin countdown
if (RC6 == 0)
{
__delay_ms(100);

if (RC6 == 0){
countDown(count);
}
}
```

```
// If value invalid set to 0
if (count > 99 || count < 0){
count = 0;
}

// show number on display
showNumber(count);

__delay_ms(1);
}

return;

}
/***************************************************************
****************
* Function: unsigned char Display(unsigned char digit)
*
* Returns: unsigned char numbers
*
* Description: Function that takes a number and returns its
index in an array
* corresponding to the hexadecimal digit
***************************************************************
**************/

unsigned char display(unsigned char digit)
{
// variable representing numbers
unsigned char numbers;

// an array of the digits 0-F
unsigned char DIGITS[] = {0x3F, 0x06, 0x5B, 0x4F, 0x66, 0x6D,
0x7D, 0x07,0x7F, 0x6F, 0x77, 0x7C, 0x39, 0x5E, 0x79, 0x71};
```

```
// assign index given by user to variable
numbers = DIGITS[digit];

// return it
return numbers;
}

/****************************************************************
****************
* Function: void countdown(unsigned char number)
*
* Returns: nothing
*
* Description: Begins a countdown based on number passed to
function
****************************************************************
**************/

void countDown(unsigned char number)
{
// loop counter
int i;

// begin countdown
for (i = number; i >= 0; i--)
{
showNumber(i);
__delay_ms(1000);
}

return;

}
```

```
/***********************************************************
****************
* Function: void shownumber(unsigned char number)
*
* Returns: nothing
*
* Description: Displays a number on the port specified
***********************************************************
**************/

void showNumber(unsigned char number)
{
// most significant digit
unsigned char MSD;

// least significant digit
unsigned char LSD;

// Get MSD and LSD
MSD = number/10;
LSD = number%10;

// Display MSD
DISPLAYPORT = display(MSD);
DIGITTWO = 1;
__delay_ms(20);
DIGITTWO = 0;

// Display LSD
DISPLAYPORT = display(LSD);
DIGITONE = 1;
__delay_ms(20);
DIGITONE = 0;

}
```

If we had covered interrupts and timers, this project would have been much more efficient and effective. Currently during the countdown, the displays flash every second. This is because, since we are using the delay function, for one second the microcontroller doesn't do anything. When you learn about timers in Chapter 8, you can revisit this project and use one of the onboard timer modules if you want.

Peripheral Pin Select

Though we will not use it in this chapter, let's take a quick look at the Peripheral Pin Select (PPS) module. On older PIC® microcontrollers, the I/O ports had fixed functions with regard to which peripherals were accessed by which pins. On newer PIC® microcontrollers, PPS was introduced to avoid this problem.

As you can see in Figure 6-8, the pins on the PIC16F1717 do not have a fixed peripheral input and output. This provides enormous possibilities with regard to board layout and circuit design. Previously to having PPS, designers had to design their circuit around the chip. While this may still be true today, the requirement is not as critical, as it is easier to adjust which pins on the chip you place your peripheral output or input. This also makes it possible to reconfigure which pins are accessed by the microcontroller at runtime and also allows an easier path to migration of legacy designs to newer ones. PPS is a very powerful feature.

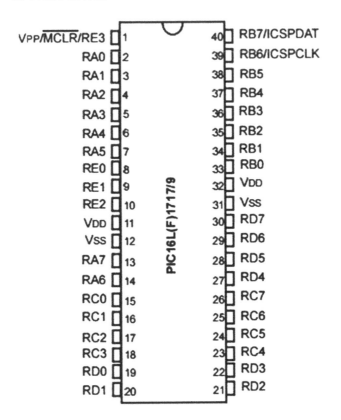

Figure 6-8. *PIC16F1717 pinout*

Conclusion

This chapter looked at how to use input and output on a PIC®
microcontroller while looking at its applications of driving LEDs, switches,
and seven segment displays. We covered display multiplexing and you saw
how to build a simple project using what you have learned so far.

CHAPTER 7

Interfacing Actuators

Introducing Actuators

So far, we have covered input and output on the PIC® microcontrollers. In this chapter, we apply the knowledge we learned thus far to control three common actuators in embedded systems—the DC motor, the stepper motor, and the servo motor. We incrementally examine these three actuators based on their ability to be controlled. We start with the DC motor, which has very coarse control of directionality (forward or backward) and is the easiest to control. Next, we look at the servo, which has a greater degree of ability to be controlled, in that it can be positioned in one of three angles. Finally, the stepper motor has the finest level of granularity with control being down to very specific degree size.

DC Motor

When introducing actuation into embedded systems, the three most common types of actuators are pneumatic, hydraulic, and electric. Of these three, electric-based actuation is the easiest and cheapest to design and prototype with. A wide spectrum of devices, from electronic locks to toy cars and robots, use electric motors. Before we look at using an electric motor, let's discuss it a bit. There are two types of electric motors. There are those that are powered by AC current and those that are DC powered. For the applications, we will look at the DC variety, specifically the brushed DC motor.

143

© Armstrong Subero 2018
A. Subero, *Programming PIC Microcontrollers with XC8*,
https://doi.org/10.1007/978-1-4842-3273-6_7

DC motors work on the principle of current flowing through a magnetic field, thereby creating a force. Electric motors are used to convert electrical energy into mechanical energy. DC motors contain two input terminals and applying a voltage across these terminals causes the motor shaft to spin. When positive voltage is applied, the motor spins in one direction; when negative voltage is applied, it spins in the other direction. In order to properly interface a DC motor to a microcontroller, we can use relays, MOSFETs, or transistors. The reason is simple:

> *If you connect a DC motor directly to the pin of your microcontroller, you will damage it!*

Mind you, PIC® microcontrollers are *very* difficult to destroy when compared to other microcontrollers. I have had PIC® microcontrollers that were smoking and then worked for years after the problem was fixed, and still work! However, to ensure that you have a happy PIC® microcontroller, do not connect the motor directly to an I/O pin.

The reason that you cannot connect a motor directly to a PIC® microcontroller is that an inductive load such as a motor requires a large amount of current. The I/O pins of a PIC® microcontroller are incapable of supplying the current required by the motor. In order to interface small DC motors, such as a small hobby motors or vibration motors commonly used for haptic feedback in embedded systems, I recommend using a simple transistor when prototyping. The reason is that when working with MOSFETs, extra precautions need to be taken to prevent static damage. So you can prototype with a transistor and use a MOSFET for your final design.

Figure 7-1 shows how you connect a DC motor to the microcontroller.

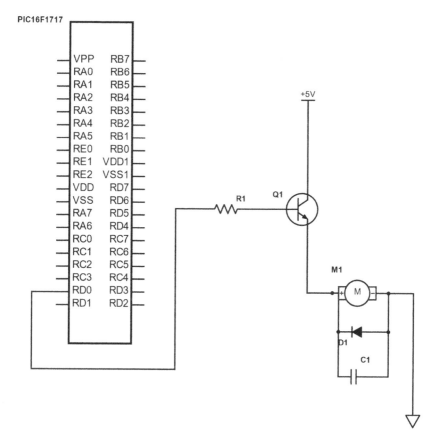

Figure 7-1. *Driving motor with PIC16F1717*

The value of the resistor, diode, and capacitors vary according to the size of the motor. For our purposes, the resistor can be 1k, the diode a standard 1N4001, and the capacitor a 0.1uF ceramic type. The transistor can be a 2n2222 or a 2n3904; however, almost any NPN transistor can be substituted. Be sure to consult the datasheet for your motor.

The code is rather simple, as shown in Listing 7-1.

145

Listing 7-1. PIC16F1717 Motor Control

```
/*
 * File: Main.c
 * Author: Armstrong Subero
 * PIC: 16F1717 w/Int OSC @ 16MHz, 5v
 * Program: 07_Motor
 * Compiler: XC8 (v1.38, MPLAX X v3.40)
 * Program Version: 1.0
 *
 *
 * Program Description: This Program Allows PIC16F1717 to Turn
 on a Motor
 *
 * Hardware Description: As per schematics
 *
 * Created November 4th, 2016, 1:00 PM
 */

/*****************************************************************
****************
*Includes and defines
*****************************************************************
**************/

#include "16F1717_Internal.h"

/*****************************************************************
****************
 * Function: void initMain()
 *
 * Returns: Nothing
 *
```

```
* Description: Contains initializations for main
*
* Usage: initMain()
****************************************************************
***************/

void initMain(){
// Run at 16 MHz
internal_16();

// Set PIN D0 as output
TRISDbits.TRISD0 = 0;

}
/****************************************************************
*******
* Function: Main
*
* Returns: Nothing
*
* Description: Program entry point
****************************************************************
******/

void main(void) {
    initMain();

  // Turn motor on for 5 seconds
    while(1){
        LATD0 = !LATD0;
        __delay_ms(5000);
    }

    return;
}
```

This should suffice for driving small motors for trivial applications. If we look at the code, the line that is responsible for actually turning the motor on is LATD0 = !LATD0. Just like in the LED program, this line drives the pin high for a period of five seconds, which turns the transistor on. When the while loop runs again, the pin outputs low, which turns the transistor off for a period of five seconds. You see even a simple application such as blinking an LED can be modified to perform other tasks in the real world. This is the power of microcontrollers. The five second on and off time is user determined and you may modify it as you see fit. If you want to have the motor turn in the other direction, you could do this by modifying the circuit and simply switching the terminals of the motor. To do so, connect the positive terminal to the ground and connect the negative terminal to the emitter of the transistor.

However, since we are using a microcontroller, I recommend that you use intelligent controls to modify the direction of the motor. In a later chapter, we will cover Pulse Width Modulation (PWM). In that same chapter, we will look at controlling a motor using the PWM on the PIC® microcontroller to control a motor driver.

Servo Motor

Now that you have a fair understanding of the DC motor, let's look at the servo motor. There are many different types and sizes of servos. There are AC servos typically used for industrial applications and DC servos commonly used for smaller applications. In fact, there are servos that are used exclusively for robots and are known as *robotic* servos. They have ridiculous torque for their size.

When we speak of *torque*, we are talking about the maximum force the servo can output. The servo typically has three wires. One wire is connected to power, the other to ground, and the last is known as the signal wire and is connected to the pin of the microcontroller. We will not go into the intricacies of the internals of how servo motors are constructed. For our purposes, all we need to know is that a servo contains control circuitry inside. Therefore, all we need to do is tell this control circuitry what position to move the servo motor to.

To tell the servo motor what position to go to, we send a pulse on the signal wire. According to the width of the pulse (essentially how long the pulse is high), the motor will turn to the desired location. A servo motor can either move to one of three angles—0 degrees, 90 degrees, or 180 degrees.

There is one exception to this, which is the continuous rotation servo. It can rotate a full 360 degrees.

The technique of varying the width of a pulse is known as *Pulse Width Modulation* and we will discuss it in later chapters. For now, just know that we control the servo by changing the duration of the pulse on its signal wire. For simple applications, I recommend metal servos, as they have more torque for their size and are more accurate and durable.

You connect the servo motor as shown in Figure 7-2.

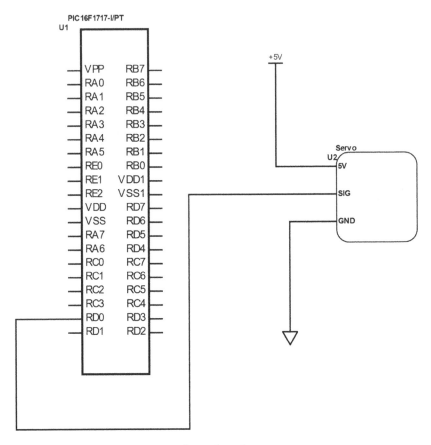

Figure 7-2. *Driving servo with PIC16F1717*

Create a file called Servo.h and use the code in Listing 7-2.

Listing 7-2. Servo Header File

```
/*
* File: Servo.h
* Author: Armstrong Subero
* PIC: 16F1717 w/Internal OSC @ 16MHz, 5v
* Program: Header file to control a standard servo
* Compiler: XC8 (v1.38, MPLAX X v3.40)
```

```
* Program Version 1.0
*
* Program Description: This program header will allow you
control a standard
* servo.
*
*
* Created on January 14th, 2017, 9:15 PM
*/

/***********************************************************
****************
*Includes and defines
***********************************************************
**************/
#include "16F1717_Internal.h"

void servoRotate0(); //0 Degree

void servoRotate90(); //90 Degree

void servoRotate180(); //180 Degree
```

Now you have to create a source file called Servo.c, which contains the code in Listing 7-3.

Listing 7-3. Servo Source File

```
/*
* File: Servo.c
* Author: Armstrong Subero
* PIC: 16F1717 w/Int OSC @ 16MHz, 5v
* Program: Library file to configure PIC16F1717
* Compiler: XC8 (v1.38, MPLAX X v3.40)
* Program Version: 1.0
*
```

151

```
* Program Description: This Library allows you to control a
standard servo
*
* Created on January 14th, 2017, 10:41 PM
*/

#include "16F1717_Internal.h"


/****************************************************************
****************
* Function: void servoRotate0()
*
* Returns: Nothing
*
* Description: Rotates servo to 0 degree position
*
*****************************************************************
***************/

void servoRotate0()
{
unsigned int i;
for(i=0;i<50;i++)
{
RD0 = 1;
__delay_us(700);
RD0 = 0;
__delay_us(19300);
}
}
```

```
/***************************************************************
****************
* Function: void servoRotate90()
*
* Returns: Nothing
*
* Description: Rotates servo to 90 degree position
*
*****************************************************************
***************/

void servoRotate90() //90 Degree
{
unsigned int i;
for(i=0;i<50;i++)
{
RD0 = 1;
__delay_us(1700);
RD0 = 0;
__delay_us(18300);
}
}

/***************************************************************
****************
* Function: void servoRotate90()
*
* Returns: Nothing
*
* Description: Rotates servo to 180 degree position
*
*****************************************************************
***************/
```

```c
void servoRotate180() //180 Degree
{
unsigned int i;
for(i=0;i<50;i++)
{
RD0 = 1;
__delay_us(2600);
RD0 = 0;
__delay_us(17400);
}
```

Listing 7-4 provides the main code.

Listing 7-4. Servo Main File

```c
/*
 * File: Main.c
 * Author: Armstrong Subero
 * PIC: 16F1717 w/Internal OSC @ 16MHz, 5v
 * Program: I02_Servo_Motor
 * Compiler: XC8 (v1.38, MPLAX X v3.40)
 * Program Version: 1.0
 *
 *
 * Program Description: This demonstrates using a servo on a pic
 microcontroller
 *
 * Hardware Description: A MG90s microservo is connected to PIN
 RD0
 *
 * Created January 14th, 2017, 10:30 PM
 */
```

```
/******************************************************************
****************
*Includes and defines
******************************************************************
**************/

#include "16F1717_Internal.h"
#include "Servo.h"

******************************************************************
***************
* Function: void initMain()
*
* Returns: Nothing
*
* Description: Contains initializations for main
*
* Usage: initMain()
******************************************************************
**************/

void initMain(){
// Run at 16 MHz
internal_16();

////////////////////
// Configure Ports
////////////////////

// Make DO Output
TRISDbits.TRISD0 = 0;

// Turn off analog
ANSELD = 0;

}
```

```
/*************************************************************
****************
* Function: Main
*
* Returns: Nothing
*
* Description: Program entry point
*************************************************************
**************/

void main(void) {
initMain();

// Rotate servo 0 - 90 - 180
while(1){

servoRotate0();
servoRotate90();
servoRotate180();

return;
}
}
```

Once all goes well, the servo shaft will move along a 180-degree arc at 90-degree increments, starting at 0 degrees.

One caveat I should mention about actually using servo motors is that if you buy the cheap variety, or even the high-quality plastic ones, they may not actually start at 0 degrees and end at 180 degrees.

Stepper Motor

The stepper motor is the next topic of our actuator trio. Stepper motors are crucial to industrial applications and robotics. Stepper motors are used in many devices, including printers and CNC control, where very precise and controlled movement is needed.

The stepper motor has multiple coils which, when organized together, are called *phases*. Each phase is turned on sequentially, causing the stepper motor to rotate. The distance between each step is known as the *step angle*. Two major windings exist for the coils of the stepper motor. One is known as the *unipolar* and the other as the *bipolar*. The basic difference between the two is that, in the unipolar stepper motor, there is coil with a center tap per phase, whereas a bipolar motor has one winding per phase. In this book, we focus on the unipolar variety.

There are three main ways to drive a stepper motor. There is the wave drive, the full-step drive, and the half-step drive.

In the wave drive mode, only a single phase is activated at a time. This results in the wave drive mode using less power than other modes, but at the cost of loss of torque. The half-step drive mode alternates between two phases on and a single phase on. This increases angular resolution but lowers the torque. The full-step drive mode allows for two phases to be on at a time, thus allowing for maximum torque.

Thus, when designing with stepper motors, there is a tradeoff between torque, power consumption, and angular resolution.

The popular method for driving stepper motors though is to use the full-step drive mode; therefore, this is the method we will use in this book. In order to drive the stepper motor, we must use a driver to give the stepper motor the power it needs. For small stepper motors, you can use H-bridges or Darlington transistor arrays. We will use the Darlington array since from my experience they are simpler to use.

The IC we will use that contains these packages is the ULN2003A. The ULN2003A contains seven Darlington pairs and will be adequate for our purposes. The ULN2003A includes fly back diodes and can work up to 50V with a single output providing 500mA. These specifications make it a popular choice for driving small stepper motors. The motor we will use in this example is a four-phase unipolar stepper motor rated at 5v. The motor also has a holding torque of 110g-cm and a step angle of 7.5 degrees and requires a current of 500mA. Motors with similar specifications can be purchased from a variety of online suppliers; just ensure you buy one where the datasheet is easily accessible; otherwise, you may not know which wire does what. The circuit in Figure 7-3 indicates how you connect a stepper motor to the microcontroller.

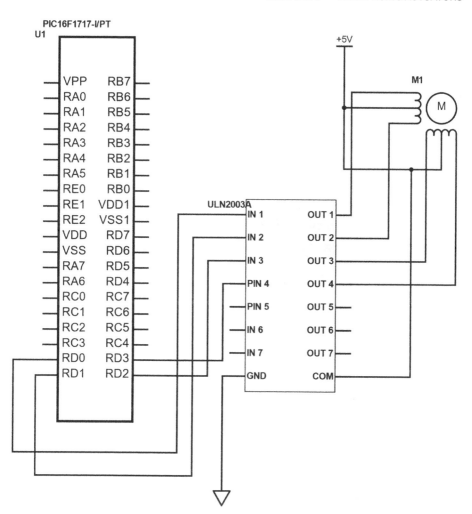

Figure 7-3. *Stepper Motor Connection*

The code in Listing 7-5 is rather straightforward and drives the stepper in full-step mode.

Listing 7-5. Stepper Main File

```
/*
* File: Main.c
* Author: Armstrong Subero
* PIC: 16F1717 w/Internal OSC @ 16MHz, 5v
* Program: IO3_Servo_Motor
* Compiler: XC8 (v1.38, MPLAX X v3.40)
* Program Version: 1.0
*
*
* Program Description: This demonstrates using a unipolar
stepper motor with a
* pic microcontroller.
*
* Hardware Description: A Sinotech 25BY4801 4 phase unipolar
stepper motor
* is connected to PORT D of the microcontroller with a
* ULN2003A darlington transistor array used as a driver
* for the stepper motor.
*
* Connections are as follows:
*
* The ULN2003A is connected to the microcontroller as
* shown below:
*
* IN1 --> RD0
* IN2 --> RD1
* IN3 --> RD2
```

```
* IN4 --> RD3
*
* The Stepper motor is connected to the ULN2003A as
* follows:
*
* White = OUT1
* Black = OUT2
* Red = OUT3
* Yellow = OUT4
*
* Created January 15th, 2017, 12:05 AM
*/

/***************************************************************
****************
*Includes and defines
*****************************************************************
**************/

#include "16F1717_Internal.h"


/***************************************************************
****************
* Function: void initMain()
*
* Returns: Nothing
*
* Description: Contains initializations for main
*
* Usage: initMain()
*****************************************************************
**************/
```

```
void initMain(){
// Run at 16 MHz
internal_16();

////////////////////
// Configure Ports
////////////////////

// Make DO Output
TRISD = 0;

// Turn off analog
ANSELD = 0;

}


/***********************************************************
****************
* Function: Main
*
* Returns: Nothing
*
* Description: Program entry point
************************************************************
**************/
void main(void) {
initMain();

while(1){
LATD = 0b00001001; // Step 1
__delay_ms(500);
LATD = 0b00000101; // Step 2
__delay_ms(500);
```

```
LATD = 0b00000110; // Step 3
  __delay_ms(500);
LATD = 0b00001010; // Step 4
  __delay_ms(500);
}
return;
}
```

If you look in the main while loop in Listing 7-5, you'll notice that the lower four bits of PORTD keep changing. In case you are wondering what is going on here, here is how it works. Remember we said that in full-drive step mode, the motor turns on two phases at a time? Well, if you revisit the schematic in Figure 7-3, you will notice that each phase of the stepper motor is connected to a pin of the microcontroller. Now I mentioned that the coils are center tapped in the unipolar variety stepper motor and, if you look at your schematic, this is shown in Figure 7-3. Therefore, two phases need to be turned on at a time, since in actuality current only flows in half the winding of the stepper motor at a time. Thus, if you look at the code, you will notice that two output pins are high at a time. This ensures that by energizing half windings of the two coils within the stepper motor alternately, you get the full 360 degree rotation of the motor.

If you are still having trouble understanding how this works, there are excellent resources on the web that go in-depth into the intricacies of the operation of stepper motors. In this book, however, you can safely ignore all the details of operation. As long as you verify with your datasheet that you have connected the stepper motor as shown in Figure 7-3, this code will work with unipolar stepper motors of any size.

Do not worry if your stepper motor runs hot. Stepper motors use a lot of current, and they use the same amount of current when they are stationary and running, so do not panic; this is completely normal.

Conclusion

This chapter looked at interfacing actuators to the PIC® microcontroller, including DC motors, stepper motors, and servo motors. These form the foundation for applications of PIC® microcontrollers in areas such as robotics and motor control.

CHAPTER 8

Interrupts, Timers, Counters, and PWM

Introduction to Interrupts

Interrupts are one of the simplest concepts related to microcontrollers. Let me explain interrupts as simply as possible by referring to everyday life. Imagine that you need to wake up at 6:00 am. There are two ways to know when you have to wake up. One way is to keep checking the clock until it's 6:00. However, if you do that, then you will not be able to focus on the task at hand, which is getting sleep. The other thing you can do is set your clock to alarm to alert you that it's 6:00. In both scenarios, you will be aware of when it's 6:00; however, the second method is more effective as you can focus on the task at hand, which is getting sleep.

Taking this analogy back to microcontrollers, the first method of continually checking your clock is the *polling method*. The second method of the clock alerting you when the time has reached is the *interrupt method*. Interrupts are assigned priorities. For example, if you are on the phone with someone and your significant other calls you, you could interrupt your call, speak with your significant other, and then resume your call. This is because your significant other is more important to you and is therefore assigned a greater priority.

165

© Armstrong Subero 2018
A. Subero, *Programming PIC Microcontrollers with XC8*,
https://doi.org/10.1007/978-1-4842-3273-6_8

In the same way, the microcontroller assigns priorities to each interrupt. An interrupt with a higher priority takes precedence over a lower priority one. The microcontroller can also mask an interrupt, which is the name given to the way a microcontroller ignores a particular interrupt call for service.

The interrupt service routine, also known as the *interrupt handler,* is essentially the piece of code that the microcontroller executes when an interrupt is invoked. The time the microcontroller takes to respond to the interrupt and begin executing its code is known as the *interrupt latency.* For the PIC16F1717, the interrupt latency is between three to five instruction cycles.

The interrupt could have many sources, that is to say things that can cause the CPU to be interrupted, and this can include timers and other onboard peripherals, even an external pin.

Now I could go into a lot of details of how interrupts work. There is a lot of information written about that and you will find a lot of resources on the Internet if you're interested. In this book, I take a pragmatic approach. Let's look at the interrupt in action, shown in Listing 8-1. In this case, we look at the external interrupt as use a pushbutton to trigger an interrupt (see Figure 8-1).

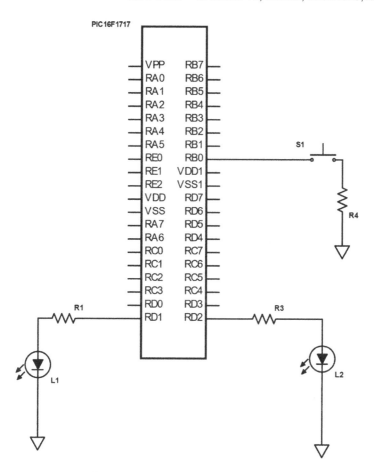

Figure 8-1. *External interrupt circuit*

Listing 8-1. External Interrupt Code

```
/*
* Fle: Main.c
* Author: Armstrong Subero
* PIC: 16F1717 w/Int OSC @ 16MHz, 5v
* Program: 07_Interrupt_External
* Compiler: XC8 (v1.38, MPLAX X v3.40)
```

```
* Program Version: 1.0
*
*
* Program Description: This Program Allows PIC16F1717 to toggle
an LED based
* on the state of a pushbutton interrupt
*
* Hardware Description: An LED is connected via a 10k resistor
to PIN D1 and
* another LED is connected to PIN D2 and a switch is
* connected to PIN B0
*
* Created November 4th, 2016, 8:10 PM
*/

/***************************************************************
****************
*Includes and defines
****************************************************************
**************/

#include "16F1717_Internal.h"

/***************************************************************
****************
* Function: void initMain()
*
* Returns: Nothing
*
* Description: Contains initializations for main
*
* Usage: initMain()
```

```
*****************************************************************
**************/

void initMain(){
// Run at 16 MHz
internal_16();

//////////////////////////
/// Configure Ports
//////////////////////////

// Set PIN D1 and D2 as output
TRISDbits.TRISD1 = 0;
TRISDbits.TRISD2 = 0;

// Turn off LED
LATDbits.LATD1 = 0;

// Set PIN B0 as input
TRISBbits.TRISB0 = 1;

// Configure ANSELB0
ANSELBbits.ANSB0 = 0;

// unlock PPS
PPSLOCK = 0x55;
PPSLOCK = 0xAA;
PPSLOCK = 0x00;

// Enable weak-pullups global
OPTION_REGbits.nWPUEN = 0;

// Enable weak-pullup on PINB0
WPUBbits.WPUB0 = 1;

//////////////////////////
```

```
/// Configure Interrupts
////////////////////////

// Set Interrupt pin to pin B0
INTPPSbits.INTPPS = 0b01000;

// lock    PPS
PPSLOCK = 0x55;
PPSLOCK = 0xAA;
PPSLOCK = 0x01;

// Trigger on falling edge
OPTION_REGbits.INTEDG = 0;

// Clear external interrupt flag
INTCONbits.INTF = 0;

//  Enable external interrupt
INTCONbits.INTE = 1;

// Enable global interrupt
ei();
}

/*************************************************************
****************
* Function: Main
*
* Returns: Nothing
*
* Description: Program entry point
*************************************************************
**************/

void main(void) {
initMain();
```

```
while(1){
LATDbits.LATD1 = ~LATDbits.LATD1;
__delay_ms(500);
}

return;

}


/****************************************************************
****************
* Function: void interrupt isr(void)
*
* Returns: Nothing
*
* Description: Interrupt triggered on pushbutton press
****************************************************************
**************/

void interrupt isr(void){
// Clear interrupt flag
INTCONbits.INTF = 0;

// Toggle led
LATDbits.LATD2 = ~LATDbits.LATD2;
}
```

Now that you have a fair understanding of how external interrupts work, we can move on to an interrupt being triggered by some internal mechanism. In this case, we will use an onboard timer to trigger the interrupt. However, we must first look at the operation of timers.

Using Timers

A *timer* on a microcontroller can count either regular clock pulses (thus making it a timer) or it can count irregular clock pulses (in this mode it is a counter). The PIC16F1717 has five timers. These are Timer 0, Timer 1, and Timers 2, 4, and 6. The timer we will use is Timer 0. We will use this timer because it is ubiquitous among 8-bit PIC® microcontrollers. Since timers can also be used as counters, we sometimes refer to them as *timer/ counters*.

The timer needs a clock pulse to tick. This clock source can either be internal or external to the microcontroller. When we feed internal clock pulses, the timer/counter is in timer mode. However, when we use an external clock pulse, the timer is in counter mode. Timer 0 on the PIC16F1717 can be used as an 8-bit timer/counter.

A Timer 0 will increment every instruction cycle unless a prescaler is used. The prescaler is responsible for slowing down the rate at which Timer 0 counts. The timer has a software selectable prescale value and has eight values from 2-256.

Timer 0 in Timer Mode

We first look at using Timer 0 in timer mode. In order to use the timer, some housekeeping needs to be done. In this mode, we need to clear the TMR0CS bit of the option register. We will then assign a prescaler and to do so, we need to clear the PSA bit of the option register. In this example, we use Timer 0 to flash an LED at precisely 1Hz. To do so, connect the LED to the microcontroller, as shown in Figure 8-2 with RD1 connected to the LED via a 1k resistor.

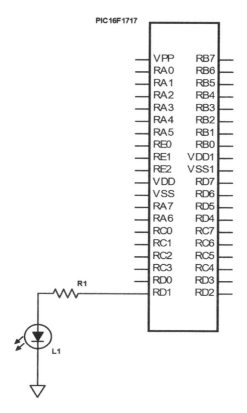

Figure 8-2. *Precise LED Flash circuit*

Listing 8-2 shows the main code.

Listing 8-2. Timer 0 Timer Mode

```
/*
* File: Main.c
* Author: Armstrong Subero
* PIC: 16F1717 w/Int OSC @ 16MHz, 5v
* Program: 04_Timer0
* Compiler: XC8 (v1.38, MPLAX X v3.40)
* Program Version: 1.0
*
*
```

```
* Program Description: This Program Allows PIC16F1717 to flash
an LED at 1 Hz
* on Timer0 overflow
*
* Hardware Description: An LED is connected via a 10k resistor
to PIN D1
*
* Created November 4th, 2016, 4:14 PM
*/

/*************************************************************
****************
*Includes and defines
*************************************************************
**************/

#include "16F1717_Internal.h"

// Counter variable
int count = 0;

/*************************************************************
****************
* Function: void initMain()
*
* Returns: Nothing
*
* Description: Contains initializations for main
*
* Usage: initMain()
*************************************************************
**************/
```

```
void initMain(){
// Run at 16 MHz
internal_16();

////////////////////////
/// Configure Ports
////////////////////////

// Set PIN D1 as output
TRISDbits.TRISD1 = 0;

// Turn off LED
LATDbits.LATD1 = 0;

// Set PIN B0 as input
TRISBbits.TRISB0 = 1;

// Configure ANSELB0
ANSELBbits.ANSB0 = 0;

////////////////////////
/// Configure Timer0
////////////////////////

// Select timer mode
OPTION_REGbits.TMR0CS = 0;

// Assign Prescaler to TIMER0
OPTION_REGbits.PSA = 0;

// Set Prescaler to 256
OPTION_REGbits.PS0 = 1;
OPTION_REGbits.PS1 = 1;
OPTION_REGbits.PS2 = 1;
```

```
// Zero Timer
TMRO = 0;
}

/************************************************************
****************
* Function: Main
*
* Returns: Nothing
*
* Description: Program entry point
************************************************************
**************/

void main(void) {
initMain();

while(1){

// When timer overflows TMRO interrupt flag will be equal to 1
while (INTCONbits.TMROIF != 1);

// Reset flag after overflow
INTCONbits.TMROIF = 0;

// Increment count
count++;

// Value = fclk / (4 * 256 * 256 * fout)
//|-- Frequency out (in Hz)
//|-- Prescaler value
// Value =  16 000 000 / (262 144)
// Value =61.04 for 1 s
```

```
// Turn on LED for 1 second on timer overflow
if (count == 61){
LATDbits.LATD1 = 1;
count = 0;
}

// Else turn LED off
else {
LATDbits.LATD1 = 0;
}

}

return;
}
```

Timer 0 in Counter Mode

Now we look at using the timer in counter mode. In order to use the timer in counter mode, we need to set the TMR0CS bit of the option register. The steps for assigning the prescaler are the same as for a timer. This code also is the first in the book to utilize the PPS. The PPS in this case is used to designate which pin will be used to count the external clock pulses. The sequence for assigning a peripheral to a pin using PPS is as follows:

1. Unlock the PPS.

2. Assign the peripheral to the pins.

3. Lock the PPS.

You must follow these steps to correctly use the PPS. The global interrupt enable must be configured appropriately, as is shown in the code in Listing 8-3. There is also a function to read Timer 0. When the counter on Timer 0 reaches a particular value, the LED is turned on.

The connections are very simple, as shown in the schematic in Figure 8-3.

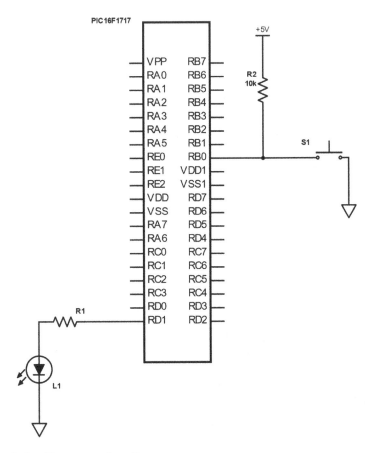

Figure 8-3. *Counter circuit*

Listing 8-3 provides the code.

Listing 8-3. Timer 0 Counter Mode

```
/*
* File: Main.c
* Author: Armstrong Subero
* PIC: 16F1717 w/Int OSC @ 16MHz, 5v
```

```
* Program: 05_Counter
* Compiler: XC8 (v1.38, MPLAX X v3.40)
* Program Version: 1.0
*
*
* Program Description: This Program Allows PIC16F1717 to turn
on an LED after
* the counter module on Time0 reaches a specified value
* which is detected from external pulses given via a
* switch on RB0.
*
* Hardware Description: An LED is connected via a 1k resistor
to pin RD1 and
* a switch is connected to pin RB0
*
* Created February 23rd, 2017, 5:22 PM
*/

/************************************************************
****************
*Includes and defines
************************************************************
**************/

#include "16F1717_Internal.h"

/************************************************************
***************
* Function: void initMain()
*
* Returns: Nothing
*
```

```
* Description: Contains initializations for main
*
* Usage: initMain()
**************************************************************
**************/

void initMain(){
// Run at 16 MHz
internal_16();

////////////////////////
/// Configure Ports
////////////////////////

// Set PIN D1 as output
TRISDbits.TRISD1 = 0;

// Turn off LED
LATDbits.LATD1 = 0;

// Set PIN B0 as input
TRISBbits.TRISB0 = 1;

// Configure ANSELB0
ANSELBbits.ANSB0 = 0;

////////////////////////
/// Configure Timer0
////////////////////////

// Select counter mode
OPTION_REGbits.TMR0CS = 1;

// Assign Prescaler to TIMER0
OPTION_REGbits.PSA = 1;
```

```
bool state = GIE;
GIE = 0;
PPSLOCK = 0x55;
PPSLOCK = 0xAA;
PPSLOCKbits.PPSLOCKED = 0x00; // unlock PPS

TOCKIPPSbits.TOCKIPPS = 0x08;   //RB0->TMR0:TOCKI;

PPSLOCK = 0x55;
PPSLOCK = 0xAA;
PPSLOCKbits.PPSLOCKED = 0x01; // lock PPS

GIE = state;

// Zero Timer
TMR0 = 0;

// Enable timer0 interrupts and clear interrupt flag
INTCONbits.TMR0IE = 1;
INTCONbits.TMR0IF = 0;
}

/****************************************************************
****************
* Function: int ReadTimer(void)
*
* Returns: int readVal;
*
* Description: Returns the value of Timer0
*
* Usage: int x;
****************************************************************
**************/
```

```c
uint8_t ReadTimer0(void)
{
// Read value variable
uint8_t readVal;

// Set variable to timer0 value
readVal = TMR0;

// return value
return readVal;
}
/*****************************************************************
****************
* Function: Main
*
* Returns: Nothing
*
* Description: Program entry point
*****************************************************************
**************/

void main(void) {
initMain();

// count variable
uint8_t count;

while(1){

// read timer with count
count = ReadTimer0();

// if counter has value of 5
if (count == 5){
```

```
// turn LED on
LATDbits.LATD1 = 1;

// short delay to see LED on
__delay_ms(2000);

// zero timer
TMR0 = 0;
}

else
{
// keep LED off
LATDbits.LATD1 = 0;
}
}

return;
}
```

Timer 0 with Interrupts

Now we look at using Timer 0 with interrupts. The code is very simple if you have been following along up to this point, and we will use it to blink an LED every second while simultaneously responding to the pushbutton to toggle another LED. This example demonstrates an important application of interrupts, performing an action in a very deterministic manner.

The circuit is shown in Figure 8-4.

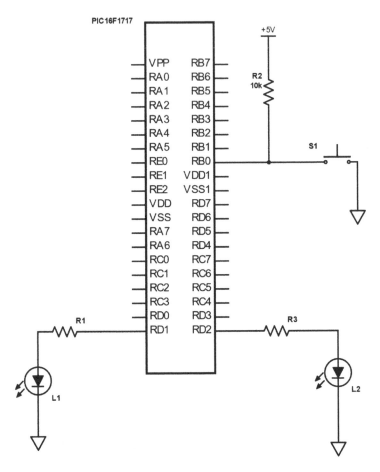

Figure 8-4. *Timer interrupt circuit*

Listing 8-4 provides the code.

Listing 8-4. Timer 0 with Interrupt

```
/*
* File: Main.c
* Author: Armstrong Subero
* PIC: 16F1717 w/Int OSC @ 16MHz, 5v
* Program: 06_Interrupts
```

```
* Compiler: XC8 (v1.38, MPLAX X v3.40)
* Program Version: 1.0
*
*
* Program Description: This Program Allows PIC16F1717 flash an
LED at a rate
* of 1 Hz while responding to a pushbutton input using
* a timer0 interrupt
*
*
* Hardware Description: An LED is connected via a 1k resistor
to PIN D1 and
* another LED connected to PIN D2 switch is connected
* to PIN B0
*
* Created November 4th, 2016, 7:15 PM
*/

/****************************************************************
****************
*Includes and defines
****************************************************************
**************/

#include "16F1717_Internal.h"

/****************************************************************
****************
* Function: void initMain()
*
* Returns: Nothing
*
```

```
* Description: Contains initializations for main
*
* Usage: initMain()
************************************************************
**************/

void initMain(){
/////////////////////
// Configure Ports
/////////////////////

// Run at 16 MHz
internal_16();

// Set PIN D1, D2 as output
TRISDbits.TRISD1 = 0;
TRISDbits.TRISD2 = 0;

// Turn off LED
LATDbits.LATD1 = 0;

// Set PIN B0 as input
TRISBbits.TRISB0 = 1;

// Configure ANSELB0
ANSELBbits.ANSB0 = 0;

/////////////////////
// Configure Timer0
/////////////////////

// Select timer mode
OPTION_REGbits.TMR0CS = 0;

// Assign Prescaler to TIMER0
OPTION_REGbits.PSA = 0;
```

```c
// Set Prescaler to 256
OPTION_REGbits.PS = 0b111;

// enable Timer0 interrupt
INTCONbits.TMR0IE = 1;

// enable global interrupts
ei();
}

/***************************************************************
****************
* Function: Main
*
* Returns: Nothing
*
* Description: Program entry point
****************************************************************
**************/

void main(void) {
initMain();

while(1){
// Toggle LED on PUSH Button
LATDbits.LATD1 = ~PORTBbits.RB0;
}

return;
}

/***************************************************************
****************
* Function: void interrupt isr(void)
*
```

```
* Returns: Nothing
*
* Description: Timer0 interrupt at a rate of 1 second
**************************************************************
**************/

void interrupt isr(void)
{
static int count = 0;

// Reset flag after overflow
INTCONbits.TMR0IF = 0;

TMR0 = 0;

// Increment count
count++;

// Value = fclk / (4 * 256 * 256 * fout)
// |-- Frequency out (in Hz)
// |-- Prescaler value
// Value =  16 000 000 / (262 144)
// Value =  61.04 for 1 s

// Turn on LED for 1 second on timer overflow
if (count == 61){
LATDbits.LATD2 = 1;
count = 0;
}

// Else keep LED off
else {
LATDbits.LATD2 = 0;
}

}
```

Using the CCP Module

The PIC16F1717 comes with onboard Capture/Compare/PWM (CCP) modules. The capture mode times the duration of an event. The compare mode triggers an external event after a certain amount of time has passed. We will focus on the PWM. If you need to utilize capture or compare functions, consult the datasheet.

In the last chapter, we briefly examined using PWM for controlling a servo. In this section, we look at using PWM with dedicated hardware.

Understanding PWM

Pulse Width Modulation (PWM) describes a type of signal that can be produced by a microcontroller. However, in order to understand PWM, we must first understand the concept of the duty cycle. A digital signal can be 5v (high) or 0v (low). The amount of time a signal is high is described as the duty cycle of that signal. This is expressed as a percentage. For example, if during a given period of time, a signal is high half of the time and low the other half, it will have a duty cycle of 50%.

Using PWM

Let's look at using the PWM on the CCP module. A timer is required to use the PWM module. Since Timer 0 is used for so many things, we will use Timer 6 to be the PWM timer.

The PWM module is very important and has a lot of uses. The most popular uses are for light dimming, motor speed control, and generating a modulated signal. In this example, we will use the PWM module to dim an LED. We will run the LED at 50% duty cycle.

Figure 8-5 shows the circuit.

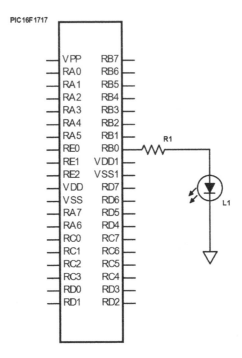

Figure 8-5. *PWM circuit*

The code is shown in Listing 8-5.

Listing 8-5. CCP PWM

```
/*
* File: Main.c
* Author: Armstrong Subero
* PIC: 16F1717 w/Int OSC @ 16MHz, 5v
* Program: 20_PWM
* Compiler: XC8 (v1.38, MPLAX X v3.40)
* Program Version: 1.0
*
*
```

```
* Program Description: This Program uses the PWM module of the
PIC16F1717
*
*
* Hardware Description: An LED is connected to PINB0
*
* Created November 7th, 2016, 5:20 PM
*/

/**************************************************************
****************
*Includes and defines
***************************************************************
**************/

#include "16F1717_Internal.h"


/**************************************************************
****************
* Function: void initMain()
*
* Returns: Nothing
*
* Description: Contains initializations for main
*
* Usage: initMain()
***************************************************************
**************/

void initMain(){
// Run at 16 MHz
internal_16();
```

```
// Setup PINB0 as output
TRISBbits.TRISB0 = 0;

/////////////////////
// Configure Timer6
/////////////////////

// Select PWM timer as Timer6
CCPTMRSbits.C1TSEL = 0b10;

// Enable timer Increments every 250 ns (16MHz clock) 1000/
(16/4)
// Period = 256 x 0.25 us = 64 us

// Crystal Frequency
// PWM Freq  = ------------------------------------------
// (PRX + 1) * (TimerX Prescaler) * 4

//PWM Frequency = 16 000 000 / 256 * 1 * 4
//PWM Frequency = 15.625 kHz

// Prescale = 1
T6CONbits.T6CKPS = 0b00;

// Enable Timer6
T6CONbits.TMR6ON = 1;

// Set timer period
PR6 = 255;

// Configure CCP1

// LSB's of PWM duty cycle = 00
CCP1CONbits.DC1B = 00;

// Select PWM mode
CCP1CONbits.CCP1M = 0b1100;
```

192

```
PPSLOCK = 0x55;
PPSLOCK = 0xAA;
PPSLOCKbits.PPSLOCKED = 0x00; // unlock PPS

// Set RB0 to PWM1
RB0PPSbits.RB0PPS = 0b01100;

PPSLOCK = 0x55;
PPSLOCK = 0xAA;
PPSLOCKbits.PPSLOCKED = 0x01; // lock PPS
}

/****************************************************************
****************
* Function: Main
*
* Returns: Nothing
*
* Description: Program entry point
****************************************************************
**************/

void main(void) {
initMain();

while(1){
// Run at 50% duty cycle @ 15.625 kHz
CCPR1L = 127;
}

return;
}
```

The code also contains a formula for calculating the frequency of the PWM module, which is important for applications such as motor control.

Project: Using PWM with a Motor Driver

In the previous chapter on interfacing actuators, we looked at a simple way of driving a motor. In this section, we look at the typical way of driving a motor, which is to use a dedicated motor driver, IC. Using a dedicated IC allows us to easily control the speed and direction of the motor and offers better general control of the motor.

The motor driver that we will use is the common SN754410, which has two H-Bridges onboard and can handle up to 36 volts at 1A per driver. In addition to having decent specs, this driver is also low cost, which makes it an attractive option for general-purpose applications.

When teaching someone to do something the first time, it is nice to provide a lot of hand-holding. After all, beginners need a lot of hand-holding to properly understand concepts. In this project, however, I let you do a little research to complete it. I provide the connections in the text as well as in the code, and your job is to connect the motor driver and motor to the microcontroller without a schematic. Think you can handle that? Let's begin!

The motor is connected as follows:

- 1: Enables motor one, connect to 5v

- 2: Connects to forward PWM channel (motor 1)

- 3: Motor 1 +

- 4-5: GND

- 6: Motor 1

- 7: Connects to reverse PWM channel (motor 1)

- 8: +VE Motor Power In

- 12-13: GND

- 16: 5v

We will run the motor for five seconds in one direction, turn it off for two seconds, and then run it again for five seconds in the other direction.

The code is provided in Listing 8-6.

Listing 8-6. PWM Motor

```
/*
* File: Main.c
* Author: Armstrong Subero
* PIC: 16F1717 w/Internal OSC @ 16MHz, 5v
* Program: I04_H_Bridge
* Compiler: XC8 (v1.38, MPLAX X v3.40)
* Program Version: 1.0
*
*
* Program Description: This demonstrates using a SN754410
H-Bridge with a
* DC motor with a PIC microcontroller.
*
* Hardware Description: A generic brushed hobby DC motor is
connected to the
* SN754410 as per standard connections. The PWM signals
* are emanating from RB0 and RB1 for forward and reverse
* signals respectively.
*
*
* Created January 15th, 2017, 11:36 AM
*/
```

```
/************************************************************
****************
*Includes and defines
************************************************************
**************/
```

```
#include "16F1717_Internal.h"
```

```
/************************************************************
****************
* Function: void initMain()
*
* Returns: Nothing
*
* Description: Contains initializations for main
*
* Usage: initMain()
************************************************************
**************/
```

```
void initMain(){
// Run at 16 MHz
internal_16();

/////////////////////
// Configure Ports
/////////////////////

// Set PIN B0 as output
TRISBbits.TRISB0 = 0;

// Set PIN B1 as output
TRISBbits.TRISB1 = 0;
```

```
// Turn off analog
ANSELB = 0;

/////////////////////
// Configure Timer6
/////////////////////

// Select PWM timer as Timer6 for CCP1 and CCP2
CCPTMRSbits.C1TSEL = 0b10;
CCPTMRSbits.C2TSEL = 0b10;

// Enable timer Increments every 250 ns (16MHz clock) 1000/
(16/4)
// Period = 256 x 0.25 us = 64 us

// Crystal Frequency
//PWM Freq   = ----------------------------------------
//(PRX + 1) * (TimerX Prescaler) * 4

//PWM Frequency = 16 000 000 / 256 * 1 * 4
//PWM Frequency = 15.625 kHz

// Prescale = 1
T6CONbits.T6CKPS = 0b00;

// Enable Timer6
T6CONbits.TMR6ON = 1;

// Set timer period
PR6 = 255;

//////////////////////////
// Configure PWM
//////////////////////////

// Configure CCP1
```

```
// LSB's of PWM duty cycle = 00
CCP1CONbits.DC1B = 00;

// Select PWM mode
CCP1CONbits.CCP1M = 0b1100;

// Configure CCP2

// LSB's of PWM duty cycle = 00
CCP2CONbits.DC2B = 00;

// Select PWM mode
CCP2CONbits.CCP2M = 0b1100;

/////////////////////////////
// Configure PPS
/////////////////////////////

PPSLOCK = 0x55;
PPSLOCK = 0xAA;
PPSLOCKbits.PPSLOCKED = 0x00; // unlock PPS

// Set RB0 to PWM1
RB0PPSbits.RB0PPS = 0b01100;

// Set RB1 to PWM2
RB1PPSbits.RB1PPS = 0b01101;

PPSLOCK = 0x55;
PPSLOCK = 0xAA;
PPSLOCKbits.PPSLOCKED = 0x01; // lock PPS

}
```

198

```
/*********************************************************
****************
* Function: Main
*
* Returns: Nothing
*
* Description: Program entry point
*********************************************************
**************/

void main(void) {
initMain();

while(1){
// Run at approx. 20% duty cycle @ 15.625 kHz for 5 sec

// Forward
CCPR1L = 192;
CCPR2L = 0;

__delay_ms(5000);

CCPR1L = 0;
CCPR2L = 0;

__delay_ms(2000);

// Reverse
CCPR1L = 0;
CCPR2L = 192;

__delay_ms(5000);

}
return;
}
```

Project: Using CCP and Dedicated PWM with RGB LED

As was previously mentioned, an important use of PWM is in lighting applications. In this project, we will use the PWM to drive a tri-color LED. A tri-color LED (RGB LED) consists of three LEDs in a single package. By varying the intensity of each of these three colors, any other color can be generated.

We will use the PWM to change the average voltage flowing through each individual LED and let our persistence of vision do the rest.

In the code in Listing 8-7, we also utilize the built-in PWM module of the PIC® microcontroller and we use a dedicated PWM3 channel.

Listing 8-7. PWM RGB

```
/*
* File: Main.c
* Author: Armstrong Subero
* PIC: 16F1717 w/Internal OSC @ 16MHz, 5v
* Program: I08_RGB_LED
* Compiler: XC8 (v1.41, MPLAX X v3.55)
* Program Version: 1.0
*
*
* Program Description: This demonstrates using a RGB LED with
PIC16F1717
*
* Hardware Description:  A RGB LED is connected as follows:
* Red - RB0
* Green – RB3
* Blue – RB2
*
```

```
*
* Created Tuesday 18th, April, 2017, 11:53 AM
*/

/****************************************************************
****************
*Includes and defines
****************************************************************
**************/

#include "16F1717_Internal.h"

/*
Value for PWM1
*/
void PWM1_LoadDutyValue(uint16_t dutyValue) {
// Writing to 8 MSBs of pwm duty cycle in CCPRL register
CCPR1L = ((dutyValue & 0x03FC) >> 2);

// Writing to 2 LSBs of pwm duty cycle in CCPCON register
CCP1CON = (CCP1CON & 0xCF) | ((dutyValue & 0x0003) << 4);
}

/*
Value for PWM2
*/
void PWM2_LoadDutyValue(uint16_t dutyValue) {
// Writing to 8 MSBs of pwm duty cycle in CCPRL register
CCPR2L = ((dutyValue & 0x03FC) >> 2);

// Writing to 2 LSBs of pwm duty cycle in CCPCON register
CCP2CON = (CCP2CON & 0xCF) | ((dutyValue & 0x0003) << 4);
}
```

```
/*
Value for PWM3
*/
void PWM3_LoadDutyValue(uint16_t dutyValue) {
// Writing to 8 MSBs of PWM duty cycle in PWMDCH register
PWM3DCH = (dutyValue & 0x03FC) >> 2;

// Writing to 2 LSBs of PWM duty cycle in PWMDCL register
PWM3DCL = (dutyValue & 0x0003) << 6;
}

/*
Value for RGB LED
*/
void RGB_LoadValue(uint16_t red, uint16_t green, uint16_t blue)
{

PWM1_LoadDutyValue(red);
PWM2_LoadDutyValue(green);
PWM3_LoadDutyValue(blue);
}

/****************************************************************
*******************
* Function: void initMain()
*
* Returns: Nothing
*
* Description: Contains initializations for main
*
* Usage: initMain()
****************************************************************
**************/
```

```
void initMain(){
// Run at 16 MHz
internal_16();

////////////////////
// Configure Ports
////////////////////

// Set PIN B0 as output
TRISBbits.TRISB0 = 0;

// Set PIN B1 as output
TRISBbits.TRISB1 = 0;

// Set PIN B2 as output
TRISBbits.TRISB2 = 0;

// Turn off analog
ANSELB = 0;

////////////////////
// Configure Timer6
////////////////////

// Select PWM timer as Timer6 for CCP1 and CCP2
CCPTMRSbits.C1TSEL = 0b10;
CCPTMRSbits.C2TSEL = 0b10;

// Enable timer Increments every 250 ns (16MHz clock) 1000/
(16/4)
// Period = 256 x 0.25 us = 64 us

// Crystal Frequency
//PWM Freq  = -----------------------------------------
//(PRX + 1) * (TimerX Prescaler) * 4
```

```
//PWM Frequency = 16 000 000 / 256 * 1 * 4
//PWM Frequency = 15.625 kHz

// Prescale = 1
T6CONbits.T6CKPS = 0b00;

// Enable Timer6
T6CONbits.TMR6ON = 1;

// Set timer period
PR6 = 255;

///////////////////////////
// Configure PWM
///////////////////////////

// Configure CCP1

// LSB's of PWM duty cycle = 00
CCP1CONbits.DC1B = 00;

// Select PWM mode
CCP1CONbits.CCP1M = 0b1100;

// Configure CCP2


// LSB's of PWM duty cycle = 00
CCP2CONbits.DC2B = 00;

// Select PWM mode
CCP2CONbits.CCP2M = 0b1100;

// Configure PWM 3

// PWM3EN enabled, PWM3POL active high
PWM3CON = 0x80;
```

```
// PWM3DCH 127
PWM3DCH = 0x7F;

// PWM3DCL 192
PWM3DCL = 0xC0;

// Select timer6
CCPTMRSbits.P3TSEL = 0b10;

///////////////////////////////
// Configure PPS
///////////////////////////////

PPSLOCK = 0x55;
PPSLOCK = 0xAA;
PPSLOCKbits.PPSLOCKED = 0x00; // unlock PPS

// Set RB0 to PWM1
RB0PPSbits.RB0PPS = 0b01100;

// Set RB1 to PWM2
RB1PPSbits.RB1PPS = 0b01101;

// Set RB2 to PWM3
RB2PPSbits.RB2PPS = 0x0E;

PPSLOCK = 0x55;
PPSLOCK = 0xAA;
PPSLOCKbits.PPSLOCKED = 0x01; // lock PPS

}
```

```
/*****************************************************************
*****************
* Function: Main
*
* Returns: Nothing
*
* Description: Program entry point
*****************************************************************
***************/

void main(void) {
initMain();

// All channels initially 0
PWM1_LoadDutyValue(0);
PWM2_LoadDutyValue(0);
PWM3_LoadDutyValue(0);

while(1){

// Red
RGB_LoadValue(512,    0,   0);
__delay_ms(1000);

// Green
RGB_LoadValue(0,    512,   0);
__delay_ms(1000);

// Blue
RGB_LoadValue(0,    0,    512);
__delay_ms(1000);

// Yellow
RGB_LoadValue(192,    192,   0);
__delay_ms(1000);
```

```
// Purple
RGB_LoadValue(192,    0,    192);
__delay_ms(1000);

// Aquamarine
RGB_LoadValue(0,    512,    512);
__delay_ms(1000);

}
return;
}
```

Conclusion

This concludes this chapter, where we looked at a few more onboard modules of the PIC® microcontroller. We looked at *interrupts*, which allow the microcontroller to instantly jump to a specific task, timers, which count regular clock pulses, *counters*, which count irregular pulses, and *PWM*, which is very useful in microcontroller applications such as lighting and motor control.

CHAPTER 9

USART, SPI, and I2C: Serial Communication Protocols

In this chapter, we look at using serial communication protocols. The most ubiquitous of these are USART, SPI, and I2C, which I will be explaining in this chapter. This is one chapter you do not want to skip, as we cover using sensors, GPS, GSM, and a host of other things. So, grab a bottle of water and sit down. This will be a long one.

Using USART (Universal Synchronous Asynchronous Receiver Transmitter)

The Universal Synchronous Asynchronous Receiver Transmitter (USART) is my favorite communication protocol. The reason it is my favorite is because it is the simplest to use. It is possible for an embedded systems designer to understand every detail of the USART protocol. Sometimes you may see USART being written as just "UART". For our applications, they do pretty much the same thing. USART is just an enhanced UART protocol, as the missing "S" (synchronous) requires clocking to be synchronous and

© Armstrong Subero 2018
A. Subero, *Programming PIC Microcontrollers with XC8*,
https://doi.org/10.1007/978-1-4842-3273-6_9

adds a little complexity to your design. Therefore, we will use the USART module asynchronously in compliance with KISS.

The USART module onboard the PIC® microcontroller can be used synchronously or asynchronously. When used asynchronously, all the communication takes place without a clock. This saves an I/O pin as in this mode only the transmit and receiver lines are required. The asynchronous mode is the type of communication we will use. Synchronous mode allows the module to be used with a clock and is not as widely used, thus we will not discuss it in this book.

An important consideration for USART is the baud rate. The baud rate of the USART specifies the rate at which the USART transfers data. A baud rate of 2400 means that the USART can transfer a maximum of 2400 bits per second.

Serial Character LCD

We begin our usage of USART by sending signals to a serial LCD module. The serial LCD module we will use is the Parallax 2x16 LCD (see Figure 9-1). In this example, we write text and commands to the LCD. The Parallax datasheet provides information about the commands that must be sent to the LCD.

This LCD module has selectable baud rates of 2400, 9600, and 19200. This LCD also includes a built-in piezo speaker and has a backlight.

Figure 9-1. *Parallax serial LCD*

Let's take a look at the code for setting up the USART module (see Listing 9-1). We first create a header file that contains several function prototypes. After you run the code in this section, download the datasheet from Parallax for the LCD and experiment using the built-in piezo speaker. I guarantee that you will be using USART like a pro in no time.

In addition, I have deliberately left out schematics for interfacing these modules so that you will download the datasheets and find out how they work. All these modules require connecting four wires to them to get them to work and the serial LCD requires connecting three. Come on, you're smart—you can figure it out!

There is one trap for beginners with USART. The TX line is connected to RX and the RX line is connected to TX.

Listing 9-1. EUSART Header

```
/*
 * File: EUSART.h
 * Author: Armstrong Subero
 * PIC: 16F1717 w/X OSC @ 16MHz, 5v
 * Program: Header file to setup PIC16F1717
 * Compiler: XC8 (v1.35, MPLAX X v3.10)
 * Program Version 1.0
 *
 * Program Description: This header sets up the EUSART module
 * Created on November 7th, 2016, 7:00 PM
 */

/**************************************************************
 * Function Prototype
 **************************************************************/

char EUSART_Initialize(const long int baudrate);
uint8_t EUSART_Read(void);
char EUSART_Read_Char(char *output);
```

```
void EUSART_Write(uint8_t txData);
void EUSART_Write_Text(char *text);
void EUSART_Read_Text(char *Output, unsigned int length);
```

Then we create the source file that implements these functions, as shown in Listing 9-2.

Listing 9-2. EUSART Source

```
/*
 * File: EUSART.c
 * Author: Armstrong Subero
 * PIC: 16F1717 w/Int OSC @ 16MHz, 5v
 * Program: Library file containing functions for the EUSART
   module
 * Compiler: XC8 (v1.38, MPLAX X v3.40)
 * Program Version: 1.1
 *              *Added additional comments
 *
 * Program Description: This Library allows you to use the
 EUSART module of the
 *                  PIC16F1717
 *
 * Created on November 7th, 2016, 7:10 PM
 */

/************************************************************
 *Includes and defines
 ************************************************************/

#include "16F1717_Internal.h"
#include "EUSART.h"
```

```
/*************************************************************
* Function: char EUSART_Initialize (const long int baudrate)
*
* Returns: Nothing
*
* Description: Initializes the EUSART module
*
* Usage: EUSART_Initialize()
*************************************************************/

char EUSART_Initialize(const long int baudrate)
{
 unsigned int x;
        x = (_XTAL_FREQ - baudrate*64)/(baudrate*64);
        if(x>255)
        {
                x = (_XTAL_FREQ - baudrate*16)/(baudrate*16);
                BRGH = 1;
        }
        if(x<256)
        {
          SPBRG = x;
          SYNC = 0;
          SPEN = 1;
          TRISC7 = 1;
          TRISC6 = 1;
          CREN = 1;
          TXEN = 1;
          return 1;
        }
        return 0;

}
```

```
/************************************************************
* Function: char EUSART_Read (void)
*
* Returns: Nothing
*
* Description: Reads the EUSART module
*
* Usage: EUSART_Read()
 ************************************************************/

uint8_t EUSART_Read(void)
{
   RC1STAbits.SREN = 1;
    while(!PIR1bits.RCIF)
    {
    }

    if(1 == RC1STAbits.OERR)
    {
        // EUSART error - restart

        RC1STAbits.SPEN = 0;
        RC1STAbits.SPEN = 1;
    }

    return RC1REG;
}

// Read Char
char EUSART_Read_Char(char *Output)
{
        Output = EUSART_Read();
        return Output;
}
```

```
/*************************************************************
* Function: char EUSART_Write (uint8_t txData)
*
* Returns: Nothing
*
* Description: Writes to the EUSART module
*
* Usage: EUSART_Write(x)
*************************************************************/

void EUSART_Write(uint8_t txData)
{
    while(0 == PIR1bits.TXIF)
    {
    }

    TX1REG = txData;    // Write the data byte to the USART.
}

void EUSART_Read_Text(char *Output, unsigned int length)
{
        int i;
        for(int i=0;i<length;i++)
                Output[i] = EUSART_Read();
}

/*************************************************************
* Function: char EUSART_Write_Text (char *text)
*
* Returns: Nothing
*
```

```
* Description: Writes text the EUSART module
*
* Usage: EUSART_Write_Text("Some String")
**************************************************************/

void EUSART_Write_Text(char *text)
{
  int i;
  for(i=0;text[i]!='\0';i++)
          EUSART_Write(text[i]);
}
```

Now we create the main file that communicates with the LCD, as shown in Listing 9-3.

Listing 9-3. Main Source

```
/*
* File: Main.c
* Author: Armstrong Subero
* PIC: 16F1717 w/Int OSC @ 16MHz, 5v
* Program: IO4_Serial_LCD
* Compiler: XC8 (v1.38, MPLAX X v3.40)
* Program Version: 1.0
*
*
* Program Description: This Program Allows PIC16F1717 to
communicate via the
* EUSART module to a 16x2 serial LCD.
*
*
* Hardware Description: A Parallax 16x2 LCD is connected to PIN
RB2 of the
```

```
* microcontroller as follows:
*
*
* Created November 7th, 2016, 7:05 PM
*/

/************************************************************
*Includes and defines
*************************************************************/

#include "16F1717_Internal.h"
#include "EUSART.h"

/************************************************************
* Function: void initMain()
*
* Returns: Nothing
*
* Description: Contains initializations for main
*
* Usage: initMain()
*************************************************************/

void initMain(){
// Run at 16 MHz
internal_16();

///////////////////////
// Setup PINS
///////////////////////

TRISBbits.TRISB2 = 0;
ANSELBbits.ANSB2 = 0;
```

```
///////////////////
// Setup EUSART
///////////////////
PPSLOCK = 0x55;
PPSLOCK = 0xAA;
PPSLOCKbits.PPSLOCKED = 0x00; // unlock PPS

RB2PPSbits.RB2PPS = 0x14 //RB2->EUSART:TX;
RXPPSbits.RXPPS = 0x0B; //RB3->EUSART:RX;

PPSLOCK = 0x55;
PPSLOCK = 0xAA;
PPSLOCKbits.PPSLOCKED = 0x01; // lock PPS
}
/************************************************************
* Function: Main
*
* Returns: Nothing
*
* Description: Program entry point
************************************************************/

void main(void) {
initMain();

// Initialize EUSART module with 19200 baud
EUSART_Initialize(19200);

while(1){

// Send command
// Turn backlight on
EUSART_Write(17);
```

```
// Send text
EUSART_Write_Text("Hello");

// Send every 2 seconds
__delay_ms(2000);
}

return;

}
```

USART to PC Communication

When you need to communicate with a PC, you can use a serial to USB converter. There are some microcontrollers that have USB onboard; however, USB communication is very complex and requires the users to write their own stack or use (sometimes unreliable) stacks provided by the manufacturer. By using a UART to USB bridge, you can avoid a lot of headaches. The CP2104 is excellent and I highly recommend it.

Text to Speech

We will now look at voice synthesis using a Text to Speech (TTS) module. The TTS modules convert text into a spoken voice. The TTS module we will use is the EMIC 2 TTS module (see Figure 9-2). This module is very easy to use. It allows the user to select many voices and produces a voice that is very simple to understand. After you have finished running the code in this section, download the datasheet for the module. Experiment with different voices and play around with the module a little. This is good practice. Once you have read the datasheets of the modules and sensors, you can create your own libraries and code, without becoming stuck if you cannot find a library online.

Figure 9-2. *EMIC 2 TTS module*

The header file remains the same. The main code is shown in Listing 9-4.

Listing 9-4. TTS Main Code

```
/*
* File: Main.c
* Author: Armstrong Subero
* PIC: 16F1717 w/Int OSC @ 16MHz, 5v
* Program: 21_EUSART
* Compiler: XC8 (v1.38, MPLAX X v3.40)
* Program Version: 1.0
*
*
* Program Description: This Program Allows PIC16F1717 to
communicate via the
* EUSART module to a EMIC 2 TTS module.
*
*
```

* Hardware Description: A EMIC 2 TTS module is connected to the PIC16F1717 as
* follows:
*
* RB2-> SIN;
* RB3-> SOUT;
*
* The other pins on the EMIC2 TTS are connected as per
* datasheet.
*
* Created February 25th, 2017, 9:55 PM
*/

/***
*Includes and defines
***/

#include "16F1717_Internal.h"
#include "EUSART.h"

/***
* Function: void initMain()
*
 Returns: Nothing
*
* Description: Contains initializations for main
*
* Usage: initMain()
***/

```c
void initMain(){
// Run at 16 MHz
internal_16();

// Setup PINS
TRISBbits.TRISB3 = 1;
ANSELBbits.ANSB3 = 0;

TRISBbits.TRISB2 = 0;
ANSELBbits.ANSB2 = 0;

///////////////////////
// Setup EUSART
///////////////////////
PPSLOCK = 0x55;
PPSLOCK = 0xAA;
PPSLOCKbits.PPSLOCKED = 0x00; // unlock PPS

RB2PPSbits.RB2PPS = 0x14; //RB2->EUSART:TX;
RXPPSbits.RXPPS = 0x0B; //RB3->EUSART:RX;

PPSLOCK = 0x55;
PPSLOCK = 0xAA;
PPSLOCKbits.PPSLOCKED = 0x01; // lock PPS
}
/************************************************************
* Function: Main
*
* Returns: Nothing
*
* Description: Program entry point
************************************************************/
```

```
void main(void) {
initMain();

char readEmic;

// Initialize EUSART module with 9600 baud
EUSART_Initialize(9600);

// give the module time to stabilize
__delay_ms(3000);

// Send CR in case system is up
EUSART_Write(13);

while(1){

// If TTS module is ready
if (EUSART_Read() == 58){

// Say something
EUSART_Write(83);
EUSART_Write_Text("Hello");
EUSART_Write(13);
__delay_ms(500);
}

}

return;

}
```

Using GPS (Global Positioning Systems)

Now we look at using GPS (Global Positioning System). GPS is a system that utilizes satellites to determine the position to a GPS receiver, which receives a signal from these satellites. I simply cannot cover GPS in its entirety in this book, since it would just confuse everything. If you want to know how GPS works in detail, browse the Internet. Once you are satisfied, come back and learn how to use the module. A good feature of GPS is that is does not require an active Internet connection or cellular network in order to work.

In this example, we look at using the U-BLOX NEO-6M GPS module, as it is very easy to use and, at the time of this writing, is widely available and extremely low cost (see Figure 9-3).

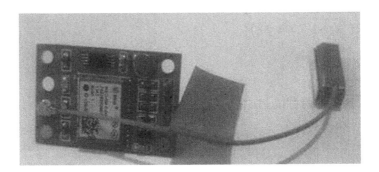

Figure 9-3. *U-BLOX NEO-6M GPS module*

NMEA Commands

In order to use the GPS module effectively, we must understand how the NMEA data transmitted by the GPS module works. NMEA stands for National Marine Electronics Association and that body produced a specification that allows the GPS receiver to give the time, position, and velocity data that the user can parse. The GPS receiver sends these commands as sentences in a particular format.

For the GPS receiver, these sentences all begin with a $ symbol followed by five letters. The first two letters are always GP followed by three other letters, which tell us what the sentence is about. For example, the sentence we are interested in is the GLL, which stands for Geographic Latitude and Longitude. The GLL type sentence has the following format:

```
$GPGLL,1123.01,N,1234.00,W,000111,A,*65
```

The $GPGLL tells us the type of NMEA sentence it is. The fragment 1123.01,N tells us a position of latitude that's 11 degrees and 23.01 minutes North. Similarly, 1234.00,W indicates a position of Longitude 12 degrees and 34.00 minutes West.

In order to extract the information about the position of the receiver, we need to create a buffer to store the information as it comes in. Then we need to eliminate any invalid data and use the C language strstr function, which is provided by XC8, to determine if the string we are looking for is present in the buffer.

I have a challenge for you. The code in Listing 9-5 has been written to display the coordinates to a HD44780 LCD (we cover this later in the chapter). Modify it to print to your serial LCD instead. (If you don't want to do this, that is understandable and you may turn to Chapter 8, where the display is covered in full.)

Listing 9-5. GPS Main Code

```
/*
* File: Main.c
* Author: Armstrong Subero
* PIC: 16F1717 w/Int OSC @ 16MHz, 5v
* Program: 21_EUSART
* Compiler: XC8 (v1.38, MPLAX X v3.40)
* Program Version: 1.0
*
*
```

```
* Program Description: This Program Allows PIC16F1717 to
communicate via the
* EUSART module to a NEO-6M GPS module and display Latitude
* and Longitude Coordinates on an LCD.
*
* Hardware Description: A NEO-6M GPS module is connected to the
PIC16F1717 as
* follows:
*
* PPS -> NC
* RXD -> TX
* TXD -> RX
* GND -> GND
* VCC -> VCC
*
*
* Created April 18th, 2017, 12:51 PM
*/

/*************************************************************
*Includes and defines
*************************************************************/

#include "16F1717_Internal.h"
#include "EUSART.h"
#include "LCD.h"
#include <string.h>

// Variables
volatile char c;
volatile char d;

char* data;
```

```c
static char uartBuffer[300];
int i;

char* terminator;
char conversionString[8];

double lat = 0.0;
double lon = 0.0;

double *longitude = &lon;
double *latitude  = &lat;

// Function prototype
void read_gps();

/************************************************************
* Function: void initMain()
*
* Returns: Nothing
*
* Description: Contains initializations for main
*
* Usage: initMain()
*************************************************************/

void initMain(){
// Run at 16 MHz
internal_16();

// Setup PINS
TRISBbits.TRISB3 = 1;
ANSELBbits.ANSB3 = 0;

TRISBbits.TRISB2 = 0;
ANSELBbits.ANSB2 = 0;
```

```c
TRISD = 0;
ANSELD = 0;
PORTD = 0;

////////////////////
// Setup EUSART
////////////////////
PPSLOCK = 0x55;
PPSLOCK = 0xAA;
PPSLOCKbits.PPSLOCKED = 0x00; // unlock PPS

RB2PPSbits.RB2PPS = 0x14; //RB2->EUSART:TX;
RXPPSbits.RXPPS = 0x0B; //RB3->EUSART:RX;

PPSLOCK = 0x55;
PPSLOCK = 0xAA;
PPSLOCKbits.PPSLOCKED = 0x01; // lock PPS

INTCONbits.GIE = 1;
INTCONbits.PEIE = 1;

// set up UART 1 receive interrupt
PIE1bits.RCIE = 1;
}

/************************************************************
* Function: Main
*
* Returns: Nothing
*
* Description: Program entry point
************************************************************/
```

```
void main(void) {
initMain();
Lcd_Init();
Lcd_Clear();

// Initialize EUSART module with 9600 baud
EUSART_Initialize(9600);

// give the module time to stabilize
__delay_ms(100);

while(1){

Lcd_Set_Cursor(1,1);

read_gps();

// Write Latitude
Lcd_Write_Float(*latitude);

Lcd_Set_Cursor(2,1);

// Write Longitude
Lcd_Write_Float(*longitude);

__delay_ms(2000);
Lcd_Clear();
}

return;

}
```

```
/*************************************************************
 * Function: void read_gps()
 *
 * Returns: Pointers to lat and lon
 *
 * Description: Function to read the GPS module
 *
 * Usage: read_gps()
 *************************************************************/

void read_gps(){

// Read characters from UART into buffer
for(i=0; i<sizeof(uartBuffer)-1; i++)
{
d = EUSART_Read_Char(c);
uartBuffer[i] = d;
}

// Last character is null terminator
uartBuffer[sizeof(uartBuffer)-1] = '\0';

// Look for needle in haystack to find string for GPGLL
data = strstr(uartBuffer, "$GPGLL");

// if null exit
if(data == NULL)
{
return;
}

// Find terminator
terminator = strstr(data,",");
```

```c
// if null exit
if(terminator == NULL)
{
return;
}

// If the first byte of the latitude field is ',', there is no info
// so exit

if(data[7] == ',')
{
return;
}

////////////////////////////////////
// Search buffer data for Latitude
// and Longitude values
////////////////////////////////////

data = terminator+1;

terminator = strstr(data,",");

if(terminator == NULL)
{
return;
}

memset(conversionString,0,sizeof(conversionString));
memcpy(conversionString, data, 2);
*latitude = atof(conversionString);

data += 2;
*terminator = '\0';
*latitude += (atof(data)/60);
```

```
data = terminator+1;
terminator = strstr(data,",");
if(terminator == NULL)
{
return;
}
if(*data == 'S')
{
*latitude *= -1;
}

data = terminator+1;
terminator = strstr(data,",");
if(terminator == NULL)
{
return;
}
memset(conversionString,0,sizeof(conversionString));
memcpy(conversionString, data, 3);
*longitude = atof(conversionString);

data += 3;
*terminator = '\0';
*longitude += (atof(data)/60);

data = terminator+1;
terminator = strstr(data,",");
if(terminator == NULL)
{
return;
}
```

```
if(*data == 'W')
{
*longitude *= -1;
}

}
```

Software USART

The PIC16F1717 only has one USART module that users can use in their applications. Now there may be situations where you need to use more than one USART module for your application. In this case, you may need to redesign your circuitry and utilize a chip that has more features. However, this is not as simple as it sounds, because you may already be familiar with the chip you are using for your application and may not want to bear the costs associated with using a larger chip. In such cases, it may be useful to use a software USART (also called a "bit-banged") implementation.

The bit-banged USART we use in this example works reliably up to about 2400 baud rate. Higher bit rates may be unstable and may not function as intended.

GSM Module

We will look at an application of the bit-banged USART using a GSM module. We will use the SIM 800L module (see Figure 9-4), which is very popular at the time of writing and is very simple to use.

Figure 9-4. SIM800L module

AT Commands

In a previous section, we looked at data structured in NMEA format, which is the type of data commonly given by GSM modules. In this section, we look at using AT (attention) commands. AT commands are commonly used to control modems. Here are some commonly used AT commands for controlling the SIM 800L module:

- AT: Check to see if the module is working correctly. If it is, it will return OK.

- AT+CREG?: Get information about network registration. If the modules returns +CREG: 0,1, then everything is fine.

- AT+IPR=9600: Change the baud rate. For example, changing the 9600 to 2400 in the example would set the baud rate to 2400.

The other AT commands are used for things like sending and receiving messages, calls, accessing the GPS features, among others. In this example, we will focus solely on sending text messages, so the commands for sending texts are shown in the code in Listing 9-6. Again another challenge—modify the code in Listing 9-6 to run with the serial LCD instead of the character LCD. If you don't want to do this, you can instead turn to the section later in this chapter entitled "Character: The Hitachi HD44780 LCD" and use the code of the character LCD in that section.

Listing 9-6. GSM Main Code

```
/*
* File: Main.c
* Author: Armstrong Subero
* PIC: 16F1717 w/Int OSC @ 16MHz, 5v
* Program: I08_GSM
Compiler: XC8 (v1.38, MPLAX X v3.40)
* Program Version: 1.0
*
*
* Program Description: This Program Allows PIC16F1717 to
communicate with a
* SIM800L GSM module and send an SMS message.
*
*
* Hardware Description: A SIM800L GSM module is connected as
follows:

*5v -> 5V
*GND -> GND
*VDD -> NC
*SIM_TXD -> RX
*SIM_RXD -> TX
*GND -> GND
*
*
* Created April 18th, 2017, 1:11 PM
*/
```

```
/*************************************************************
*Includes and defines
*************************************************************/

#include "16F1717_Internal.h"
#include "LCD.h"

// Setup for soft UART
#define Baudrate 2400 //bps
#define OneBitDelay (1000000/Baudrate)
#define DataBitCount 8 // no parity, no flow control
#define UART_RX LATEbits.LATE0// UART RX pin
#define UART_TX LATEbits.LATE1 // UART TX pin
#define UART_RX_DIR TRISE0// UART RX pin direction register
#define UART_TX_DIR TRISE1 // UART TX pin direction register

//Function Declarations
void InitSoftUART(void);
unsigned char UART_Receive(void);
void UART_Transmit(const char);
void SUART_Write_Text(char *text);
void SUART_Write_Char(char a);
void SUART_Read_Text(char *Output, unsigned int length);

/*************************************************************
* Function: void initMain()
*
* Returns: Nothing
*
* Description: Contains initializations for main
*
* Usage: initMain()
*************************************************************/
```

```c
void initMain(){
// Run at 16 MHz
internal_16();

// Setup pins
TRISD = 0x00;
ANSELD = 0x00;
PORTD = 0x00;

TRISE = 0;
ANSELE = 0;
}

/*************************************************************
* Function: Main
*
* Returns: Nothing
*
* Description: Program entry point
*************************************************************/

void main(void) {
initMain();

Lcd_Init();
__delay_ms(1000);

InitSoftUART(); // Initialize Soft UART
__delay_ms(1000);

while(1){

// Send commands to module
SUART_Write_Text("AT+CMGF=1\r\n");
__delay_ms(1000);
```

```
SUART_Write_Text("AT+CMGS=\"0009999\"\r\n"); // replace number
__delay_ms(1000);

// Message to send
SUART_Write_Text("Test");
__delay_ms(1000);

UART_Transmit((char)26);
__delay_ms(1000);

// Notify user message sent
Lcd_Clear();
Lcd_Set_Cursor(1,1);
__delay_ms(100);

// Write String
Lcd_Write_String("Sent");

__delay_ms(2000);

}

return;
}

/*
* Init SW UART
*/
void InitSoftUART(void) // Initialize UART pins to proper
values
{
UART_TX = 1; // TX pin is high in idle state

UART_RX_DIR = 1; // Input
UART_TX_DIR = 0; // Output
}
```

```c
/*
* Receive via SW UART
*/
unsigned char UART_Receive(void)
{
// Pin Configurations
// GP1 is UART RX Pin

unsigned char DataValue = 0;

//wait for start bit
while(UART_RX==1);

__delay_us(OneBitDelay);
__delay_us(OneBitDelay/2); // Take sample value in the mid of
bit duration

for ( unsigned char i = 0; i < DataBitCount; i++ )
{
if ( UART_RX == 1 ) //if received bit is high
{
DataValue += (1<<i);
}

__delay_us(OneBitDelay);
}

// Check for stop bit
if ( UART_RX == 1 ) //Stop bit should be high
{
__delay_us(OneBitDelay/2);
return DataValue;
}
else //some error occurred !
```

```
{
__delay_us(OneBitDelay/2);
return 0x000;
}
}

/*
* Transmit via SW UART
*/
void UART_Transmit(const char DataValue)
{
/* Basic Logic
```

TX pin is usually high. A high to low bit is the starting bit and a low to high bit is the ending bit. No parity bit. No flow control. BitCount is the number of bits to transmit. Data is transmitted LSB first.

```
*/

// Send Start Bit
UART_TX = 0;
__delay_us(OneBitDelay);

for ( unsigned char i = 0; i < DataBitCount; i++ )
{
//Set Data pin according to the DataValue
if(((DataValue>>i)&0x1) == 0x1 ) //if Bit is high
{
UART_TX = 1;
}
```

```
else //if Bit is low
{
UART_TX = 0;
}

__delay_us(OneBitDelay);
}

//Send Stop Bit
UART_TX = 1;
__delay_us(OneBitDelay);
}
/*
 * Write text via SW UART
 */
void SUART_Write_Text(char *text)
{
int i;

for(i=0;text[i]!='\0';i++)
UART_Transmit(text[i]);
}
/*
 * Read text via SW UART
 */
void SUART_Read_Text(char *Output, unsigned int length)
{
int i;
for(int i=0;i<length;i++)
```

```
{
    Output[i] = UART_Receive();
}
}

/*
* Write Char via SW UART
*/
void SUART_Write_Char(char a)
{
UART_Transmit(a - 0x128);
}
```

Using SPI (Serial Peripheral Interface)

Serial Peripheral Interface (SPI) is another type of serial communication protocol commonly used in embedded systems and present on the PIC® microcontroller. SPI is a very important protocol and is widely implemented on a variety of sensors. Unlike USART, where very few applications require a clock, in SPI a clock is present in all applications because SPI uses synchronous data transfer.

The device in the SPI communication that generates the clock is known as the *master* and the other is known as the *slave*. SPI always only has one master device, although there can be many slaves. SPI has several lines: Serial Clock (SCK), Master Out Slave In (MOSI), Master In Slave Out (MISO), and Slave Select (SS). If there is only one slave device connected to the SPI bus, then this line may be left low as SPI is active low.

One of the major disadvantages of SPI is that it uses a lot of I/O lines. Although SCK, MOSI, and MISO remain the same regardless of the number of slave devices on the bus, an additional SS line must be used for each slave device that is connected to the bus. The advantage of SPI is that it can transfer millions of bytes of data per second and is useful when interacting with devices such as SD cards, which would require data transfer at very high speeds.

In learning to use the SPI peripheral available on the PIC® microcontroller, we will use an MCP4131 digital potentiometer with the PIC® microcontroller.

The code for the SPI was generated using the Microchip Code Configurator. There are a lot of tutorials on how to use the MCC, so I leave it up to you to learn on your own. I also leave you to figure out how to connect the SPI lines. Here's a hint though—read the datasheet of the MCP4131. You need to make a few modifications to the names of the functions as per the header file. You must modify the names to match those as shown in the header file.

Listing 9-7 shows the modified header file from MCC for the SPI.

Listing 9-7. SPI Header

```
/*
 * File: SPI.h
 * Author: Armstrong Subero
 * PIC: 16F1717 w/X OSC @ 16MHz, 5v
 * Program: Header file for SPI module
 * Compiler: XC8 (v1.38, MPLAX X v3.40)
 *
 * Program Version 1.0
 *
 * Program Description: This program header provides function
 prototypes for
 * SPI module on PIC16F1717
 *
 *
 *
 * Created on November 7th, 2016, 5:45 PM
 */
```

243

```
/*************************************************************
*Includes and defines
*************************************************************/

#include "16F1717_Internal.h"
#define DUMMY_DATA 0x0

void SPI_Initialize(void);
uint8_t SPI_Exchange8bit(uint8_t data);
uint8_t SPI_Exchange8bitBuffer(uint8_t *dataIn, uint8_t bufLen,
uint8_t *dataOut\
);
bool SPI_IsBufferFull(void);
bool SPI_HasWriteCollisionOccured(void);
void SPI_ClearWriteCollisionStatus(void);
```

Digital Potentiometer

The digital potentiometer we use to demonstrate the use of the SPI bus is the MCP4131. The MCP4131 is a 7-bit device, giving a total of 129 different values, and is controlled via SPI. In this example, we send commands to the device and the device adjusts its resistance. The change in resistance is visible by connecting the POW pin of the device to an LED via a 1k resistor. The resistor will then vary in brightness.

Listing 9-8 provides the main code.

Listing 9-8. Main Code

```
/*
 * File: Main.c
 * Author: Armstrong Subero
 * PIC: 16F1717 w/Int OSC @ 16MHz, 5v
 * Program: 22_SPI
 * Compiler: XC8 (v1.38, MPLAX X v3.40)
```

```
* Program Version: 1.0
*
*
* Program Description: This Program Allows PIC16F1717 to
communicate via the
* SPI interface
*
*
* Hardware Description: A HD44780 LCD is connected via PORTD
and a MCP4131
* digital potentiometer is connected as follows:
*
* Vss --> Vss
* Vdd --> Vdd
* SS  --> RD1
* SCK --> RC3
* SDI --> RC5
* POB --> GND
* POW --> LED via 1k resistor
* POA --> Vdd
*
*
* Created November 10th, 2016, 4:42 PM
*/

/***************************************************************
*Includes and defines
***************************************************************/

#include "16F1717_Internal.h"
#include "LCD.h"
#include "SPI.h"
```

```c
void digiPot_write(int i);

/*************************************************************
* Function: void initMain()
*
* Returns: Nothing
*
* Description: Contains initializations for main
*
* Usage: initMain()
*************************************************************/

void initMain(){
// Run at 16 MHz
internal_16();

// Set PIN D1 as output
TRISDbits.TRISD1 = 0;

// Turn off LED
LATDbits.LATD1 = 0;

// Setup PORTD
TRISD = 0;
ANSELD = 0;

// Initialize LCD
Lcd_Init();
__delay_ms(100);
Lcd_Clear();

// Setup PORTC for SPI
ANSELCbits.ANSC3 = 0;
ANSELCbits.ANSC4 = 0;
```

```c
ANSELCbits.ANSC5 = 0;

TRISCbits.TRISC3 = 0;
TRISCbits.TRISC4 = 1;
TRISCbits.TRISC5 = 0;

PPSLOCK = 0x55;
PPSLOCK = 0xAA;
PPSLOCKbits.PPSLOCKED = 0x00; // unlock PPS

SSPDATPPSbits.SSPDATPPS = 0x14;    //RC4->MSSP:SDI;
RC3PPSbits.RC3PPS =0x10; //RC3->MSSP:SCK;
RC5PPSbits.RC5PPS =0x11; //RC5->MSSP:SDO;

PPSLOCK = 0x55;
PPSLOCK = 0xAA;
PPSLOCKbits.PPSLOCKED = 0x01; // lock PPS

// Initialize SPI
SPI_Initialize();

}
/**************************************************************
* Function: Main
*
* Returns: Nothing
*
* Description: Program entry point
**************************************************************/

void main(void) {
initMain();

// Digipot variable
int i;
```

```
Lcd_Set_Cursor(1,1);
__delay_ms(5);
Lcd_Write_String("SPI Ready");
__delay_ms(1000);
Lcd_Clear();

while(1){

// Seven bit resolution
for (i = 0; i <= 128; i++){
// Write Value
digiPot_write(i);

// Write to LCD
Lcd_Set_Cursor(1,1);
__delay_ms(5);
Lcd_Write_Integer(i);
__delay_ms(250);
Lcd_Clear();
}
}

return;

}

/**************************************************************
* Function: Main
*
* Returns: Nothing
*
* Description: Writes a particular value to a MCP4131 digital
potentiometer
*
* Usage: digiPot_write(x);
**************************************************************/
```

```
void digiPot_write(int i){
// Set SS Low
LATDbits.LATD1 = 0;

// Slave address
SPI_Exchange8bit(0x00);

// Data
SPI_Exchange8bit(i);

// Set SS High
LATDbits.LATD1 = 1;
}
```

Character Display

Although the focus of the next chapter is displays, we utilize a simple character LCD to demonstrate the I2C protocol.

Character: The Hitachi HD44780 LCD

The Hitachi HD44780 is known as the industry standard character LCD. The reason is simple—the HD44780 is very easy to use. The LCD is used to display characters to users. The most commonly used display type is the 2x16 variety, which displays up to 16 characters on two lines. The LCD is essential for any embedded toolbox and makes an excellent prototyping display.

The LCD commonly has 14 pins; however, LCDs that have a backlight have 16 pins. I recommend the version with the backlight. Download the datasheet for your particular display to determine which version display you have.

Let's look at the code for using the HD44780 LCD.

First, Listing 9-9 shows the header file.

Listing 9-9. HD44780 Header File

```
/*
* File: LCD.h
* Author: Armstrong Subero
* PIC: 16F1717 w/X OSC @ 16MHz, 5v
* Program: Header file to
* Compiler: XC8 (v1.38, MPLAX X v3.40)
* Program Version 1.1
* *Added additional comments
*
* Program Description: This program header provides routines
for controlling
* a STD HITACHI HD44780 and compatible LCDs
*
* Hardware Description:
*
* RS ---> RD2
* R/W ---> GND
* EN ---> RD3
* D4 ---> RD4
* D5 ---> RD5
* D6 ---> RD6
* D7 ---> RD7
*
*
* Created on November 7th, 2016, 11:56 PM
*/
```

```
/************************************************************
*Includes and defines
*************************************************************/
// STD XC8 include
#include <xc.h>

#define RS RD2   //Register Select (Character or Instruction)
#define EN RD3   //LCD Clock Enable PIN, Falling Edge Triggered

// 4 bit operation
#define D4 RD4   //Bit 4
#define D5 RD5   //Bit 5
#define D6 RD6   //Bit 6
#define D7 RD7   //Bit 7

// function prototypes
void Lcd_Port(char a);
void Lcd_Cmd(char a);
void Lcd_Clear();
void Lcd_Set_Cursor(char a, char b);
void Lcd_Init();
void Lcd_Write_Char(char a);
void Lcd_Write_String(const char *a);
void Lcd_Shift_Right();
void Lcd_Shift_Left();
void Lcd_Write_Integer(int v);
void Lcd_Write_Float(float f);
```

Next is the source file, provided in Listing 9-10.

Listing 9-10. HD44780 Source File

```
/*
 * File: LCD.c
 * Author: Armstrong Subero
 * PIC: 16F1717 w/Int OSC @ 16MHz, 5v
 * Program: Library file to configure PIC16F1717
 * Compiler: XC8 (v1.38, MPLAX X v3.40)
 * Program Version: 1.1
 * *Added additional comments
 *
 * Program Description: This Library allows you to interface
 HD44780 and
 * compatible LCDs
 *
 * Created on November 7th, 2016, 11:55 AM
 */

#include "LCD.h"
#include "16F1717_Internal.h"

/*************************************************************
 * Function: void Lcd_Port (char a)
 *
 * Returns: Nothing
 *
 * Description: LCD Setup Routines
 *************************************************************/

void Lcd_Port(char a)
{
if(a & 1)
D4 = 1;
```

```
else
D4 = 0;

if(a & 2)
D5 = 1;
else
D5 = 0;

if(a & 4)
D6 = 1;
else
D6 = 0;

if(a & 8)
D7 = 1;
else
D7 = 0;
}

/****************************************************************
* Function: void Lcd_Cmd (char a)
*
* Returns: Nothing
*
* Description: Sets LCD command
****************************************************************/

void Lcd_Cmd(char a)
{
RS = 0;    // => RS = 0
Lcd_Port(a);
EN = 1;    // => E = 1
__delay_ms(1);
EN = 0;    // => E = 0
}
```

```
/************************************************************
* Function: void Lcd_Clear()
*
* Returns: Nothing
*
* Description: Clears the LCD
*************************************************************/

void Lcd_Clear()
{
Lcd_Cmd(0);
Lcd_Cmd(1);
}

/************************************************************
* Function: void Lcd_Set_Cursor(char a, char b)
*
* Returns: Nothing
*
* Description: Sets the LCD cursor position
*************************************************************/

void Lcd_Set_Cursor(char a, char b)
{
char temp,z,y;
if(a == 1)
{
temp = 0x80 + b - 1;
z = temp>>4;
y = temp & 0x0F;
Lcd_Cmd(z);
Lcd_Cmd(y);
}
```

```
else if(a == 2)
{
temp = 0xC0 + b - 1;
z = temp>>4;
y = temp & 0x0F;
Lcd_Cmd(z);
Lcd_Cmd(y);
}
}

/****************************************************************
* Function: void Lcd_Init()
*
* Returns: Nothing
*
* Description: Initializes the LCD
****************************************************************/

void Lcd_Init()
{
Lcd_Port(0x00);
__delay_ms(10);
Lcd_Cmd(0x03);
__delay_ms(3);
Lcd_Cmd(0x03);
__delay_ms(10);
Lcd_Cmd(0x03);
/////////////////////////////////////////////////////
Lcd_Cmd(0x02);
Lcd_Cmd(0x02);
Lcd_Cmd(0x08);
Lcd_Cmd(0x00);
```

```
Lcd_Cmd(0x0C);
Lcd_Cmd(0x00);
Lcd_Cmd(0x06);
}

/***************************************************************
* Function: void Lcd_Write_Char (char a)
*
* Returns: Nothing
*
* Description: Writes a character to the LCD
***************************************************************/

void Lcd_Write_Char(char a)
{
char temp,y;
temp = a&0x0F;
y = a&0xF0;
RS = 1; // => RS = 1
Lcd_Port(y>>4); //Data transfer
EN = 1;
__delay_us(20);
EN = 0;
Lcd_Port(temp);
EN = 1;
__delay_us(20);
EN = 0;
}
```

```
/**************************************************************
 * Function: void Lcd_Write_String (const char *a)
 *
 * Returns: Nothing
 *
 * Description: Writes a string to the LCD
 **************************************************************/
void Lcd_Write_String(const char *a)
{
int i;
for(i=0;a[i]!='\0';i++)
Lcd_Write_Char(a[i]);
}

/**************************************************************
 * Function: void Lcd_Shift_Right()
 *
 * Returns: Nothing
 *
 * Description: Shifts text on the LCD right
 **************************************************************/
void Lcd_Shift_Right()
{
Lcd_Cmd(0x01);
Lcd_Cmd(0x0C);
}
```

```
/*************************************************************
* Function: void Lcd_Shift_Left()
*
* Returns: Nothing
*
* Description: Shifts text on the LCD left
*************************************************************/

void Lcd_Shift_Left()
{
Lcd_Cmd(0x01);
Lcd_Cmd(0x08);
}

/*************************************************************
* Function: void Lcd_Write_Integer(int v)
*
* Returns: Nothing
*
* Description: Converts a string to an integer
*************************************************************/

void Lcd_Write_Integer(int v)
{
unsigned char buf[8];

Lcd_Write_String(itoa(buf, v, 10));
}
```

```
/****************************************************************
 * Function: void Lcd_Write_Float(float f)
 *
 * Returns: Nothing
 *
 * Description: Converts a string to a float
 ****************************************************************/
void Lcd_Write_Float(float f)
{
char* buf11;
int status;

buf11 = ftoa(f, &status);

Lcd_Write_String(buf11);
}
```

Finally, Listing 9-11 provides the source code that goes through all the routines.

Listing 9-11. HD44780 Main

```
/*
 * File: Main.c
 * Author: Armstrong Subero
 * PIC: 16F1717 w/Int OSC @ 16MHz, 5v
 * Program: 15_HD44780_LCD
 * Compiler: XC8 (v1.38, MPLAX X v3.40)
 * Program Version: 1.0
 *
 *
```

```
* Program Description: This Program Allows PIC16F1717 to
interface to
* HD44780 and compatible LCDs
*
* Hardware Description: An HD44780 compatible LCD is connected
to PORTD of
* the microcontroller as follows:
*
* RS ---> RD2
* R/W ---> GND
* EN ---> RD3
* D4---> RD4
* D5---> RD5
* D6---> RD6
* D7---> RD7
*
*
* Created November 7th, 2016, 11:05 AM
*/

/***********************************************************
*Includes and defines
***********************************************************/

#include "16F1717_Internal.h"
#include "LCD.h"

/***********************************************************
* Function: void initMain()
*
* Returns: Nothing
*
```

```
 * Description: Contains initializations for main
 *
 * Usage: initMain()
 ***************************************************************/

void initMain(){
// Run at 16 MHz
internal_16();

TRISD = 0x00;
ANSELD = 0x00;
PORTD = 0x00;
}

/***************************************************************
 * Function: Main
 *
 * Returns: Nothing
 *
 * Description: Program entry point
 ***************************************************************/

void main(void) {
initMain();
Lcd_Init();

int a;
int c;
float b;

while(1){
Lcd_Clear();
Lcd_Set_Cursor(1,1);
```

```
// Write String
Lcd_Write_String("PIC16F1717");

// Shift it left
for(a=0;a<15;a++)
{
__delay_ms(500);
Lcd_Shift_Left();
}

// Shift it right
for(a=0;a<15;a++)
{
__delay_ms(500);
Lcd_Shift_Right();
}

Lcd_Clear();
Lcd_Set_Cursor(1,1);

// Write Integer
for (c = 0; c < 100; c++){
Lcd_Write_Integer(c);
__delay_ms(300);
Lcd_Clear();
__delay_ms(15);

}

// Write Float
for (b = 0.0; b <= 5; b+= 0.5)
{
Lcd_Write_Float(b);
__delay_ms(300);
Lcd_Clear();
```

```
    __delay_ms(15);
}

    __delay_ms(1000);
}

return;
}
```

The Samsung KS0066U

The code in Listing 9-11 works on HD44780 and compatible LCDs, including the Samsung KS0066U and was tested on both displays.

Using the I2C (Inter-Integrated Circuit) Protocol

We now look at the final protocol presented in this chapter, the I2C (Inter-Integrated Circuit) protocol. There are a lot of tutorials that go in depth into the I2C protocol and thus I will not attempt to give a detailed explanation of it. There are some things that you must first know in order to use this protocol effectively.

The I2C protocol is widely used. When compared to SPI, I2C uses fewer (only two) lines but communication occurs at a slower rate and it is a very complex protocol. The example we look at is reading and writing an EEPROM. This is an important application because the PIC16F1717 does not have an onboard EEPROM.

I2C is unique when compared to the other protocols we have discussed so far in that only one line is used for data flow. On the I2C bus, the device known as the master is used to communicate with another device, known as the slave. The master can communicate with the slave because each device on the slave has its own address.

The lines used for the communication with the slave are the serial clock line (SCL) and serial data line (SDA). In order for I2C to work, the lines must be connected to VCC using pull-up resistors. There are calculations that can be used to determine the value of these resistors by working out the capacity of the lines. In practice, however, I have found that either 4.7K or 1 K resistors do the job quite adequately.

These pull-up resistors are required because I2C devices pull the signal line low but cannot drive it high, and the pull-up resistors are there to restore the signal line to high.

The speed most I2C devices use to communicate is either 100kHz or 400kHz. The protocol transmits information via frames. There are two types of frames available—an address frame, which informs the bus which slave devices will receive the message, followed by data frames containing the actual 8-bit data. Every frame has a 9th bit, called the acknowledge (ACK) or not acknowledge (NACK) bit, which is used to indicate whether the slave device reads the transmission.

Every I2C communication from the master starts with the master pulling the SDA line low and leaving the SCL line high. This is known as the *start* condition. Similarly, there is a *stop* condition, where there is a low-to-high transition on SDA after a low-to-high transition on SCL with SCL being high.

EEPROM

The example we use for I2C is interfacing the microcontroller with an I2C based EEPROM device. The header file is shown in Listing 9-12.

Listing 9-12. I2C Header

```
/*
 * File: I2C.h
 * Author: Armstrong Subero
 * PIC: 16F1717 w/X OSC @ 16MHz, 5v
```

```
* Program: Header file to setup PIC16F1717 I2C
* Compiler: XC8 (v1.35, MPLAX X v3.10)
* Program Version 1.2
* Separated file into Header and C source file
* Used non-mcc code
*
*
* Program Description: This program header will allows set up
of I2C
*
* Created on September 12th, 2016, 7:00 PM
*/

/***************************************************************
*Includes and defines
***************************************************************/

#include "16F1717_Internal.h"

void I2C_Init(void);
void Send_I2C_Data(unsigned int databyte);
unsigned int Read_I2C_Data(void);
void Send_I2C_ControlByte(unsigned int BlockAddress,unsigned
int RW_bit);
void Send_I2C_StartBit(void);
void Send_I2C_StopBit(void);
void Send_I2C_ACK(void);
void Send_I2C_NAK(void);
```

The source file is shown in Listing 9-13.

Listing 9-13. I2C Source

```
/*
 * File: I2C.c
 * Author: Armstrong Subero
 * PIC: 16F1717 w/Int OSC @ 16MHz, 5v
 * Program: Library file to configure PIC16F1717 I2C module
 * Compiler: XC8 (v1.38, MPLAX X v3.40)
 * Program Version: 1.1
 * *Added additional comments
 *
 * Program Description: This Library allows you to control
PIC16F1717 I2C
 *
 * Created on November 12th, 2016, 7:05 AM
 */

#include "I2C.h"

void I2C_Init(void){

//**********************************************************\
********
// Setup MSSP as I2C Master mode, clock rate of 100Khz
//**********************************************************\
********

SSPCONbits.SSPM=0x08;// I2C Master mode, clock = Fosc/(4 * (SSPADD+1))
SSPCONbits.SSPEN=1; // enable MSSP port
```

```
// ********************************************************\
************

// The SSPADD register value is used to determine the clock
rate for I2C
// communication.
// Equation for I2C clock rate:   Fclock = Fosc/[(SSPADD +1)*4]
//
// For this example we want the the standard 100Khz I2C clock
rate and our
// internal Fosc is 16Mhz so we get: 100000 = 16000000/
[(SSPADD+1)*4]
// or solving for SSPADD = [(16000000/100000)-4]/4
// and we get SSPADD = 39

SSPADD = 39; // set Baud rate clock divider
// *********************************************************\
************

__delay_ms(10); // let everything settle.
}

//**********************************************************\
********
// Send one byte to SEE
//**********************************************************\
********
void Send_I2C_Data(unsigned int databyte)
{
PIR1bits.SSP1IF=0; // clear SSP interrupt bit
SSPBUF = databyte; // send databyte
while(!PIR1bits.SSP1IF); // Wait for interrupt flag to go high
indicating transmission is complete
}
```

```
//*********************************************************\
********

// Read one byte from SEE
//*********************************************************\
********

unsigned int Read_I2C_Data(void)
{
PIR1bits.SSP1IF=0; // clear SSP interrupt bit
SSPCON2bits.RCEN=1;// set the receive enable bit to initiate a read
of 8 bits from the serial EEPROM
while(!PIR1bits.SSP1IF);// Wait for interrupt flag to go high
indicating transmission is complete
return (SSPBUF); // Data from EEPROM is now in the SSPBUF so
return that value
}

//*********************************************************\
********

// Send control byte to SEE (this includes 4 bits of device
code, block select bits and the R/W bit)
//*********************************************************
***************\
********

// Notes:
// 1) The device code for serial EEPROMs is defined as '1010'
which we are using in this example
// 2) RW_bit can only be a one or zero
// 3) Block address is only used for SEE devices larger than 4K,
however on
// some other devices these bits may become the hardware
address bits that
```

```
// allow you to put multiple devices of the same type on the
same bus.
// Read the datasheet on your particular serial EEPROM device
to be sure.
//*********************************************************\
********

void Send_I2C_ControlByte(unsigned int BlockAddress,unsigned
int RW_bit)
{
PIR1bits.SSP1IF=0; // clear SSP interrupt bit

// Assemble the control byte from device code, block address
bits and R/W bit
// so it looks like this: CCCCBBBR
// where 'CCCC' is the device control code
// 'BBB' is the block address
// and 'R' is the Read/Write bit

SSPBUF = (((0b1010 << 4) | (BlockAddress <<1)) + RW_bit);
// send the control byte

while(!PIR1bits.SSP1IF);// Wait for interrupt flag to go high
indicating transmission is complete
}

//*********************************************************\
********

// Send start bit to SEE
//*********************************************************\
********
```

```
void Send_I2C_StartBit(void)
{
PIR1bits.SSP1IF=0; // clear SSP interrupt bit
SSPCON2bits.SEN=1; // send start bit
while(!PIR1bits.SSP1IF); // Wait for the SSPIF bit to go back
high before we load the data buffer
}

//***********************************************************\
********
// Send stop bit to SEE
//***********************************************************\
********
void Send_I2C_StopBit(void)
{
PIR1bits.SSP1IF=0; // clear SSP interrupt bit
SSPCON2bits.PEN=1; // send stop bit
while(!PIR1bits.SSP1IF);// Wait for interrupt flag to go high
indicating\
transmission is complete
}

//***********************************************************\
********
// Send ACK bit to SEE
//***********************************************************\
********
```

```c
void Send_I2C_ACK(void)
{
PIR1bits.SSP1IF=0; // clear SSP interrupt bit
SSPCON2bits.ACKDT=0; // clear the Acknowledge Data Bit - this
means we are sending an Acknowledge or 'ACK'
SSPCON2bits.ACKEN=1; // set the ACK enable bit to initiate
transmission of the ACK bit to the serial EEPROM
while(!PIR1bits.SSP1IF); // Wait for interrupt flag to go high
indicating transmission is complete
}

//***********************************************************\
********
// Send NAK bit to SEE
//***********************************************************\
********

void Send_I2C_NAK(void)
{
PIR1bits.SSP1IF=0; // clear SSP interrupt bit
SSPCON2bits.ACKDT=1; // set the Acknowledge Data Bit- this
means we are sending a No-Ack or 'NAK'
SSPCON2bits.ACKEN=1; // set the ACK enable bit to initiate
transmissi on of the ACK bit to the serial EEPROM
while(!PIR1bits.SSP1IF); // Wait for interrupt flag to go high
indicating transmission is complete
}
```

Now for at the main code, shown in Listing 9-14.

Listing 9-14. Main File

```
/*
 * File: Main.c
 * Author: Armstrong Subero
 * PIC: 16F1717 w/Int OSC @ 16MHz, 5v
 * Program: 24_I2C
 * Compiler: XC8 (v1.38, MPLAX X v3.40)
 * Program Version: 1.0
 *
 *
 * Program Description: This Program Allows PIC16F1717 to
communicate via the
 * I2C interface
 *
 *
 * Hardware Description: A HD44780 LCD is connected via PORTD
and a 24LC16B
 * EEPROM chip is connected to the I2C bus
 *
 *
 * Created November 10th, 2016, 8:02 PM
 */

/***********************************************************
*Includes and defines
***********************************************************/

#include "16F1717_Internal.h"
#include "LCD.h"
#include "I2C.h"
```

```
/*************************************************************
*Includes and defines
*************************************************************/

int block_address = 0x00;    // Set the EEPROM block address
                                that we will write the data to
int word_address = 0x00;     // Set the EEPROM word address that
                                we will write the data to
int eeprom_data = 0x09;      // This is the data we are going to write
int incoming_data;

/*************************************************************
* Function: void initmain(void)
*
* Returns: Nothing
*
* Description: Initializations for main
*************************************************************/

void initmain(void){
internal_16();

// Setup pins for I2C
ANSELCbits.ANSC4 = 0;
ANSELCbits.ANSC5 = 0;

TRISCbits.TRISC4 = 1;
TRISCbits.TRISC5 = 1;

PPSLOCK = 0x55;
PPSLOCK = 0xAA;
PPSLOCKbits.PPSLOCKED = 0x00; // unlock PPS

RC4PPSbits.RC4PPS =0x0011; //RC4->MSSP:SDA;
SSPDATPPSbits.SSPDATPPS =0x0014; //RC4->MSSP:SDA;
```

```
SSPCLKPPSbits.SSPCLKPPS =0x0015; //RC5->MSSP:SCL;
RC5PPSbits.RC5PPS =0x0010; //RC5->MSSP:SCL;

PPSLOCK = 0x55;
PPSLOCK = 0xAA;
PPSLOCKbits.PPSLOCKED = 0x01; // lock PPS
//Setup for LCD
TRISD = 0;
ANSELD = 0;

//Setup LCD
Lcd_Init();
__delay_ms(1000);
Lcd_Clear();

}
/************************************************************
* Function: void main(void)
*
* Returns: Nothing
*
* Description: Program entry point
************************************************************/

void main(void)
{
initmain();
I2C_Init();

Lcd_Set_Cursor(1,1);
Lcd_Write_String("I2C Ready");
__delay_ms(1000);
Lcd_Clear();
```

```
while (1)
{
/////////////////////////
// Write EEPROM
/////////////////////////

Lcd_Set_Cursor(1,1);
Lcd_Write_String("Write");
__delay_ms(1000);
Lcd_Clear();

Send_I2C_StartBit(); // send start bit
Send_I2C_ControlByte(block_address,0);  // send control byte
with R/W bit\
set low
Send_I2C_Data(word_address); // send word address
Send_I2C_Data(eeprom_data); // send data byte
Send_I2C_StopBit();// send stop bit
__delay_ms(200);

/////////////////////////
// Read EEPROM
/////////////////////////

Lcd_Set_Cursor(1,1);
Lcd_Write_String("Read");
__delay_ms(1000);
Lcd_Clear();

Send_I2C_StartBit();    // send start bit
Send_I2C_ControlByte(block_address,0);  // send control byte
                                        with R/W bit set low
Send_I2C_Data(word_address);    // send word address
```

```
Send_I2C_StartBit();    // send start bit
Send_I2C_ControlByte(block_address,1); // send control byte
                                    with R/W bit set high
incoming_data = Read_I2C_Data(); // read data coming back from
                                    the EEPROM
Send_I2C_NAK();   // send NACK to tell EEPROM we don't want any
                more data
Send_I2C_StopBit();

Lcd_Set_Cursor(1,1);

Lcd_Write_Integer(incoming_data);
__delay_ms(1000);

Lcd_Clear();
}
}
```

Conclusion

In this chapter, we looked at USART, SPI, and I2C, which are the fundamental communication protocols of microcontroller-based systems. We also looked at GPS, GSM, LCDs, and a host of other things. Once you understand these communication protocols, you can easily interface your microcontroller to a host of sensors. At this point you can do quite a lot; however, keep reading because the next few chapters will take your skills to another level.

CHAPTER 10

Interfacing Displays

Displays

So far we have looked at using LEDs, seven segment displays, serial character LCDs, and parallel character LCDs to relay information to users. To design modern embedded systems, users demand more. Many users, thanks to the smartphone revolution, expect to be able to interact with their devices using touch displays. In addition, OLED technology is rapidly replacing LCD technology. For these reasons, this chapter looks at going a bit further and using OLEDs and touch screen LCDs (see Figure 10-1).

Figure 10-1. *Modern smartphone*

© Armstrong Subero 2018
A. Subero, *Programming PIC Microcontrollers with XC8,*
https://doi.org/10.1007/978-1-4842-3273-6_10

OLED Displays

We begin the chapter by looking at the use of the Organic Light Emitting Diode (OLED) displays. OLEDs are my favorite type of displays. This is because they have high contrast, use relatively little power, and do not require extra power considerations for backlighting. We use the SSD1306 in this chapter (see Figure 10-2); it is a small LCD that is rather simple to interface. It also consumes relatively little power. In fact, using this display with a PIC16F1717, LED, and logic-level converter, I have been able to get power readings as low as 5mA! In practice, I have found it to use less power than a HD44780 LCD with backlighting. In addition, it uses less I/O because it's a serial LCD using the I2C protocol, so it uses only two I/O lines.

In order to use the display, we need to provide a sequence of commands. This will initialize the display. The sequence in the code will enable the OLED to turn on. Enabling the charge pump is very important, and initially when I was developing the library, this caused a lot of problems. The sequence provided in the example code works.

Next, we will set the row and column coordinates of the OLED. The other functions draw characters and strings and contain functions for displaying integers and floating point numbers.

Most libraries for the SSD1306 utilize a buffer. However, the PIC16F1717 does not have the RAM, as a buffer would require 1024 bytes of RAM. The total RAM of the PIC16F1717 is 1024 bytes, so such a buffer is out of the question. This means that graphics are not available without a proper buffer. However, that is not necessary, as most applications with a small display do not require graphics. Displaying text and characters works great on the OLED.

Figure 10-2. *The SSD1306 OLED*

Listing 10-1 provides the header file.

Listing 10-1. OLED Header File

```
/*
* File: oled.h
* Author: Armstrong Subero
* PIC: 16F1717 w/X OSC @ 16MHz, 5v
* Program: Header file to setup PIC16F1717 I2C
* Compiler: XC8 (v1.35, MPLAX X v3.10)
* Program Version 1.3
* Separated file into Header and C source
* Replace fixed hex with macros
* Added additional comments
*
*
* Program Description: This program header will allow setup of
SSD 1306 OLEDs
*
```

```
* Created on March 10th, 2017, 8:00 PM
*/

// Define OLED dimensions
#define OLED_WIDTH 128
#define OLED_HEIGHT 64

// Define command macros
#define OLED_SETCONTRAST 0x81
#define OLED_DISPLAYALLON_RESUME 0xA4
#define OLED_DISPLAYALLON 0xA5
#define OLED_NORMALDISPLAY 0xA6
#define OLED_INVERTDISPLAY 0xA7
#define OLED_DISPLAYOFF 0xAE
#define OLED_DISPLAYON 0xAF
#define OLED_SETDISPLAYOFFSET 0xD3
#define OLED_SETCOMPINS 0xDA
#define OLED_SETVCOMDETECT 0xDB
#define OLED_SETDISPLAYCLOCKDIV 0xD5
#define OLED_SETPRECHARGE 0xD9
#define OLED_SETMULTIPLEX 0xA8
#define OLED_SETLOWCOLUMN 0x00
#define OLED_SETHIGHCOLUMN 0x10
#define OLED_SETSTARTLINE 0x40
#define OLED_MEMORYMODE 0x20
#define OLED_COLUMNADDR 0x21
#define OLED_PAGEADDR    0x22
#define OLED_COMSCANINC 0xC0
#define OLED_COMSCANDEC 0xC8
#define OLED_SEGREMAP 0xA0
#define OLED_CHARGEPUMP 0x8D

// Header file
#include "16F1717_Internal.h"
```

```
// Function declarations
void OLED_Command( uint8_t temp);
void OLED_Data( uint8_t temp);
void OLED_Init();
void OLED_YX(unsigned char Row, unsigned char Column);
// *warning!* max 4 rows
void OLED_PutChar( char ch );
void OLED_Clear();
void OLED_Write_String( char *s );
void OLED_Write_Integer(uint8_t i);
void OLED_Write_Float(float f);
```

Listing 10-2 provides the source for the display driver.

Listing 10-2. OLED Source

```
/*
* File: oled.c
* Author: Armstrong Subero
* PIC: 16F1717 w/Int OSC @ 16MHz, 5v
* Program: Library file for SSD 1306 OLED
* Compiler: XC8 (v1.38, MPLAX X v3.40)
* Program Version: 1.1
* *Added additional comments
*
* Program Description: This Library allows you to control the
SSD 1306 OLED
*
* Created on March 10th, 2017, 8:05 PM
*/

#include "oled.h"
#include "I2C.h"
#include <string.h>
```

```
/*****************************************************************
*****************
* Function: const uint8_t OledFont[][8]
*
* Returns: Nothing
*
* Description: 2 Dimensional array containing the the ASCII
characters
*
*****************************************************************
**************/

const uint8_t OledFont[][8] =
{
{0x00,0x00,0x00,0x00,0x00,0x00,0x00,0x00},
{0x00,0x00,0x5F,0x00,0x00,0x00,0x00,0x00},
{0x00,0x00,0x07,0x00,0x07,0x00,0x00,0x00},
{0x00,0x14,0x7F,0x14,0x7F,0x14,0x00,0x00},
{0x00,0x24,0x2A,0x7F,0x2A,0x12,0x00,0x00},
{0x00,0x23,0x13,0x08,0x64,0x62,0x00,0x00},
{0x00,0x36,0x49,0x55,0x22,0x50,0x00,0x00},
{0x00,0x00,0x05,0x03,0x00,0x00,0x00,0x00},
{0x00,0x1C,0x22,0x41,0x00,0x00,0x00,0x00},
{0x00,0x41,0x22,0x1C,0x00,0x00,0x00,0x00},
{0x00,0x08,0x2A,0x1C,0x2A,0x08,0x00,0x00},
{0x00,0x08,0x08,0x3E,0x08,0x08,0x00,0x00},
{0x00,0xA0,0x60,0x00,0x00,0x00,0x00,0x00},
{0x00,0x08,0x08,0x08,0x08,0x08,0x00,0x00},
{0x00,0x60,0x60,0x00,0x00,0x00,0x00,0x00},
{0x00,0x20,0x10,0x08,0x04,0x02,0x00,0x00},
{0x00,0x3E,0x51,0x49,0x45,0x3E,0x00,0x00},
{0x00,0x00,0x42,0x7F,0x40,0x00,0x00,0x00},
```

```
{0x00,0x62,0x51,0x49,0x49,0x46,0x00,0x00},
{0x00,0x22,0x41,0x49,0x49,0x36,0x00,0x00},
{0x00,0x18,0x14,0x12,0x7F,0x10,0x00,0x00},
{0x00,0x27,0x45,0x45,0x45,0x39,0x00,0x00},
{0x00,0x3C,0x4A,0x49,0x49,0x30,0x00,0x00},
{0x00,0x01,0x71,0x09,0x05,0x03,0x00,0x00},
{0x00,0x36,0x49,0x49,0x49,0x36,0x00,0x00},
{0x00,0x06,0x49,0x49,0x29,0x1E,0x00,0x00},
{0x00,0x00,0x36,0x36,0x00,0x00,0x00,0x00},
{0x00,0x00,0xAC,0x6C,0x00,0x00,0x00,0x00},
{0x00,0x08,0x14,0x22,0x41,0x00,0x00,0x00},
{0x00,0x14,0x14,0x14,0x14,0x14,0x00,0x00},
{0x00,0x41,0x22,0x14,0x08,0x00,0x00,0x00},
{0x00,0x02,0x01,0x51,0x09,0x06,0x00,0x00},
{0x00,0x32,0x49,0x79,0x41,0x3E,0x00,0x00},
{0x00,0x7E,0x09,0x09,0x09,0x7E,0x00,0x00},
{0x00,0x7F,0x49,0x49,0x49,0x36,0x00,0x00},
{0x00,0x3E,0x41,0x41,0x41,0x22,0x00,0x00},
{0x00,0x7F,0x41,0x41,0x22,0x1C,0x00,0x00},
{0x00,0x7F,0x49,0x49,0x49,0x41,0x00,0x00},
{0x00,0x7F,0x09,0x09,0x09,0x01,0x00,0x00},
{0x00,0x3E,0x41,0x41,0x51,0x72,0x00,0x00},
{0x00,0x7F,0x08,0x08,0x08,0x7F,0x00,0x00},
{0x00,0x41,0x7F,0x41,0x00,0x00,0x00,0x00},
{0x00,0x20,0x40,0x41,0x3F,0x01,0x00,0x00},
{0x00,0x7F,0x08,0x14,0x22,0x41,0x00,0x00},
{0x00,0x7F,0x40,0x40,0x40,0x40,0x00,0x00},
{0x00,0x7F,0x02,0x0C,0x02,0x7F,0x00,0x00},
{0x00,0x7F,0x04,0x08,0x10,0x7F,0x00,0x00},
{0x00,0x3E,0x41,0x41,0x41,0x3E,0x00,0x00},
{0x00,0x7F,0x09,0x09,0x09,0x06,0x00,0x00},
```

```
{0x00,0x3E,0x41,0x51,0x21,0x5E,0x00,0x00},
{0x00,0x7F,0x09,0x19,0x29,0x46,0x00,0x00},
{0x00,0x26,0x49,0x49,0x49,0x32,0x00,0x00},
{0x00,0x01,0x01,0x7F,0x01,0x01,0x00,0x00},
{0x00,0x3F,0x40,0x40,0x40,0x3F,0x00,0x00},
{0x00,0x1F,0x20,0x40,0x20,0x1F,0x00,0x00},
{0x00,0x3F,0x40,0x38,0x40,0x3F,0x00,0x00},
{0x00,0x63,0x14,0x08,0x14,0x63,0x00,0x00},
{0x00,0x03,0x04,0x78,0x04,0x03,0x00,0x00},
{0x00,0x61,0x51,0x49,0x45,0x43,0x00,0x00},
{0x00,0x7F,0x41,0x41,0x00,0x00,0x00,0x00},
{0x00,0x02,0x04,0x08,0x10,0x20,0x00,0x00},
{0x00,0x41,0x41,0x7F,0x00,0x00,0x00,0x00},
{0x00,0x04,0x02,0x01,0x02,0x04,0x00,0x00},
{0x00,0x80,0x80,0x80,0x80,0x80,0x00,0x00},
{0x00,0x01,0x02,0x04,0x00,0x00,0x00,0x00},
{0x00,0x20,0x54,0x54,0x54,0x78,0x00,0x00},
{0x00,0x7F,0x48,0x44,0x44,0x38,0x00,0x00},
{0x00,0x38,0x44,0x44,0x28,0x00,0x00,0x00},
{0x00,0x38,0x44,0x44,0x48,0x7F,0x00,0x00},
{0x00,0x38,0x54,0x54,0x54,0x18,0x00,0x00},
{0x00,0x08,0x7E,0x09,0x02,0x00,0x00,0x00},
{0x00,0x18,0xA4,0xA4,0xA4,0x7C,0x00,0x00},
{0x00,0x7F,0x08,0x04,0x04,0x78,0x00,0x00},
{0x00,0x00,0x7D,0x00,0x00,0x00,0x00,0x00},
{0x00,0x80,0x84,0x7D,0x00,0x00,0x00,0x00},
{0x00,0x7F,0x10,0x28,0x44,0x00,0x00,0x00},
{0x00,0x41,0x7F,0x40,0x00,0x00,0x00,0x00},
{0x00,0x7C,0x04,0x18,0x04,0x78,0x00,0x00},
{0x00,0x7C,0x08,0x04,0x7C,0x00,0x00,0x00},
{0x00,0x38,0x44,0x44,0x38,0x00,0x00,0x00},
{0x00,0xFC,0x24,0x24,0x18,0x00,0x00,0x00},
```

284

```
{0x00,0x18,0x24,0x24,0xFC,0x00,0x00,0x00},
{0x00,0x00,0x7C,0x08,0x04,0x00,0x00,0x00},
{0x00,0x48,0x54,0x54,0x24,0x00,0x00,0x00},
{0x00,0x04,0x7F,0x44,0x00,0x00,0x00,0x00},
{0x00,0x3C,0x40,0x40,0x7C,0x00,0x00,0x00},
{0x00,0x1C,0x20,0x40,0x20,0x1C,0x00,0x00},
{0x00,0x3C,0x40,0x30,0x40,0x3C,0x00,0x00},
{0x00,0x44,0x28,0x10,0x28,0x44,0x00,0x00},
{0x00,0x1C,0xA0,0xA0,0x7C,0x00,0x00,0x00},
{0x00,0x44,0x64,0x54,0x4C,0x44,0x00,0x00},
{0x00,0x08,0x36,0x41,0x00,0x00,0x00,0x00},
{0x00,0x00,0x7F,0x00,0x00,0x00,0x00,0x00},
{0x00,0x41,0x36,0x08,0x00,0x00,0x00,0x00},
{0x00,0x02,0x01,0x01,0x02,0x01,0x00,0x00},
{0x00,0x02,0x05,0x05,0x02,0x00,0x00,0x00},
};

/****************************************************************
****************
* Function: void OLED_Command( uint8_t temp)
*
* Returns: Nothing
*
* Description: sends commands to the OLED
*
*****************************************************************
**************/

void OLED_Command( uint8_t temp){

Send_I2C_StartBit();    // send start bit
Send_I2C_Data(0x3C << 1);   // send word address
Send_I2C_Data(0x00);
```

285

```
Send_I2C_Data(temp);    // send data byte
Send_I2C_StopBit();    // send stop bit
}

/***************************************************************
***************
* Function: void OLED_Data ( uint8_t temp)
*
* Returns: Nothing
*
* Description: sends data to the OLED
*
***************************************************************
**************/

void OLED_Data( uint8_t temp){

Send_I2C_StartBit();    // send start bit
Send_I2C_Data(0x3C << 1);    // send word address
Send_I2C_Data(0x40);
Send_I2C_Data(temp);    // send data byte
Send_I2C_StopBit();    // send stop bit
}

/***************************************************************
***************
* Function: void OLED_Init ()
*
* Returns: Nothing
*
* Description: Initializes OLED
*
```

```
****************************************************************
***************/

void OLED_Init() {

OLED_Command(OLED_DISPLAYOFF);    // 0xAE
OLED_Command(OLED_SETDISPLAYCLOCKDIV);    // 0xD5
OLED_Command(0x80);    // the suggested ratio 0x80
OLED_Command(OLED_SETMULTIPLEX);    //0xA8
OLED_Command(0x1F);
OLED_Command(OLED_SETDISPLAYOFFSET);    // 0xD3
OLED_Command(0x0);    // no offset
OLED_Command(OLED_SETSTARTLINE | 0x0); // line #0
OLED_Command(OLED_CHARGEPUMP);    // 0x8D
OLED_Command(0xAF);
OLED_Command(OLED_MEMORYMODE);    //0x20
OLED_Command(0x00);    //0x0 act like ks0108
OLED_Command(OLED_SEGREMAP | 0x1);
OLED_Command(OLED_COMSCANDEC);
OLED_Command(OLED_SETCOMPINS);    // 0xDA
OLED_Command(0x02);
OLED_Command(OLED_SETCONTRAST);    // 0x81
OLED_Command(0x8F);
OLED_Command(OLED_SETPRECHARGE);    // 0xd9
OLED_Command(0xF1);
OLED_Command(OLED_SETVCOMDETECT);    // 0xDB
OLED_Command(0x40);
OLED_Command(OLED_DISPLAYALLON_RESUME);    // 0xA4
OLED_Command(OLED_NORMALDISPLAY);    // 0xA6
OLED_Command(OLED_DISPLAYON);    //--turn on oled panel

}
```

```
/*************************************************************
****************
* Function: void OLED_YX(unsigned char Row, unsigned char
Column)
*
* Returns: Nothing
*
* Description: Sets the X and Y coordinates
*
*************************************************************
**************/

void OLED_YX(unsigned char Row, unsigned char Column)
{
OLED_Command( 0xB0 + Row);
OLED_Command( 0x00 + (8*Column & 0x0F) );
OLED_Command( 0x10 + ((8*Column>>4)&0x0F) );
}

/*************************************************************
****************
* Function: void OLED_PutChar(char ch)
*
* Returns: Nothing
*
* Description: Writes a character to the OLED
*
*************************************************************
**************/

void OLED_PutChar( char ch )
{
```

```c
if ( ( ch < 32 ) || ( ch > 127 ) ){
ch = ' ';
}

const uint8_t *base = &OledFont[ch - 32][0];

uint8_t bytes[9];
bytes[0] = 0x40;
memmove( bytes + 1, base, 8 );

Send_I2C_StartBit();   // send start bit
Send_I2C_Data(0x3C << 1);   // send word address
Send_I2C_Data(0x40);

int i;

for (i = 1; i <= 8; i++){
Send_I2C_Data(bytes[i]);
}

Send_I2C_StopBit();   // send stop bit
}
/****************************************************************
****************
* Function: void OLED_Clear()
*
* Returns: Nothing
*
* Description: Clears the OLED
*
****************************************************************
**************/
```

```
void OLED_Clear()
{
for ( uint16_t row = 0; row < 8; row++ ) {
for ( uint16_t col = 0; col < 16; col++ ) {
}
}
}
```

```
/****************************************************************
****************
* Function:  void OLED_Write_String( char *s )
*
* Returns: Nothing
*
* Description: Writes a string to the OLED
*
****************************************************************
**************/
```

```
void OLED_Write_String( char *s )
{
while (*s) OLED_PutChar( *s++);
}
```

```
/****************************************************************
****************
* Function:  void OLED_Write_Integer ( uint8_t i )
*
* Returns: Nothing
*
* Description: Writes an integer to the OLED
*
```

```
**************************************************************
**************/

void OLED_Write_Integer(uint8_t i)
{
char s[20];
itoa( s, i, 10 );
OLED_Write_String( s );
OLED_Write_String( "" );
}
/**************************************************************
****************
* Function:  void OLED_Write_Float( float f )
*
* Returns: Nothing
*
* Description: Writes a float to the OLED
*
**************************************************************
**************/

void OLED_Write_Float(float f)
{
char* buf11;
int status;

buf11 = ftoa(f, &status);

OLED_Write_String(buf11);
OLED_Write_String( "" );
}
```

Finally, we have the main code, shown in Listing 10-3.

Listing 10-3. Main Code

```
/*
* File: Main.c
* Author: Armstrong Subero
* PIC: 16F1717 w/Int OSC @ 16MHz, 5v
* Program: I08_SSD1306
* Compiler: XC8 (v1.38, MPLAX X v3.40)
* Program Version: 1.0
*
* Program Description: This Program Allows PIC16F1717 to be
connected to a
* SSD1306 via the I2C bus. It demonstrates writing strings
* together with writing integers and floating point
* numbers.
*
* Hardware Description: A SSD1306 based OLED is connected to a
PIC16F1717 via
* a logic level converter to a SSD1306 based OLED as
* follows:
*
* GND --> GND
* VCC --> VCC
* SCL --> RC5
* SDA --> RC4
*
* Created Friday 10th March, 2017, 8:05 PM
*/
```

```
/**********************************************************
****************
*Includes and defines
**********************************************************
**************/

#include "16F1717_Internal.h"
#include "I2C.h"
#include "oled.h"
#include <string.h>

/**********************************************************
***************
* Function: void initMain()
*
* Returns: Nothing
*
* Description: Contains initializations for main
*
* Usage: initMain()
**********************************************************
**************/

void initMain(){

// Run at 16 MHz
internal_16();

////////////////////
// Setup I2C
////////////////////

// Setup pins for I2C
ANSELCbits.ANSC4 = 0;
ANSELCbits.ANSC5 = 0;
```

```c
TRISCbits.TRISC4 = 1;
TRISCbits.TRISC5 = 1;

PPSLOCK = 0x55;
PPSLOCK = 0xAA;
PPSLOCKbits.PPSLOCKED = 0x00; // unlock PPS

RC4PPSbits.RC4PPS = 0x0011;   //RC4->MSSP:SDA;
SSPDATPPSbits.SSPDATPPS = 0x0014;   //RC4->MSSP:SDA;
//RC5->MSSP:SCL;

PPSLOCK = 0x55;
PPSLOCK = 0xAA;
PPSLOCKbits.PPSLOCKED = 0x01; // lock PPS
}

/*************************************************************
****************
* Function: Main
*
* Returns: Nothing
*
* Description: Program entry point
*************************************************************
**************/

void main(void) {
initMain();

// Initialize I2C
I2C_Init();

__delay_ms(100);

// Initialize OLED
OLED_Init();
```

```
// clear OLED
OLED_Clear();

// variables for counting
int count = 0;
float dec = 0.0;

while ( 1 ) {

////////////////////
// Strings
////////////////////

__delay_ms(100);
}

__delay_ms(100);
OLED_Clear();
}

return;

}
```

Touch Screen LCD

Thanks to the smartphone revolution, every user wants a screen that they can touch and interact with. It is for this very reason that I chose to include interfacing touch screens in this book. Smartphones have encouraged wide availability of touch screens. Many people think that you need a lot of processing power to use touch screens. In the past this was true, but with the advent of intelligent display modules, this is no longer the case. Intelligent displays have a processor onboard that handles drawing and updating the display. The application processor can thus interact with the display using simple commands. What this means is that even 8-bit microcontroller solutions can utilize a touch screen display.

When integrating touch-based displays into your design, it is important to consider the following factors:

- The touch screen must have a GUI interface that can be developed *quickly*.

- The touch screen must be *easy* to integrate into your projects.

- The touch screen must be *cost-effective*.

In addition to these factors, we must also examine the types of touch displays that are available on the market today. There are two main types of touch displays available—resistive touch screens and capacitive touch screens. We take a look at each of these types of displays in the next sections.

Resistive Touch

The resistive touch screen essentially consists of two layers of flexible sheets, which are then placed on a piece of glass. These sheets are clad in a substance that has a certain resistance and kept apart by small dots. When a part of the screen is pressed, the two layers are pressed together and this change in resistance at that touch point is measured.

Resistive touch screens require a hard object to press them together, such as a stylus, fingernail, or a sufficiently hard object. A major advantage of a resistive touch screens is that they can be used through electrically insulating materials such as when wearing gloves. A major disadvantage is that they are not as responsive as capacitive touch screens.

Capacitive Touch

The human body is known to have electrical properties. One of these properties is the fact that the human body is a conductor. Capacitive touch screens exploit this aspect of the human body. The capacitive touch screen consist of glass covered with a conductive material. When the material is touched, it produces a change in capacitance, which is measured and used to determine where the touch took place.

A major advantage of capacitive touch screens is that they are very responsive and a major disadvantage is that, unlike resistive touch screens, they cannot be used through electrically insulating materials.

Selecting a Touch Screen LCD

Now that you have a basic understanding of the factors to be determined when selecting a touch screen and have learned about the types of touch screens, you can select a touch screen to use in your project. The Nextion series of displays (see Figure 10-3) were chosen for this example because they have an editor tool that enables you to quickly develop the GUI. They also communicate via the ubiquitous UART protocol and are some of the lowest cost displays available on the market today. They are resistive touch screens. Before you continue with this section, I highly recommend you go through the tutorials on the Nextion web site at `https://nextion.itead.cc/`.

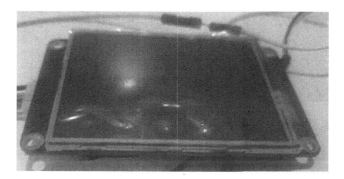

Figure 10-3. *Nextion display*

297

Using the Touch LCD

Here are the steps required to use the Nextion type displays:

1. Create the layout in your photo editor of choice.

2. Add widgets to your layout with the Nextion Editor.

3. Add code to those widgets via Nextion Editor.

4. Read information sent from the display by the microcontroller.

Creating a Layout

The first step is to create the layout of your choice (see Figure 10-4). If you want to use solid colors only in your design, you do not need to use any photo editing software to create a layout. However, if you plan on adding a decent looking background to your design, you will need images. I recommend that you purchase images from the many sites available that provide such a service. This will ensure that you are not violating any copyrights and you will have high-quality images.

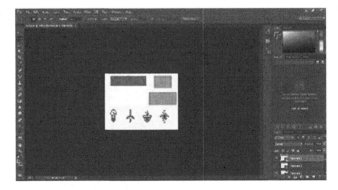

Figure 10-4. *Layout of the design*

Adding Widgets

The next important step in working with a touch screen is adding widgets to your application (see Figure 10-5). This can be done in the editor. We will add text and use a checkbox, although other types of widgets are available. Using the editor is very straightforward, and if you need to learn how to use it, there are a lot of tutorials on the web.

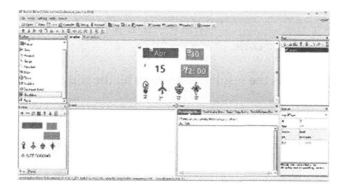

Figure 10-5. *Adding widgets*

Adding Code

The touch screens we are using are intelligent displays. Thus, code can be written on the display itself and sent to the microcontroller. The Nextion editor includes a section for adding code to the display. If you are unsure how to add code, you can follow along with the tutorials on the web site to learn how to do so.

The code is added to each widget (see Figure 10-6). The `print` command in the editor allows you to print a string of characters when a particular touch event of that particular widget is triggered. In this example they are `blulbpressed`, `motopressed`, `planpressed`, and `connpressed`. So, to add bulbpressed, for example, you would type `print bulbpressed` in the editor.

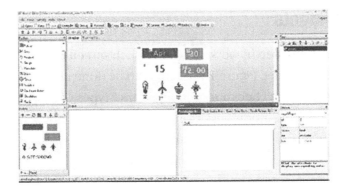

Figure 10-6. *Adding code*

Figure 10-7 shows the result you get after all the widgets have been added to your design.

Figure 10-7. *Final result*

Reading on the Microcontroller

Next on the microcontroller side, we will read the code sent by the display (see Listing 10-4).

Listing 10-4. Touch Screen Code

```
/*
* File: Main.c
* Author: Armstrong Subero
* PIC: 16F1717 w/Int OSC @ 16MHz, 5v
* Program: 31_Touchscreen
* Compiler: XC8 (v1.41, MPLAX X v3.55)
* Program Version: 1.0
*
*
* Program Description: This Program Allows PIC16F1717 to
communicate with a
* NX3224T024_0112.4 inch Nextion Display. The display
* communicates with the microcontroller via UART and
* sends messages to the microcontroller which is displayed
* on the SSD1306 OLED
*
* Hardware Description: A Nextion 2.4 inch touch screen and
SSD1306 OLED is
* connected to the microcontroller as per header file.
*
* Created April 15th, 2017, 9:30 PM
*/
```

```c
/****************************************************************
****************
*Includes and defines
****************************************************************
**************/

#include "16F1717_Internal.h"
#include "EUSART.h"
#include "oled.h"
#include <string.h>
#include <stdbool.h>

// buffer for UART
char buf[50];

// Function prototypes
void touchscreen_command(char* string);

void moto_func(char* buf);
void plan_func(char* buf);
void conn_func(char* buf);
void bulb_func(char* buf);

//////////////////////////
// Bool support
//////////////////////////

typedef unsigned char bool;

#define true 1
#define false 0

// boolean for current state
bool on = false;
```

```
/***************************************************************
****************
* Function: void initMain()
*
* Returns: Nothing
*
* Description: Contains initializations for main
*
* Usage: initMain()
****************************************************************
**************/

void initMain(){
// Run at 16 MHz
internal_16();

// Setup pins for EUSART
TRISBbits.TRISB2 = 0;
ANSELBbits.ANSB2 = 0;

TRISBbits.TRISB3 = 1;
ANSELBbits.ANSB3 = 0;

// Setup pins for I2C
ANSELCbits.ANSC4 = 0;
ANSELCbits.ANSC5 = 0;

TRISCbits.TRISC4 = 1;
TRISCbits.TRISC5 = 1;

///////////////////////
// Setup Serial Comms
///////////////////////
PPSLOCK = 0x55;
```

```
PPSLOCK = 0xAA;
PPSLOCKbits.PPSLOCKED = 0x00; // unlock PPS

RC4PPSbits.RC4PPS = 0x0011;    //RC4->MSSP:SDA;
SSPDATPPSbits.SSPDATPPS =0x0014;    //RC4->MSSP:SDA;
SSPCLKPPSbits.SSPCLKPPS =0x0015;    //RC5->MSSP:SCL;
RC5PPSbits.RC5PPS = 0x0010;    //RC5->MSSP:SCL;
RB2PPSbits.RB2PPS = 0x14;
//RB2->EUSART:TX;
RXPPSbits.RXPPS = 0x0B;    //RB3->EUSART:RX;

PPSLOCK = 0x55;
PPSLOCK = 0xAA;
PPSLOCKbits.PPSLOCKED = 0x01; // lock PPS
}
/****************************************************************
****************
* Function: Main
*
* Returns: Nothing
*
* Description: Program entry point
*****************************************************************
**************/

void main(void) {
initMain();

// Initialize I2C
I2C_Init();
__delay_ms(500);

// Initialize OLED
OLED_Init();
```

```
// clear OLED
OLED_Clear();

__delay_ms(1000);

// Initialize EUSART module with 9600 baud
EUSART_Initialize(9600);
__delay_ms(2000);

// Dim Touchscreen
OLED_YX(0, 0);
OLED_Write_String("Dim Screen");

touchscreen_command("dim=30");

// Update Touchscreen
OLED_YX(0, 0);
OLED_Write_String("Update Screen");

touchscreen_command("t3.txt=\"16\"");

OLED_Clear();

while(1){

// Read EUSART
EUSART_Read_Text(buf, 11);

// Check for which checkbox triggered
bulb_func(buf);
moto_func(buf);
plan_func(buf);
conn_func(buf);
}

return;
}
```

```
/*
Send commands to Touchscreen
*/
void touchscreen_command(char* string)
{
EUSART_Write_Text(string);
EUSART_Write(0xFF);
EUSART_Write(0xFF);
EUSART_Write(0xFF);
__delay_ms(1000);
}

/*
Bulb Function Routines
*/
void bulb_func(char* buf)
{
char* bulb1;

bulb1 = strstr(buf, "bulb");

if (bulb1 == NULL)
{
return;
}

else
{
if (!on){
OLED_YX(0, 0);
OLED_Write_String("Bulb On");
__delay_ms(1000);
OLED_Clear();
```

```c
on = true;
}

else {
OLED_YX(0, 0);
OLED_Write_String("Bulb Off");
__delay_ms(1000);
OLED_Clear();

on = false;
}
}
}
/*
Motor function Routines
*/
void moto_func(char* buf)
{
char* moto1;

moto1 = strstr(buf, "moto");

if (moto1 == NULL)
{
return;
}

else
{
if (!on){
OLED_YX(0, 0);
OLED_Write_String("Motor On");
```

```
__delay_ms(1000);
OLED_Clear();

on = true;
}

else {
OLED_YX(0, 0);
OLED_Write_String("Motor Off");
__delay_ms(1000);
OLED_Clear();

on = false;
}
}
}
/*
Plant function routines
*/
void plan_func(char* buf)
{
char* plant1;

plant1 = strstr(buf, "plan");

if (plant1 == NULL)
{
return;
}
else
{
if (!on){
```

```c
OLED_YX(0, 0);
OLED_Write_String("Plant On");
__delay_ms(1000);
OLED_Clear();

on = true;
}

else {
OLED_YX(0, 0);
OLED_Write_String("Plant Off");
__delay_ms(1000);
OLED_Clear();

on = false;
}
}
}

/*
Connection Function Routines
*/
void conn_func(char* buf)
{
char* conn1;

conn1 = strstr(buf, "conn");

if (conn1 == NULL)
{
return;
}
```

```
else
{
if (!on){
OLED_YX(0, 0);
OLED_Write_String("Connected");
__delay_ms(1000);
OLED_Clear();

on = true;
}
else {
OLED_YX(0, 0);
OLED_Write_String("Disconnected");
__delay_ms(1000);
OLED_Clear();

on = false;
}
}
}
```

Conclusion

In this chapter, we looked at using OLED and touch screen displays. Although other types of displays are available, users now expect to be able to touch their displays to interact with them. In addition, OLED technology is rapidly taking the place of traditional LCD displays. At this point, I am confident that you can interface your microcontroller to any type of display that will be thrown at you.

CHAPTER 11

ADC and DAC

Data Conversion

Many times when you're working with microcontrollers, you might need to use analog to digital and digital to analog converters. Devices that are responsible for data conversion between digital and analog forms are ubiquitous in our modern world. Devices like smartphones, drones, and televisions depend on data conversion to work. Converters are crucial to the operation of most modern devices.

ADC (Analog to Digital Conversion)

Analog to digital conversion (ADC) is one of the most important onboard modules of the PIC® microcontroller. The reason is very simple—we live in an analog world. Computers process all their information in digital format; however many transducers, which when electronic are called sensors, output their values as voltage. The ADC converts these analog voltages into a digital representation that the processor can understand.

The ADC has a specific number of bits of resolution. These can be from 8 to 32 bits. The higher the resolution of the ADC, the greater the number of steps there will be from the minimum voltage to the maximum voltage. The PIC16F1717 has a 10-bit resolution ADC. What this means is

© Armstrong Subero 2018
A. Subero, *Programming PIC Microcontrollers with XC8*,
https://doi.org/10.1007/978-1-4842-3273-6_11

that the ADC can read a voltage in steps from 0 to 1023. Here is the code to interface the ADC:

In this example, we use a potentiometer connected to the microcontroller to demonstrate the use of the ADC module. The potentiometer will vary the voltage between 5v (step 1023) down to 0v (step 0), which is connected to a pin that has been configured for analog input on the PIC® microcontroller.

Listing 11-1 provides the code to interface the ADC.

Listing 11-1. ADC Source

```
/*
* File: Main.c
* Author: Armstrong Subero
* PIC: 16F1717 w/Int OSC @ 16MHz, 5v
* Program: 16_ADC
* Compiler: XC8 (v1.38, MPLAX X v3.40)
* Program Version: 1.0
*
*
* Program Description: This Program Allows PIC16F1717 to
demonstrate the on
* board 10 bit ADC module. A 10k potentiometer is
* connected to PIN RA0 and a 10 bit ( 0 - 1023) conversion
* result is displayed on the LCD.
*
*
* Hardware Description: An HD44780 compatible LCD is connected
to PORTD of the
* microcontroller as follows:
*
* RS ---> RD2
* R/W ---> GND
```

```
* EN ---> RD3
* D4 ---> RD4
* D5 ---> RD5
* D6 ---> RD6
* D7 ---> RD7
*
* A 10k pot is connected to PIN RA0.
*
*
* Created November 7th, 2016, 11:05 AM
*/

/****************************************************************
****************
*Includes and defines
****************************************************************
**************/

#include "16F1717_Internal.h"
#include "LCD.h"

/****************************************************************
****************
* Function: void initMain()
*
* Returns: Nothing
*
* Description: Contains initializations for main
*
* Usage: initMain()
****************************************************************
**************/
```

```
void initMain(){
// Run at 16 MHz
internal_16();

// Set PIN D1 as output
TRISDbits.TRISD1 = 0;

// Turn off LED
LATDbits.LATD1 = 0;

// Setup PORTD
TRISD = 0;
ANSELD = 0;

// Set PIN B0 as input
TRISBbits.TRISB0 = 1;

// Configure ANSELB0
ANSELBbits.ANSB0 = 0;

// Set A0 as input
TRISAbits.TRISA0 = 1;

// Set A0 as analog
ANSELAbits.ANSA0 = 1;

///////////////////
// Configure ADC
///////////////////

// Fosc/32 ADC conversion time is 2.0 us
ADCON1bits.ADCS = 0b010;

// Right justified
ADCON1bits.ADFM = 1;

// Vref- is Vss
ADCON1bits.ADNREF = 0;
```

```c
// Vref+ is Vdd
ADCON1bits.ADPREF = 0b00;

// Set input channel to AN0
ADCON0bits.CHS = 0b00000;

// Zero ADRESL and ADRESH
ADRESL = 0;
ADRESH = 0;

// Initialize LCD
Lcd_Init();
__delay_ms(100);
Lcd_Clear();
}

/****************************************************************
****************
* Function: Main
*
* Returns: Nothing
*
* Description: Program entry point
****************************************************************
**************/

void main(void) {
initMain();

// variable to store conversion result
int result;

while(1){

// Turn ADC on
ADCON0bits.ADON = 1;
```

```
// Sample CH0
__delay_us(10);
ADCON0bits.GO = 1;
while (ADCON0bits.GO_nDONE);

// Store ADC result
result = ((ADRESH<<8)+ADRESL);

// Write result to LCD
Lcd_Set_Cursor(1,1);
__delay_ms(5);
Lcd_Write_Integer(result);

// Update every second
__delay_ms(1000);
Lcd_Clear();
}

return;

}
```

Project: Digital Thermometer

In this section, we look at building a digital thermometer using the PIC®
microcontroller. The ADC onboard the microcontroller will read the
LM34 temperature sensor and output the corresponding voltage (see
Figure 11-1). The LM34 has a scale factor of 1 degree Fahrenheit for every
10 millivolts. Thus, in order to convert the voltage to temperature, there are
three stages. The steps are as follows:

1. Get the results according to the scale factor.

2. Convert that result to Fahrenheit.

3. Convert Fahrenheit to Celsius.

The code is pretty straightforward, as shown in Listing 11-2.

Listing 11-2. Temperature Code

```
/*
* File: Main.c
* Author: Armstrong Subero
* PIC: 16F1717 w/Int OSC @ 16MHz, 5v
* Program: P01_Temperature
* Compiler: XC8 (v1.41, MPLAX X v3.55)
* Program Version: 1.0
*
*
*Program Description: This Program gives a reading in Celsius
based on the
* output of a LM34 temperature sensor. The output is
* displayed on an OLED.
*
* Hardware Description: A LM34 is connected to PIN E0 and a
SSD1306 OLED is
* connected to the I2C bus.

*
*
* Created March 22nd, 2017, 8:15 PM
*/

/************************************************************
****************
*Includes and defines
************************************************************
**************/
```

```
#include "16F1717_Internal.h"
#include "I2C.h"
#include "oled.h"

/***************************************************************
****************
* Function: void initMain()
*
* Returns: Nothing
*
* Description: Contains initializations for main
*
* Usage: initMain()
****************************************************************
**************/

void initMain(){
// Run at 16 MHz
internal_16();

//////////////////////
// Setup I2C
//////////////////

// Setup pins for I2C
ANSELCbits.ANSC4 = 0;
ANSELCbits.ANSC5 = 0;

TRISCbits.TRISC4 = 1;
TRISCbits.TRISC5 = 1;

PPSLOCK = 0x55;
PPSLOCK = 0xAA;
PPSLOCKbits.PPSLOCKED = 0x00; // unlock PPS
```

```
RC4PPSbits.RC4PPS =0x0011;    //RC4->MSSP:SDA;
SSPDATPPSbits.SSPDATPPS =0x0014;    //RC4->MSSP:SDA;
SSPCLKPPSbits.SSPCLKPPS =0x0015;    //RC5->MSSP:SCL;
RC5PPSbits.RC5PPS =0x0010;    //RC5->MSSP:SCL;

PPSLOCK = 0x55;
PPSLOCK = 0xAA;
PPSLOCKbits.PPSLOCKED = 0x01; // lock PPS

///////////////////
// Configure ADC
///////////////////

// Fosc/32 ADC conversion time is 2.0 us
ADCON1bits.ADCS = 0b010;

// Right justified
ADCON1bits.ADFM = 1;

// Vref- is Vss
ADCON1bits.ADNREF = 0;

// Vref+ is Vdd
ADCON1bits.ADPREF = 0b00;

// Set input channel to AN0
ADCON0bits.CHS = 0x05;

// Zero ADRESL and ADRESH
ADRESL = 0;
ADRESH = 0;

ANSELEbits.ANSE0 = 1;

}
```

```
/*************************************************************
****************
* Function: Main
*
* Returns: Nothing
*
* Description: Program entry point
*************************************************************
**************/

void main(void) {
initMain();

// Initialize I2C
I2C_Init();

// Initialize OLED
OLED_Init();

// clear OLED
OLED_Clear();

// result to store ADC conversion
float result;

// variables for conversion
float conversion10;
float farenheit;
float celsius;

while(1){

// Turn ADC on
ADCONObits.ADON = 1;
```

```
// Sample CH0
__delay_us(10);
ADCON0bits.GO = 1;
while (ADCON0bits.GO_nDONE);

// Store ADC result
result = ((ADRESH<<8)+ADRESL);

// 10 bit conversion
conversion10 = (result * 5000)/1024 ;

// to Fahrenheit
farenheit = conversion10 / 10;

// to Celsius
celsius = (farenheit - 32) * 5/9;

// Display temperature
OLED_YX(0, 0);
OLED_Write_String("Temp: ");

OLED_YX(1, 0);
OLED_Write_Integer((int)celsius);

// Update every second
__delay_ms(2000);

}

return;

}
```

Figure 11-1. *Temperature results*

DAC (Digital to Analog Converter)

In addition to an ADC module, the PIC16F1717 also provides a DAC onboard. The digital to analog converter (DAC) is the brother of the ADC, except it does the exact opposite. Instead of converting an analog signal to a digital one, as its name suggests, it converts a digital signal to an analog one. The PIC16F1717 has two onboard DACs and they include an 8-bit DAC and a 5 bit-DAC. In this example, we use the 8-bit DAC to output a waveform on pin RA2, which can be viewed with an oscilloscope.

Listing 11-3 shows the code to use the DAC onboard the PIC16F1717 and generate a waveform.

Listing 11-3. DAC Source

```
/*
 * File: Main.c
 * Author: Armstrong Subero
 * PIC: 16F1717 w/Int OSC @ 16MHz, 5v
 * Program: 14_DAC_8_Bit
 * Compiler: XC8 (v1.38, MPLAX X v3.40)
 * Program Version: 1.0
 *
 *
 * Program Description: This Program Allows PIC16F1717 DAC1 to
generate a
 * waveform on PIN RA2
 *
 *
 * Hardware Description: An Oscilloscope probe is connected to
pin RA2
 *
 *
 * Created November 7th, 2016, 10:08 AM
 */

/****************************************************************
****************
*Includes and defines
*****************************************************************
**************/

#include "16F1717_Internal.h"

/****************************************************************
****************
```

```
* Function: void initMain()
*
* Returns: Nothing
*
* Description: Contains initializations for main
*
* Usage: initMain()
****************************************************************
**************/
void initMain(){
// Run at 16 MHz
internal_16();

// Set PIN D1 as output
TRISDbits.TRISD1 = 0;
TRISDbits.TRISD2 = 0;

// Turn off LED
LATDbits.LATD1 = 0;
LATDbits.LATD1 = 0;

/////////////////////
// Configure DAC
/////////////////////

// DAC enabled
DAC1CONobits.DAC1EN = 1;

// DACOUT pin enabled
DAC1CONobits.DAC1OE1 = 1;

// +ve source is Vdd
DAC1CONobits.DAC1PSS = 0;
```

```
// -ve source is Vss
DAC1CON0bits.DAC1NSS = 0;

// Initial output is 0v
DAC1CON1bits.DAC1R = 0;
}

/*************************************************************
****************
* Function: Main
*
* Returns: Nothing
*
* Description: Program entry point
*************************************************************
**************/
void main(void) {
initMain();

while(1){
DAC1CON1++;

}

return;

}
```

Conclusion

This chapter looked at using the onboard ADC and DAC of the PIC®
microcontroller. You saw how to used these modules to create a
thermometer and generate a simple waveform.

CHAPTER 12

NCO, Comparator, and FVR

CLC (Configurable Logic Cell)

The Configurable Logic Cell (CLC) is a module designed by Microchip that provides basic configurable logic for PIC® microcontrollers. This includes the basic gates and D and JK flip-flops and D and SR latches. This means that with the CLC, you can combine logic internal and external to the chip to produce a particular function. The CLC can even wake the microcontroller up from sleep.

Microchip provides many examples to use the CLC and they will not be repeated in this book; instead, we look at a simple example. In this example, we demonstrate the CLC by configuring it as a four-input AND gate.

The inputs of the CLC are each connected to switches. If any of the switches is pressed, the respective input of the AND gate becomes a logic low and the LED is switched off.

We will begin by selecting the CLC option from the MCC Device Resources (see Figure 12-1).

© Armstrong Subero 2018
A. Subero, *Programming PIC Microcontrollers with XC8*,
https://doi.org/10.1007/978-1-4842-3273-6_12

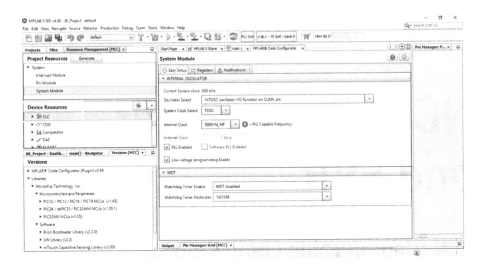

Figure 12-1. *MCC screen*

Next, double-click the CLC peripherals option from the Project
Resources tab. Set the mode to 4-input AND and ensure that the output is
not inverted. At each of the four OR gates, you will notice four lines marked
with X. Click the first, second, third, and fourth of these and select the
inputs as CLCIN1, CLCIN2, CLCIN3, and CLCIN4, respectively, as shown
in Figure 12-2.

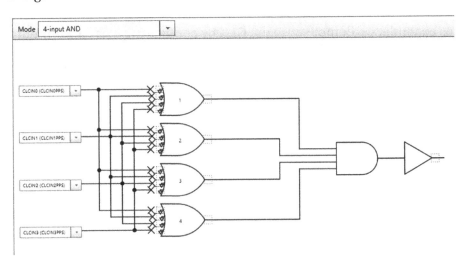

Figure 12-2. *Selecting inputs*

Figure 12-3 shows the finished setup.

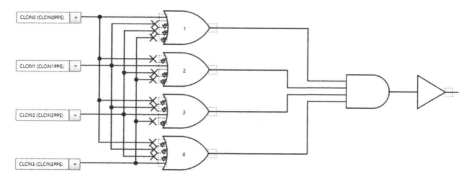

Figure 12-3. *Finished setup*

Choose Pin Manager: Package and Pin Manager: Grid and select your input and output pins, as shown in Figure 12-4.

Output	Pin Manager: Grid [MCC] ×																																										
Package:	PDIP40	▾	Pin No:	2	3	4	5	6	7	14	13	33	34	35	36	37	38	39	40	15	16	17	18	23	24	25	26	19	20	21	22	27	28	29	30	8	9	10
					Port A ▾								Port B ▾								Port C ▾								Port D ▾								Port E ▾		
Module	Function	Direction	0	1	2	3	4	5	6	7	0	1	2	3	4	5	6	7	0	1	2	3	4	5	6	7	0	1	2	3	4	5	6	7	0	1	2	
CLC1	CLC1OUT	output	ⓑ	ⓑ	ⓑ	ⓑ	ⓑ	ⓑ	ⓑ	ⓑ									ⓐ	ⓑ	ⓑ	ⓑ	ⓑ	ⓑ	ⓑ	ⓑ											
CLCx ▾	CLCIN0	input	ⓑ	ⓑ	ⓑ	ⓑ	ⓑ	ⓑ	ⓑ	ⓑ									ⓑ	ⓐ	ⓑ	ⓑ	ⓑ	ⓑ	ⓑ	ⓑ											
	CLCIN1	input	ⓑ	ⓑ	ⓑ	ⓑ	ⓑ	ⓑ	ⓑ	ⓑ									ⓑ	ⓑ	ⓐ	ⓑ	ⓑ	ⓑ	ⓑ	ⓑ											
	CLCIN2	input									ⓑ	ⓑ	ⓑ	ⓑ	ⓑ	ⓑ	ⓑ	ⓑ									ⓐ	ⓑ	ⓑ	ⓑ	ⓑ	ⓑ	ⓑ	ⓑ			
	CLCIN3	input									ⓑ	ⓑ	ⓑ	ⓑ	ⓑ	ⓑ	ⓑ	ⓑ									ⓑ	ⓐ	ⓑ	ⓑ	ⓑ	ⓑ	ⓑ	ⓑ			
OSC	CLKOUT	output					ⓑ																														

Figure 12-4. *Selecting pins*

Click Generate and program! That's it! There is no main code to be written by the developer. The MCC makes it very easy for a developer; however, in this book I deliberately avoided the use of the MCC to allow you to get a good understanding of the underlying hardware. In the case of the CLC, the MCC has a visual configuration tool that is very simple to use.

NCO (Numerically Controlled Oscillator)

The PIC® microcontroller has always been a cut above the rest in matters relating to onboard peripherals. The Numerically Controlled Oscillator (NCO) is one such peripheral that was introduced to PIC® microcontrollers. The output of the NCO is a square wave that's dependent on the input clock and the value given for the increment postscaler.

The NCO, like the CLC, operates independently from the core, which means that once it is set up in this example, we won't have any code to write. All you have to do to see this square wave is connect the probe to the output pin. This process is really straightforward. If you have never used an oscilloscope, it's best to consult you user manual. There are also plenty of resources on the web showing you how to use your oscilloscope. If you are using a Velleman pocket oscilloscope, connect the ground to the ground rail first and leave the attenuation at 1x. The scope will do the rest.

Let's write some code to generate a square wave, as shown in Listing 12-1.

Listing 12-1. NCO Source

```
/*
* File: Main.c
* Author: Armstrong Subero
* PIC: 16F1717 w/Int OSC @ 16MHz, 5v
* Program: 27_NCO
* Compiler: XC8 (v1.38, MPLAX X v3.40)
* Program Version: 1.0
*
*
* Program Description: This Program Allows PIC16F1717 to use
the NCO
*
```

```
* Hardware Description: An oscilloscope probe is connected to
PIN CO
*
* Created November 4th, 2016, 1:00 PM
*/

/****************************************************************
****************
*Includes and defines
****************************************************************
**************/

#include "16F1717_Internal.h"


/****************************************************************
****************
* Function: void initMain()
*
* Returns: Nothing
*
* Description: Contains initializations for main
*
* Usage: initMain()
****************************************************************
**************/

void initMain(){
// Run at 16 MHz
internal_16();

/////////////////
// Set UP NCO
/////////////////
```

```
TRISCbits.TRISC0 = 0x00; // Port C as digital output port
ANSELC = 0;

bool state = GIE;
GIE = 0;
PPSLOCK = 0x55;
PPSLOCK = 0xAA;
PPSLOCKbits.PPSLOCKED = 0x00; // unlock PPS

RC0PPSbits.RC0PPS = 0x03;    //RC0->NCO1:NCO1OUT;

PPSLOCK = 0x55;
PPSLOCK = 0xAA;
PPSLOCKbits.PPSLOCKED = 0x01; // lock PPS

GIE = state;

LATCbits.LATC0 = 0;

// Enable NCO
NCO1CONbits.N1EN = 1;

// Operate in Fixed Duty cycle mode
NCO1CONbits.N1PFM = 0;

// Output signal active high
NCO1CONbits.N1POL = 0;

// Clock is 16 MHz
NCO1CLKbits.N1CKS = 0b01;

// NCO increment
NCO1INC =0x3334;

}
```

```
/**************************************************************
****************
* Function: Main
*
* Returns: Nothing
*
* Description: Program entry point
***************************************************************
**************/

void main(void) {
initMain();

while(1){
// Connect scope to RCO
}

return;

}
```

Comparator

A *comparator* is a device that compares two analog voltages and outputs the difference between them. Essentially, a comparator outputs either a high or a low based on the voltages as its inputs. A comparator can be thought of as a crude 1-bit analog to digital converter since it is converting an analog representation of voltages into a format that can be interpreted by a digital system.

The PIC® microcontroller has a comparator onboard. This comparator operates independently. In the following example, we put the CPU to sleep while the comparator is running. The comparator can also have its output directed internally or externally. In the example in Listing 12-2, we make the comparator output externally available.

Listing 12-2. Comparator Source

```
/*
* File: Main.c
* Author: Armstrong Subero
* PIC: 16F1717 w/Int OSC @ 16MHz, 5v
* Program: 12_Comparator
* Compiler: XC8 (v1.41, MPLAX X v3.55)
* Program Version: 1.0
*
*
* Program Description: This Program uses the onboard comparator
module of
* the PIC microcontroller. When the voltage at Vin+ is
* more than the voltage at Vin- the comparator outputs a
* logic level high and vice versa.
*
* Hardware Description: An LED is connected via a 10k resistor
to PIN RA3 and
* the output of a 1k voltage divider is fed into the
* - input (PIN RA0) of the comparator with the + input
* (PIN RA2) being the output of a 10k pot is fed into
* the positive end.
*
* Created March 24th, 2017, 12:48 PM
*/

/****************************************************************
****************
*Includes and defines
****************************************************************
**************/
#include "16F1717_Internal.h"
```

```
/******************************************************
****************
* Function: void initMain()
*
* Returns: Nothing
*
* Description: Contains initializations for main
*
* Usage: initMain()
******************************************************
**************/

void initMain(){
// Run at 16 MHz
internal_16();

/////////////////////
// Setup Comparator1
/////////////////////

//_____
// RA0 = C1IN0-
//_____

// Set as input
TRISAbits.TRISA0 = 1;

// Set analog mode on
ANSELAbits.ANSA0 = 1;

//_____
// RA2 = C1IN0+
//_____

// Set as input
TRISAbits.TRISA2 = 1;
```

```
// Set analog mode on
ANSELAbits.ANSA2 = 1;

TRISAbits.TRISA3 = 0;


//_____
// RA3 = C1OUT
//_____

PPSLOCK = 0x55;
PPSLOCK = 0xAA;
PPSLOCKbits.PPSLOCKED = 0x00; // unlock PPS

RA3PPSbits.RA3PPS = 0x16;    //RA3->CMP1:C1OUT;

PPSLOCK = 0x55;
PPSLOCK = 0xAA;
PPSLOCKbits.PPSLOCKED = 0x01; // lock PPS

TRISAbits.TRISA3 = 0;

//////////////////////////
// configure comparator1
//////////////////////////

// enable comparator
CM1CONobits.C1ON = 1;

// output not inverted
CM1CONobits.C1POL = 0;

// normal power mode
CM1CONobits.C1SP = 1;

// asynchronous output
CM1CONobits.C1SYNC = 0;
```

```c
// turn on zero latency filter
CM1CON0bits.C1ZLF = 1;

//Enable comparator hysteresis (45 mV)
CM1CON0bits.C1HYS = 1;

// + in = C1IN+ pin
CM1CON1bits.C1PCH = 0b00;

// - in = C1IN- PIN
CM1CON1bits.C1NCH = 0b00;
}

/****************************************************************
****************
* Function: Main
*
* Returns: Nothing
*
* Description: Program entry point
****************************************************************
**************/

void main(void) {
    initMain();

    while(1){
    // Have the CPU sleep!
    SLEEP();
    }

    return;

}
```

FVR (Fixed Voltage Reference)

The next module we look at is the Fixed Voltage Reference (FVR). The FVR provides a stable voltage reference that is independent of the voltage source. The FVR can be configured as a voltage to a number of modules onboard the PIC® microcontroller. However, in the example in Listing 12-3, we use the FVR as an input into the positive reference of the onboard comparator.

In this case, we reconfigure the comparator to accept its positive voltage input to the FVR, which has been set to provide an output of 2.048v. If the voltage drops below this value, the change is reflected on an LED connected to the comparator output.

Listing 12-3. FVR Source

```
/*
 * File: Main.c
 * Author: Armstrong Subero
 * PIC: 16F1717 w/Int OSC @ 16MHz, 5v
 * Program: 13_FVR
 * Compiler: XC8 (v1.38, MPLAX X v3.40)
 * Program Version: 1.0
 *
 *
 * Program Description: This Program utilizes the FVR to provide
 a reference for
 * the positive input of the comparator.
 *
 * Hardware Description: An LED is connected via a 10k resistor
 to PIN RA3 and
 * the output of a 10k pot is fed into the - input
 * (PIN RA0) of the comparator.
 *
```

```
* Created March 24th, 2017, 1:30 PM
*/

/****************************************************************
****************
*Includes and defines
****************************************************************
**************/

#include "16F1717_Internal.h"


/****************************************************************
****************
* Function: void initMain()
*
* Returns: Nothing
*
* Description: Contains initializations for main
*
* Usage: initMain()
****************************************************************
**************/

void initMain(){
// Run at 16 MHz
internal_16();

/////////////////////
// Setup Comparator1
/////////////////////

//_____
// RA1 = C1IN1-
//_____
```

```
// Set as input
TRISAbits.TRISA0 = 1;

// Set analog mode on
ANSELAbits.ANSA0 = 1;

//_____
// RA3 = C1OUT
//_____

PPSLOCK = 0x55;
PPSLOCK = 0xAA;
PPSLOCKbits.PPSLOCKED = 0x00; // unlock PPS

RA3PPSbits.RA3PPS = 0x16;    //RA3->CMP1:C1OUT;
PPSLOCK = 0x55;
PPSLOCK = 0xAA;
PPSLOCKbits.PPSLOCKED = 0x01; // lock PPS

TRISAbits.TRISA3 = 0;

/////////////////////////
// configure comparator1
/////////////////////////

// enable comparator
CM1CONobits.C1ON = 1;

// output not inverted
CM1CONobits.C1POL = 1;

// normal power mode
CM1CONobits.C1SP = 1;

// hysteresis disabled
CM1CONobits.C1HYS =0;
```

340

```
// asynchronous output
CM1CONobits.C1SYNC = 0;

// turn on zero latency filter
CM1CONobits.C1ZLF = 1;

// Set IN+ to fixed voltage reference
CM1CON1bits.C1PCH = 0b110;

// - in = C1IN- PIN (C1OUT = 1 if < 2.048v)
CM1CON1bits.C1NCH = 0b00;

/////////////////////////////
// Configure FVR
/////////////////////////////

// Enable the FVR
FVRCONbits.FVREN = 1;

// Output 2.048v to comparators
FVRCONbits.CDAFVR = 0b10;
}

/****************************************************************
****************
* Function: Main
*
* Returns: Nothing
*
* Description: Program entry point
****************************************************************
**************/

void main(void) {
initMain();
```

```
while(1){
// Put the CPU to sleep!
SLEEP();
}

return;

}
```

Conclusion

This chapter looked at some of the important new peripherals that are onboard the PIC® microcontroller. These include the Configurable Logic Cell (CLC), Numerically Controlled Oscillator (NCO), Comparator, and Fixed Voltage Reference (FVR).

CHAPTER 13

Wi-Fi and Bluetooth

Low-Cost Wireless Connectivity

In this chapter, we look at the basics of Bluetooth with the low-cost HC05 Bluetooth module. The chapter also discusses using Wi-Fi and the device that took the embedded market by storm, the ESP8266.

Integrating Wi-Fi

Wi-Fi is a type of protocol used for wireless networking. Wi-Fi allows a device to communicate over TCP/IP wirelessly. The most important parts of the Wi-Fi network are the Wireless Access Point (AP), which is the epicenter of the communications, and a *station*, which is a device that has the ability to connect to an access point. In your home or office, this access point usually allows you to connect to the Internet.

Each device on your Wi-Fi network is assigned a MAC address, which is a unique 48-bit value that allows a particular node on a network to distinguish itself from another node.

One of the benefits of Wi-Fi is that it allows you to set up a network more cheaply and easily than when using a wired network. In the embedded systems context, it is easier to integrate Wi-Fi into your systems versus Ethernet since the Wi-Fi module we will examine is readily available. Writing your own TCP/IP tasks takes a lot of work.

In this section, we examine one of the simplest ways to integrate networking into your embedded systems.

343

© Armstrong Subero 2018
A. Subero, *Programming PIC Microcontrollers with XC8*,
https://doi.org/10.1007/978-1-4842-3273-6_13

Using the ESP8266

The ESP8266 is a little device that can be used for Wi-Fi communication. This little part is very inexpensive and is ridiculously inexpensive on the Chinese market. The ESP8266 can act as an access point or as a station within a Wi-Fi network. The ESP8266 was revolutionary in that it allowed embedded designers and makers to add wireless connectivity to their devices at a very low cost, with nothing else in that price range existing at the time it appeared.

Testing the ESP8266

The ESP8266 has a built-in processor that allows you to communicate with it via AT commands. Let's look at some of these commands, which can be used to control the ESP8266.

Table 13-1 lists some commands that you can use to test your ESP8266.

Table 13-1. Some ESP8266 AT Commands

Command	Function
AT	Tests if the AT system works OK.
AT+RST	Resets the module.
AT+GMR	Prints the version of the firmware installed on the ESP8266.
AT+CWMODE?	Wi-Fi mode of the ESP8266.
AT+CWJAP = SSID, PWD	Connects to SSID with the password specified.
AT+CWLAP	Lists all available access points.

Project: Wi-Fi Data Logger

In this project, we use the PIC16F1717 to send wireless data over Wi-Fi, which can be viewed in any web browser. We will set up the ESP8266 in server mode for a single connection. The PIC16F1717 does not have the RAM, ROM, or processing power to build a full web page. Since it only uses a baud rate of 9600 to communicate with the ESP8266, it would take too long to send a full web page and perform all the necessary checks to ensure that the ESP8266 is receiving commands. A web page would also use a good portion of the onboard storage of the microcontroller.

To compensate for this limitation, we will send the minimum commands necessary to set up the ESP8266 as a web server. We will also use the watchdog timer. The WDT will be used initially at a timeout of 4 seconds to ensure that the server starts up properly. Parsing all the required strings sent by the ESP8266 would add extra overhead. After the server is set up, the watchdog timer will be set to have a higher timeout of 128 seconds, up from the original 4 seconds.

The output of the ESP8266 can be viewed in any web browser once you get the IP address via your router. In your web address bar, type the IP of the device followed by :80/ and wait for it to load.

The schematics are shown in Figure 13-1.

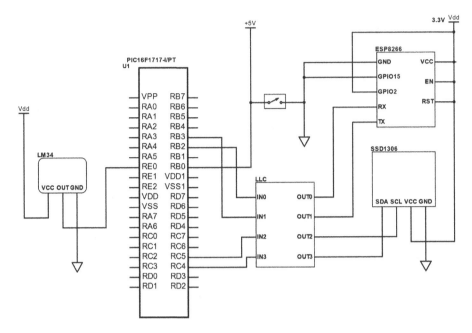

Figure 13-1. *Wi-Fi logger schematics*

Take a look at the code in Listing 13-1.

Listing 13-1. Wi-Fi Logger Source

```
/*
* File: Main.c
* Author: Armstrong Subero
* PIC: 16F1717 w/Int OSC @ 16MHz, 5v
* Program: P03_IoT_WiFi
* Compiler: XC8 (v1.41, MPLAX X v3.55)
* Program Version: 1.0
*
*
* Program Description: This Program gives a reading in Celsius
based on the
* output of a LM34 temperature sensor which is then sent
```

```
* via WiFi using the ESP8266 ESP-12-F the output of which
* can be read in a web browser. The program uses the
* watchdog timer initially with a timeout of 4s then
* once the server is operational has a timeout of 128s
* after which the server will reboot.
*
* Hardware Description: A LM34 is connected to PIN EO and a
SSD1306 OLED is
* connected to the I2C bus. The ESP8266 is connected as
* follows:
* VCC-> VCC
* TX-> RB3
* RD-> RB2
* GPIO15-> GND
* GPIO2-> VCC
* REST-> VCC
* EN-> VCC
* VC-> VCC
*
* External interrupt is connected to PINB0
*
* Created March 31st, 2017, 10:57 AM
*/

/****************************************************************
****************
*Includes and defines
****************************************************************
**************/

#include "16F1717_Internal.h"
#include "I2C.h"
#include "oled.h"
```

```c
#include "EUSART.h"
#include <string.h>

// Buffer for UART transactions
char buf[50];

// Function prototypes
float Read_Temperature();
void server_Initialize();

/****************************************************************
****************
* Function: void initMain()
*
* Returns: Nothing
*
* Description: Contains initializations for main
*
* Usage: initMain()
****************************************************************
***************/

void initMain(){
// Run at 16 MHz
internal_16();

////////////////////
// Set up All Serial
////////////////////

// Set up pins for I2C
ANSELCbits.ANSC4 = 0;
ANSELCbits.ANSC5 = 0;

TRISCbits.TRISC4 = 1;
TRISCbits.TRISC5 = 1;
```

```
PPSLOCK = 0x55;
PPSLOCK = 0xAA;
PPSLOCKbits.PPSLOCKED = 0x00; // unlock PPS

RC4PPSbits.RC4PPS =0x0011; //RC4->MSSP:SDA;
SSPDATPPSbits.SSPDATPPS =0x0014; //RC4->MSSP:SDA;
SSPCLKPPSbits.SSPCLKPPS =0x0015; //RC5->MSSP:SCL;
RC5PPSbits.RC5PPS =0x0010; //RC5->MSSP:SCL;

// Set up pins for EUSART
RB2PPSbits.RB2PPS = 0x14; //RB2->EUSART:TX;
RXPPSbits.RXPPS = 0x0B; //RB3->EUSART:RX;

PPSLOCK = 0x55;
PPSLOCK = 0xAA;
PPSLOCKbits.PPSLOCKED = 0x01; // lock PPS

///////////////////
// Configure ADC
///////////////////

// Fosc/32 ADC conversion time is 2.0 us
ADCON1bits.ADCS = 0b010;

// Right justified
ADCON1bits.ADFM = 1;

// Vref- is Vss
ADCON1bits.ADNREF = 0;

// Vref+ is Vdd
ADCON1bits.ADPREF = 0b00;

// Set input channel to AN0
ADCON0bits.CHS = 0x05;
```

```
// Zero ADRESL and ADRESH
ADRESL = 0;
ADRESH = 0;

// Set E0 as ADC input channel5
ANSELEbits.ANSE0 = 1;

//////////////////////
// Set up EUSART Pins
//////////////////////

// Set up PINS
TRISBbits.TRISB3 = 1;
ANSELBbits.ANSB3 = 0;

TRISBbits.TRISB2 = 0;
ANSELBbits.ANSB2 = 0;

//////////////////////////////////
// Configure watchdog timer
//////////////////////////////////

// Set watchdog timeout for 4 seconds
WDTCONbits.WDTPS = 0b01100;

TRISDbits.TRISD1 = 1;
ANSELDbits.ANSD1 = 1;

// Set PIN B0 as input
TRISBbits.TRISB0 = 1;

// Configure ANSELB0
ANSELBbits.ANSB0 = 0;

//////////////////////////
/// Configure Interrupts
//////////////////////////
```

```
// unlock PPS
PPSLOCK = 0x55;
PPSLOCK = 0xAA;
PPSLOCK = 0x00;

// Set Interrupt pin to pin B0
INTPPSbits.INTPPS = 0b01000;

// lock    PPS
PPSLOCK = 0x55;
PPSLOCK = 0xAA;
PPSLOCK = 0x01;

// Trigger on falling edge
OPTION_REGbits.INTEDG = 0;

// Clear external interrupt flag
INTCONbits.INTF = 0;

//  Enable external interrupt
INTCONbits.INTE = 1;

// Enable global interrupt
ei();

}

/****************************************************************
****************
* Function: Main
*
* Returns: Nothing
*
* Description: Program entry point
****************************************************************
**************/
```

```
void main(void) {
initMain();

// Initialize I2C
I2C_Init();
__delay_ms(500);

// Initialize OLED
OLED_Init();

// clear OLED
OLED_Clear();

__delay_ms(1000);

CLRWDT();

// Initialize EUSART
EUSART_Initialize(9600);

// Indicate start of server
OLED_YX(0, 0);
OLED_Write_String("START SERVER");
__delay_ms(2000);

CLRWDT();

// Initialize the sever
server_Initialize();

// temperature variable
float temp;

while(1){

// Clear OLED
OLED_Clear();
```

```
/////////////////////////////
// Read and Display temperature
/////////////////////////////
temp = Read_Temperature();

OLED_YX(0, 0);
OLED_Write_String("Temperature:");
OLED_YX(1, 0);
OLED_Write_Integer(temp);
__delay_ms(1000);
OLED_Clear();

/////////////////////////////
// Convert temperature to string
/////////////////////////////
char* buff11;
int status;

buff11 = itoa(&status, temp, 10);
strcat(buff11, "\r\n");

/////////////////////////////
// Wait for connection request
/////////////////////////////
EUSART_Read_Text(buf, 20);

///////////////////////////////////
// Display some of the received data
///////////////////////////////////
OLED_YX(1, 0);
OLED_Write_String(buf);
__delay_ms(3000);
OLED_Clear();
```

```
/////////////////////////////////////////
// Send the temperature as 2 bytes of data
/////////////////////////////////////////
OLED_YX(0, 0);
OLED_Write_String("Sending Data");
EUSART_Write_Text("AT+CIPSEND=0,2\r\n");
__delay_ms(5000);

EUSART_Write_Text(buff11);

EUSART_Read_Text(buf, 10);
OLED_YX(1, 0);
OLED_Write_String(buf);
__delay_ms(3000);
OLED_Clear();

//////////////////////////
// Close connection
//////////////////////////

EUSART_Write_Text("AT+CIPCLOSE=0\r\n");
__delay_ms(1000);

EUSART_Read_Text(buf, 10);
OLED_YX(1, 0);
OLED_Write_String(buf);
__delay_ms(3000);
OLED_Clear();

// Reset EUSART
RC1STAbits.SPEN = 0;
RC1STAbits.SPEN = 1;

// one this is complete clear watchdog
CLRWDT();
}
```

return;
}

```
/****************************************************************
****************
* Function: void interrupt isr(void)
*
* Returns: Nothing
*
* Description: Interrupt triggered on pushbutton press
****************************************************************
**************/

void interrupt isr(void){
// Clear interrupt flag
INTCONbits.INTF = 0;

// Set watchdog timeout for 4 seconds
WDTCONbits.WDTPS = 0b01100;

// Re-initialize server
server_Initialize();
}

/****************************************************************
****************
* Function: void server_Initialize(void)
*
* Returns: Nothing
*
* Description: Sets up ESP8266 as single connection server on
port 80
****************************************************************
**************/
```

```
float Read_Temperature()
{
float conversion10;
float farenheit;
float celsius;
float result;

// Turn ADC on
ADCONobits.ADON = 1;

// Sample CHO
__delay_us(10);
ADCONobits.GO = 1;
while (ADCONobits.GO_nDONE);

// Store ADC result
result = ((ADRESH<<8)+ADRESL);

// 10 bit conversion
conversion10 = (result * 5000)/1024 ;

// to Fahrenheit
farenheit = conversion10 / 10;

// to Celsius
celsius = (farenheit - 32) * 5/9;

return celsius;
}
/****************************************************************
****************
* Function: void server_Initialize(void)
*
* Returns: Nothing
*
* Description: Sets up ESP8266 as single connection server on port 80
```

```
*************************************************************
**************/

void server_Initialize()
{
//////////////////////
// Send AT Command
//////////////////////
CLRWDT();
OLED_YX(0, 0);
OLED_Write_String("Sending AT");
EUSART_Write_Text("AT\r\n");
EUSART_Read_Text(buf, 11);

OLED_YX(1, 0);
OLED_Write_String(buf);
__delay_ms(3000);
OLED_Clear();

////////////////////////////////
// Enable Single Connection
////////////////////////////////

CLRWDT();
OLED_YX(0, 0);
OLED_Write_String("Sending CIPMUX");
EUSART_Write_Text("AT+CIPMUX=0\r\n");
EUSART_Read_Text(buf, 15);

OLED_YX(1, 0);
OLED_Write_String(buf);
__delay_ms(3000);
OLED_Clear();

CLRWDT();
```

```
///////////////////////////////
// Configure as server on port 80
///////////////////////////////
OLED_YX(0, 0);
OLED_Write_String("Sending CIPSERVER");
EUSART_Write_Text("AT+CIPSERVER=1,80\r\n");

EUSART_Read_Text(buf, 15);

OLED_YX(1, 0);
OLED_Write_String(buf);

__delay_ms(3000);
OLED_Clear();

CLRWDT();


// Set watchdog timeout for 128 seconds
WDTCONbits.WDTPS = 0b10001;
}
```

The output to the web browser is shown in Figure 13-2.

Figure 13-2. *Output to the web browser*

Integrating Bluetooth

Bluetooth is another wireless protocol we will examine. Bluetooth can replace wired communication between electronic devices with the attributes of low-power consumption and low cost. These traits make it lucrative for the embedded systems designer, since they go hand in hand with general embedded development.

A few years ago, it would have been very expensive to add Bluetooth connectivity to your system, because the modules available to the average developer were relatively expensive. Thanks to its popularity, the cost of adding Bluetooth connectivity to a project has rapidly declined.

The primary reason for this is due to the creation of low-cost Bluetooth modules by companies and manufacturers in the Chinese market. One such low-cost module is the HC05 Bluetooth module, shown in Figure 13-3.

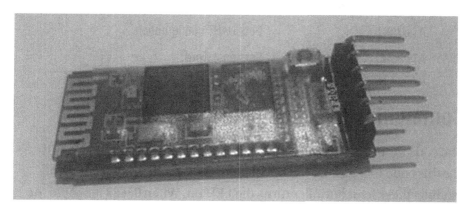

Figure 13-3. *HC05 Bluetooth module*

Using the HC05 Bluetooth Module

Using the HC05 is very simple. You simply connect the RX and TX pins of the module to the microcontroller through a logic-level converter. The Vcc and GND pins of the HC05 are connected to 5v and GND, respectively.

AT Mode

It is possible to place the HC05 in AT mode by pressing the small button on the module while it is powering on. Older versions of the modules enter the AT mode in a different way; therefore, I recommend you check the method that works for your particular module. Note that the baud rate for AT mode is 38400. Table 13-2 shows some AT commands for your module.

Table 13-2. *Some HC05 AT Commands*

Command	Function
AT	Checks to ensure module is working.
AT+VERSION?	Gets version.
AT+ORGL	Restores to original state.
AT+NAME="MYNAME"	Sets device name.
AT+UART	Gets UART configuration.
AT+PSWD="1234"	Sets password.

Communicating via Bluetooth

The code for receiving commands for the HC05 is very simple. We will use this code to toggle an LED. When the ONPR command is sent to the module, the microcontroller turns the LED on. When OFFPR is sent to the module, the microcontroller turns the LED off. We will use the C needle in a haystack command, called `strstr`, to search the received command for ON or OFF.

The commands can be sent from a PC or a mobile device. On a PC or Android, when pairing the device, enter the default passcode 1234. On a PC, the device shows up as a COM port. I recommend the Termite program by CompuPhase to communicate via Bluetooth. On Android, there are a lot of Bluetooth terminals; however, I recommend an app named Bluetooth

Terminal HC05, which works quite well and has preset buttons to make things simple. This module does not work with iOS.

Listing 13-2 provides the code.

Listing 13-2. Bluetooth Control Source

```
/*
* File: Main.c
* Author: Armstrong Subero
* PIC: 16F1717 w/Int OSC @ 16MHz, 5v
* Program: I19_Bluetooth_HC05
* Compiler: XC8 (v1.41, MPLAX X v3.61)
* Program Version: 1.0
*
*
* Program Description: This Program Allows PIC16F1717 to
communicate via
*
*
* Hardware Description: A HC-06 is connected to the PIC16F1717
as follows:
*
* RX->RB3
* TX->RB2
*
* Created May 15th, 2017, 5:00 PM
*/

/***************************************************************
****************
*Includes and defines
***************************************************************
**************/
```

```
#include "16F1717_Internal.h"
#include "EUSART.h"
#include <string.h>

#define LED LATDbits.LATD1


/*************************************************************
****************
* Function: void initMain()
*
* Returns: Nothing
*
* Description: Contains initializations for main
*
* Usage: initMain()
*************************************************************
**************/

void initMain(){
// Run at 16 MHz
internal_16();

// Set PIN D1 as output
TRISDbits.TRISD1 = 0;

// Turn off LED
LATDbits.LATD1 = 0;

// Set up PORTD
TRISD = 0;
ANSELD = 0;

// Set up pins for EUSART
TRISBbits.TRISB2 = 0;
ANSELBbits.ANSB2 = 0;
```

```
TRISBbits.TRISB3 = 1;
ANSELBbits.ANSB3 = 0;

///////////////////////
// Set up EUSART
///////////////////////
PPSLOCK = 0x55;
PPSLOCK = 0xAA;
PPSLOCKbits.PPSLOCKED = 0x00; // unlock PPS

RB2PPSbits.RB2PPS = 0x14; //RB2->EUSART:TX;
RXPPSbits.RXPPS = 0x0B; //RB3->EUSART:RX;

PPSLOCK = 0x55;
PPSLOCK = 0xAA;
PPSLOCKbits.PPSLOCKED = 0x01; // lock PPS

}


/****************************************************************
****************
* Function: Main
*
* Returns: Nothing
*
* Description: Program entry point
****************************************************************
**************/

void main(void) {
initMain();

// Initialize EUSART module with 9600 baud
EUSART_Initialize(9600);
```

```
char buf[20];
char* ON;
char* OFF;

while(1){

// Send start so we'll know it's working
EUSART_Write_Text("Start");

// Read UART messages
EUSART_Read_Text(buf, 4);

// Test received string
ON = strstr(buf, "ON");
OFF = strstr(buf, "OFF");

// If ON string, turn LED on
if (ON)
{
EUSART_Write_Text("LED ON");
LED = 1;
}

// If OFF string, turn LED off
else if(OFF)
{
EUSART_Write_Text("LED OFF");
LED = 0;
}
}

return;

}
```

Conclusion

This chapter looked at using Bluetooth and Wi-Fi and using the PIC®
microcontroller with the ESP8266. Bluetooth and Wi-Fi are arguably two
of the most important wireless protocols available today. The information
presented in this chapter was just enough so that you will be able to add
these protocols to your own systems.

CHAPTER 14

Watchdog Timer and Low Power

Low Power 8-Bit vs 32-Bit

One cannot write a book on 8-bit microcontrollers without writing a little about low power. The argument has always been that 8-bit microcontrollers are superior to 32-bit ones in relation to low power. The reason is simple. A 32-bit microcontroller has more transistors, thus it requires more power to work. The argument for the 32-bit microcontroller is that if it is a computationally intensive task, then the 32-bit microcontroller would have an advantage, as it will take less time to do the processing. I say that you don't need to use a machete to peel an orange. Yes, it will get the job done, but it is not the right tool for the task—in fact, it is over-engineering. Being a good embedded systems designer means using the right tool for the task. Problem solving involves applying the most relevant tool for the task to the problem at hand. In many instances, we do not need the power of a 32-bit microcontroller and in such cases using an 8-bit microcontroller is the logical choice.

The PIC® microcontroller has Microchip's Extreme Low Power (XLP) technology built-in. What this means is that there are modes on the PIC® microcontroller that allow it to enter a very low power state.

367
© Armstrong Subero 2018
A. Subero, *Programming PIC Microcontrollers with XC8,*
https://doi.org/10.1007/978-1-4842-3273-6_14

Sleep Mode

The PIC® microcontroller can be put into sleep mode by using the SLEEP instruction. When this happens, the microcontroller enters a low power mode and conserves power. We will write an application that utilizes the SLEEP instruction of the PIC16F1717 (see Listing 14-1). In this application, the microcontroller will turn an LED on for five seconds, and then go to sleep. The microcontroller will then be woken up by using an external interrupt on PINB0.

By waking up the microcontroller only when we want it to perform some function and then putting it back to sleep, we can reduce power consumption. This is important in cases where devices are battery powered. A remote control is a good application of this, since the user only uses it when he wants to turn something on or off and then puts it back down. In such cases, it is not feasible to keep the microcontroller energized, and putting the microcontroller into sleep and then having it turn on when the user pushes a button will save a considerable amount of power.

Using the Sleep function is not limited only to battery-powered devices. Another application of this circuit is in devices where there is an ecofriendly button. You too can make ecofriendly devices by having a device go into sleep mode after a certain period of inactivity. For example, after someone uses a printer, it may be unnecessary to have it running and consuming power. The printer can be made ecofriendly by powering down after a certain amount of time, which is done via timers that you already know about. The printer can then be turned on again using the ecofriendly button.

Listing 14-1. Sleep Demonstration

```
/*
* File: Main.c
* Author: Armstrong Subero
* PIC: 16F1717 w/Int OSC @ 16MHz, 5v
* Program: 08_Sleep
* Compiler: XC8 (v1.38, MPLAX X v3.40)
* Program Version: 1.0
*
*
* Program Description: This demonstrates sleep mode on a
PIC16F1717 using
* an external interrupt to wake from sleep mode
*
* Hardware Description: An LED is connected via a 10k resistor
to PIN D1 and
* another LED is connected to PIN D2 and a switch is
* connected to PIN B0
*
* Created November 4th, 2016, 8:43 PM
*/


/************************************************************
****************
*Includes and defines
*************************************************************
**************/

#include "16F1717_Internal.h"


/************************************************************
****************
```

```
* Function: void initMain()
*
* Returns: Nothing
*
* Description: Contains initializations for main
*
* Usage: initMain()
***********************************************************
**************/

void initMain(){
// Run at 16 MHz
internal_16();

////////////////////////
/// Configure Ports
////////////////////////

// Set PIN D1 as output
TRISDbits.TRISD1 = 0;
TRISDbits.TRISD2 = 0;

// Turn off LED
LATDbits.LATD1 = 0;

// Set PIN B0 as input
TRISBbits.TRISB0 = 1;

// Configure ANSELB0
ANSELBbits.ANSB0 = 0;

// unlock PPS
PPSLOCK = 0x55;
PPSLOCK = 0xAA;
PPSLOCK = 0x00;
```

```
// Enable weak-pullups global
OPTION_REGbits.nWPUEN = 0;

// Enable weak-pullup on PINB0
WPUBbits.WPUB0 = 1;

/////////////////////////
/// Configure Interrupts
/////////////////////////

// Set Interrupt pin to pin B0
INTPPSbits.INTPPS = 0b01000;

// lock    PPS
PPSLOCK = 0x55;
PPSLOCK = 0xAA;
PPSLOCK = 0x01;

// Trigger on falling edge
OPTION_REGbits.INTEDG = 0;

// Clear external interrupt flag
INTCONbits.INTF = 0;

//  Enable external interrupt
INTCONbits.INTE = 1;

// Enable global interrupt
ei();
}

/****************************************************************
****************
* Function: Main
*
* Returns: Nothing
```

```
 *
 * Description: Program entry point
 ***************************************************************
 **************/

void main(void) {
initMain();

int x;
while(1){

// Turn LED on for 5 seconds
LATDbits.LATD1 = 1;
__delay_ms(5000);

LATDbits.LATD1 = 0;

// Sleep
SLEEP();
}

return;

}


/***************************************************************
****************

* Function: void interrupt isr(void)
*
* Returns: Nothing
*
* Description: Interrupt triggered on pushbutton press
 ***************************************************************
 **************/
```

```
void interrupt isr(void){
// Clear interrupt flag
INTCONbits.INTF = 0;

// Toggle led
LATDbits.LATD2 = ~LATDbits.LATD2;
}
```

Watchdog Timer

The watchdog timer (WDT) is a type of timer onboard PIC®
microcontrollers that periodically reset the device. What this means is that
the watchdog timer, like any other timer, will count a particular period of
time. When the CLRWDT (clear watchdog timer) command is issued, the
watchdog timer will not reset the microcontroller. If a certain amount of
time passes as determined by the user, and the WDT is not cleared, then
the device will be reset.

The WDT is very important for systems that are inaccessible or are
very difficult for a person to get to in case of a malfunction. For example,
in space applications it would be impossible for a human to interact with
a robot that is exploring the surface of a planet or the moon. In such cases,
the onus is on the device to reset itself to ensure continual operation.

It is important to note that improper use of the watchdog timer can be
the source of a lot of system bugs. For example, if you use another timer to
reset the watchdog timer, the system will not reset as expected on failure,
as the other timers will run independent of the CPU.

It is also important, when designing with the watchdog timer, to set the
interval at which the timer resets to the shortest possible value. This will
ensure that your system is back to proper operation as soon as possible.

The code example in Listing 14-2 shows how we use the watchdog timer. It is very similar to the sleep example, except we use the WDT to break the microcontroller out of an infinite while loop. To prove that the program is working, a heartbeat LED flashes and an external interrupt can be used to flash the WDT LED. The watchdog timer runs in the background and, when it is reset, it turns on another LED.

Listing 14-2. WDT Demonstration

```
/*
* File: Main.c
* Author: Armstrong Subero
* PIC: 16F1717 w/Int OSC @ 16MHz, 5v
* Program: 09_Watchdog_Timer
* Compiler: XC8 (v1.38, MPLAX X v3.40)
* Program Version: 1.0
*
*
* Program Description: This demonstrates using the watchdog
timer on a
* PIC16F1717 to break out of an infinite loop
*
*
* Hardware Description: An LED is connected via a 10k resistor
to PIN D1 and
* another LED is connected to PIN D2 and a switch is
* connected to PIN B0
*
* Created November 4th, 2016, 9:04 PM
*/
```

```
/**************************************************************
****************
*Includes and defines
**************************************************************
**************/

#include "16F1717_Internal.h"


/**************************************************************
****************
* Function: void initMain()
*
* Returns: Nothing
*
* Description: Contains initializations for main
*
* Usage: initMain()
**************************************************************
**************/

void initMain(){
// Run at 16 MHz
internal_16();

/////////////////////////
/// Configure Ports
/////////////////////////

// Set PIN D1 as output
TRISDbits.TRISD1 = 0;
TRISDbits.TRISD2 = 0;

// Turn off LED
LATDbits.LATD1 = 0;
```

```
// Set PIN B0 as input
TRISBbits.TRISB0 = 1;

// Configure ANSELB0
ANSELBbits.ANSB0 = 0;

// unlock PPS
PPSLOCK = 0x55;
PPSLOCK = 0xAA;
PPSLOCK = 0x00;

// Enable weak-pullups global
OPTION_REGbits.nWPUEN = 0;

// Enable weak-pullup on PINB0
WPUBbits.WPUB0 = 1;

////////////////////////
/// Configure Interrupts
////////////////////////

// Set Interrupt pin to pin B0
INTPPSbits.INTPPS = 0b01000;

// lock   PPS
PPSLOCK = 0x55;
PPSLOCK = 0xAA;
PPSLOCK = 0x01;

// Trigger on falling edge
OPTION_REGbits.INTEDG = 0;

// Clear external interrupt flag
INTCONbits.INTF = 0;

//  Enable external interrupt
INTCONbits.INTE = 1;
```

```c
// Enable global interrupt
ei();

////////////////////////////////
// Configure watchdog timer
////////////////////////////////

// Set watchdog timeout for 2 seconds (prescale = 65536)
WDTCONbits.WDTPS = 0b01011;
}

/****************************************************************
****************
* Function: Main
*
* Returns: Nothing
*
* Description: Program entry point
****************************************************************
**************/

void main(void) {
initMain();

int x;
while(1){

// If WDT timeout occurred turn on error LED
if (!STATUSbits.nTO){
}

// flash heartbeat LED
LATDbits.LATD2 = 1;
__delay_ms(1000);
LATDbits.LATD2 = 0;
```

```
for(;;){
// infinite loop
}

}

return;

}


/****************************************************************
****************
* Function: void interrupt isr(void)
*
* Returns: Nothing
*
* Description: Interrupt triggered on pushbutton press
*****************************************************************
**************/

void interrupt isr(void){
// Clear interrupt flag
INTCONbits.INTF = 0;

// Toggle led
LATDbits.LATD2 = ~LATDbits.LATD2;
}
```

Other Ways to Conserve Power

In this section, we look at other ways to conserve power on PIC®
microcontrollers. We take several steps to reduce power consumption. We
look at three universally applicable ways to reduce power consumption
of embedded devices. These three methods are tried and true and are

guaranteed to lower power consumption. In fact, the first two methods can also be applied to general-purpose processors as well. Many people use over-clocking, under-clocking, and under-voltage to reduce power consumption, usually with relatively little performance losses.

Reduce the Clock Frequency

To reduce the power consumption on the microcontroller, consider running the microcontroller at 31kHz. Running the device at such low power reduces power consumption for tasks that are not computationally intensive. If a particular application requires a lot of CPU power, then running it at a low clock speed may actually be counterproductive since it will take a long time to complete its task and thus will be on for longer. It is an art to find the balance between computational speed and power consumption. Generally, however, the lower the clock speed, the lower the power consumption.

Reduce the Operating Voltage

Another way to reduce the power consumption on the microcontroller is to reduce the power from the usual 5 volts to 3.3 volts. That way, the microcontroller consumes less power as the voltage is lower. The disadvantage is that if your system has sensors that run at a higher voltage, you may need to add logic-level converters, which increases the design complexity.

Power External Devices from I/O Lines

If the power consumption of the device is less than the maximum the microcontroller can source, it's best to drive the devices directly from the microcontroller. This method reduces power consumption; however, it is at the tradeoff of utilizing I/O pins.

Conclusion

This chapter looked at specific ways to reduce power consumption on the PIC® microcontroller, including using sleep mode as well as using the watchdog timer.

CHAPTER 15

PIC® Microcontroller Projects

In this chapter, we look at building two projects using the PIC® microcontroller. The first is a classic microcontroller project involving a temperature controlled fan. The second project shows how far microcontroller technology has progressed and what is now possible with 8-bit bare metal systems by building a simple touch screen clock, a project that a few years ago would have required a 32-bit microcontroller.

Project: Temperature Controlled Fan

The first project involves building a temperature controlled fan. The LM34 temperature sensor output is converted to Celsius values, and when a particular threshold voltage is reached, the microcontroller turns on the fan. Once the temperature is within the normal values, the string "Temp OK" is displayed on the OLED. When the temperature crosses a certain value, the string "Warning!!" is displayed on the OLED.

Figure 15-1 shows the schematics of the temperature controlled fan.

381

© Armstrong Subero 2018
A. Subero, *Programming PIC Microcontrollers with XC8*,
https://doi.org/10.1007/978-1-4842-3273-6_15

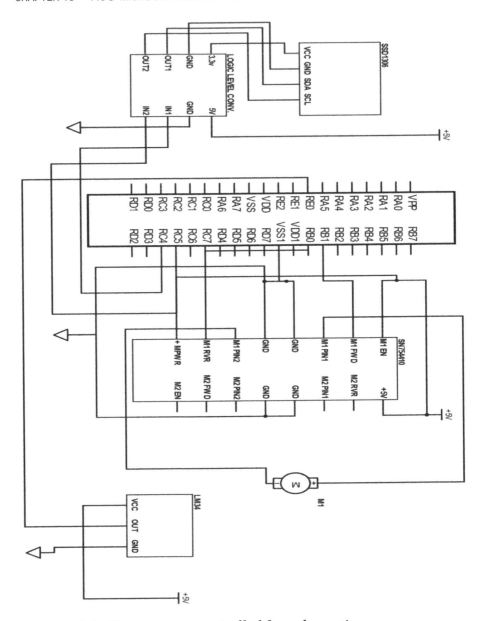

Figure 15-1. *Temperature controlled fan schematics*

Listing 15-1 shows the main code for the temperature controlled fan.

Listing 15-1. Temperature Controlled Fan

```
/*
 * File: Main.c
 * Author: Armstrong Subero
 * PIC: 16F1717 w/Internal OSC @ 16MHz, 5v
 * Program: P04_Temp_Fan
 * Compiler: XC8 (v1.41, MPLAX X v3.55)
 * Program Version: 1.0
 *
 * Program Description: This project builds a temperature
controlled fan. When
 * the temperature rises above 35 Celsius a fan turns on
 * until the temperature drops to 35 Celsius or below.
 *
 * Hardware Description: A generic brushed hobby DC motor is
connected to the
 * SN754410 as per standard connections. The PWM signals
 * are emanating from RB0 and RB1. The LM34 temperature
 * sensor is connected to PIN RE0 and an SSD1306 based
 * OLED is connected as per header file.
 *
 *
 * Created April 18th, 2017, 4:36 PM
 */

/****************************************************************
****************
*Includes and defines
*****************************************************************
**************/
```

```
#include "16F1717_Internal.h"
#include "I2C.h"
#include "oled.h"

/****************************************************************
****************
* Function: void initMain()
*
* Returns: Nothing
*
* Description: Contains initializations for main
*
* Usage: initMain()
****************************************************************
**************/

void initMain(){
// Run at 16 MHz
internal_16();

/////////////////////////
// Configure PWM Ports
/////////////////////////

// Set PIN B0 as output
TRISBbits.TRISB0 = 0;

// Set PIN B1 as output
TRISBbits.TRISB1 = 0;

// Turn off analog on PORTB
ANSELB = 0;
```

```
///////////////////////
// Configure Timer6
///////////////////////

// Select PWM timer as Timer6 for CCP1 and CCP2
CCPTMRSbits.C1TSEL = 0b10;
CCPTMRSbits.C2TSEL = 0b10;

// Enable timer Increments every 250 ns (16MHz clock) 1000/
(16/4)
// Period = 256 x 0.25 us = 64 us

// Crystal Frequency
//PWM Freq   = ------------------------------------------
//(PRX + 1) * (TimerX Prescaler) * 4

//PWM Frequency = 16 000 000 / 256 * 1 * 4
//PWM Frequency = 15.625 kHz

// Prescale = 1
T6CONbits.T6CKPS = 0b00;

// Enable Timer6
T6CONbits.TMR6ON = 1;

// Set timer period
PR6 = 255;

///////////////////////////
// Configure PWM
///////////////////////////

// Configure CCP1

// LSB's of PWM duty cycle = 00
CCP1CONbits.DC1B = 00;
```

385

```
// Select PWM mode
CCP1CONbits.CCP1M = 0b1100;

// Configure CCP2

// LSB's of PWM duty cycle = 00
CCP2CONbits.DC2B = 00;

// Select PWM mode
CCP2CONbits.CCP2M = 0b1100;

//////////////////
// Setup I2C
//////////////////

// Setup pins for I2C
ANSELCbits.ANSC4 = 0;
ANSELCbits.ANSC5 = 0;

TRISCbits.TRISC4 = 1;
TRISCbits.TRISC5 = 1;

//////////////////////////////
// Configure PPS
//////////////////////////////

PPSLOCK = 0x55;
PPSLOCK = 0xAA;
PPSLOCKbits.PPSLOCKED = 0x00; // unlock PPS

// Set RB0 to PWM1
RB0PPSbits.RB0PPS = 0b01100;

// Set RB1 to PWM2
RB1PPSbits.RB1PPS = 0b01101;
```

```
RC4PPSbits.RC4PPS =0x0011; //RC4->MSSP:SDA;
SSPDATPPSbits.SSPDATPPS =0x0014; //RC4->MSSP:SDA;
SSPCLKPPSbits.SSPCLKPPS =0x0015; //RC5->MSSP:SCL;
RC5PPSbits.RC5PPS =0x0010; //RC5->MSSP:SCL;

PPSLOCK = 0x55;
PPSLOCK = 0xAA;
PPSLOCKbits.PPSLOCKED = 0x01; // lock PPS

////////////////////
// Configure ADC
////////////////////

// Fosc/32 ADC conversion time is 2.0 us
ADCON1bits.ADCS = 0b010;

// Right justified
ADCON1bits.ADFM = 1;

// Vref- is Vss
ADCON1bits.ADNREF = 0;

// Vref+ is Vdd
ADCON1bits.ADPREF = 0b00;

// Set input channel to AN0
ADCON0bits.CHS = 0x05;

// Zero ADRESL and ADRESH
ADRESL = 0;
ADRESH = 0;

// ADC Input channel PIN E0
ANSELEbits.ANSE0 = 1;
}
```

```c
/*************************************************************
****************
* Function: Main
*
* Returns: Nothing
*
* Description: Program entry point
*************************************************************
**************/

void main(void) {
initMain();

// Initialize I2C
I2C_Init();

__delay_ms(500);

// Initialize OLED
OLED_Init();

__delay_ms(1000);

// clear OLED
OLED_Clear();

// result to store ADC conversion
float result;

// variables for conversion
float conversion10;
float farenheit;
float celsius;
```

```
// PWM Off
CCPR1L = 0;
CCPR2L = 0;

OLED_YX(0, 0);
OLED_Write_String("Init");

while(1){

// Turn ADC on
ADCON0bits.ADON = 1;

// Sample CH0
__delay_us(10);
ADCON0bits.GO = 1;
while (ADCON0bits.GO_nDONE);

// Store ADC result
result = ((ADRESH<<8)+ADRESL);

// 10 bit conversion
conversion10 = (result * 5000)/1024 ;

// to Fahrenheit
farenheit = conversion10 / 10;

// to Celsius
celsius = (farenheit - 32) * 5/9;

// Display temperature

OLED_YX(1, 0);
OLED_Write_Integer((int)celsius);

// Update every second
__delay_ms(2000);
```

```
// If temperature is more than 35C turn on fan
if ((int)celsius > 35){

// Forward
CCPR1L = 127;
CCPR2L = 0;

// clear OLED
OLED_Clear();

OLED_YX(0, 0);
OLED_Write_String("Warning!!");
}

// If less turn off fan
else{
OLED_YX(0, 0);
OLED_Write_String("Temp OK");
CCPR1L =0;
CCPR2L =0;
}

}
return;
}
```

Project: Touch Screen Clock

In this section, we make a basic touch screen clock. We use the DS1302 timekeeper. Though there are many modern Real Time Clock Calendar (RTCC) ICs on the market, the beauty of the DS1302 is that it uses a non-standard protocol. The DS1302 uses a protocol called the "three wire interface". This is not necessarily a bad thing, because if your I2C and SPI bus are occupied, you can used this RTCC on any available pin.

We will use the Nextion 2.4 touch LCD as the display. The interrupt on the PIC® will update the time on the display every five seconds. This is acceptable as it gives the microcontroller sufficient time for the touch screen to react to other user events.

The clock consists of two screens. The first screen will display the time and date to the user. The second screen will allow the user to set the time and date.

Let's create the first screen, as shown in Figure 15-2.

Figure 15-2. *Screen 1*

Now create the second one, as shown in Figure 15-3.

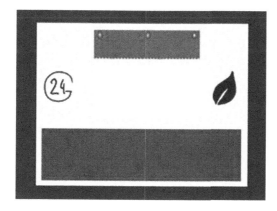

Figure 15-3. *Screen 2*

Open the Nextion Editor and add touch hotspots, as shown on screen 1 in Figure 15-4.

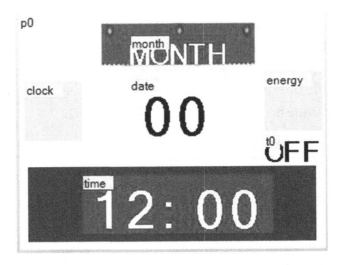

Figure 15-4. *Nextion Editor on screen 1*

The clock hotspot opens the second page. The green (leaf) icon sends the text enerpressed and the text under it keeps the default label t0. The other text labels are added and renamed month, date, and time. Feel free to customize the layout according to your needs.

Use the editor to make screen 2 look like Figure 15-5.

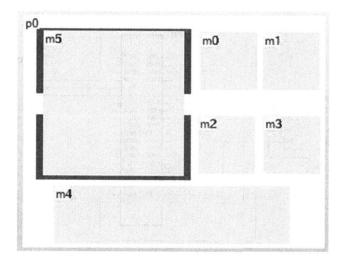

Figure 15-5. *Nextion Editor Screen 2*

The second screen has text views t0, t1, t2, and t3, representing the hours, minutes, date, and month. Each is overlaid by hotspots that send m0, m1, m2, and m3, which send hourpressed, minspressed, datepressed, and monthpressed, respectively. The hotspot at the bottom (m4) is used to set the current time. It is very important and sends the text setppressed (not a typo; be sure to use the double p).

Figure 15-6 shows the schematics for this project.

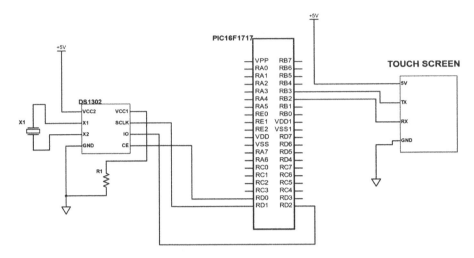

Figure 15-6. *Clock schematics*

This project contains a lot of code. Let's break it down. The first thing we need to add is a header file for bool support, as shown in Listing 15-2.

Listing 15-2. Bool Support

```
/*
* File: bool_support.h
* Author: Armstrong Subero
* PIC: 16F1717 w/X OSC @ 16MHz, 5v
* Program: Header file to setup PIC16F1717 I2C
* Compiler: XC8 (v1.35, MPLAX X v3.10)
* Program Version 1.0
*
* Program Description: This program header will allow addition
of simple bool
* support to XC8
*
* Created on March 10th, 2017, 8:00 PM
*/
```

```
//////////////////////////
// Bool support
//////////////////////////
```

typedef unsigned char bool;

```
#define true 1
#define false 0

// boolean for current state
```
bool on = false;

Next, we add a header file for setup, as shown in Listing 15-3. This is necessary. Due to the size of the program, we will separate the initialization from the main file.

Listing 15-3. Setup Header

```
/*
* File: setup.h
* Author: Armstrong Subero
* PIC: 16F1717 w/X OSC @ 16MHz, 5v
* Program: Header file to setup PIC16F1717 I2C
* Compiler: XC8 (v1.40, MPLAX X v3.55)
* Program Version 1.0
*
* Program Description: This program header will allow setup of
SSD 1306 OLEDs
*
* Created on April 21st, 2017, 2:25 PM
*/

#include "16F1717_Internal.h"
```

void initMain();

The next step is to create a header file for the touch screen, as shown in Listing 15-4.

Listing 15-4. Touch Screen Header

```
/*
 * File: touchscreen.h
 * Author: Armstrong Subero
 * PIC: 16F1717 w/X OSC @ 16MHz, 5v
 * Program: Header file to setup PIC16F1717 I2C
 * Compiler: XC8 (v1.40, MPLAX X v3.55)
 * Program Version 1.0
 *
 * Program Description: This program header provide function
prototypes for
 * sending commands to a Nextion Touch Display
 *
 * Created on April 21st, 2017, 2:25 PM
 */

#include "16F1717_Internal.h"
#include <string.h>

// Function prototypes
void touchscreen_command(char* string);
void touchscreen_data(char* cmd, char* string2);
```

The RTCC header (see Listing 15-5) and source (see Listing 15-6) are created. Notice that the three-wire interface can be used on any pin. The DS1302 provides its data in BCD format. It is necessary therefore to create functions to allow the conversion to and from that format.

Listing 15-5. DS1302 Header

```
/*
* File: ds1302.h
* Author: Armstrong Subero
* PIC: 16F1717 w/X OSC @ 16MHz, 5v
* Program: Header file to setup PIC16F1717 I2C
* Compiler: XC8 (v1.41, MPLAX X v3.55)
* Program Version 1.0
*
* Program Description: This program header allows the control
of a DS1302
* time keeper chip
*
* Created on April 18th, 2017, 11:40 PM
*/

#include "16F1717_Internal.h"

#define CE RD0
#define SCLK RD1
#define IO RD2
#define Data_Tris TRISD2

typedef unsigned char byte;

void DS1302_Reset();
void DS1302_WriteByte(unsigned char W_Byte);
unsigned char DS1302_ReadByte();
void DS1302_Initialize(byte sec, byte min, byte hr, byte day,
byte date, byte mth, byte year);
unsigned char get_bcd(unsigned char data);
unsigned char get_dec(byte var);
```

Listing 15-6. DS1302 Source

```c
/*
* File: ds1302.c
* Author: Armstrong Subero
 PIC: 16F1717 w/Int OSC @ 16MHz, 5v
* Program: Library file for ds1302 RTCC
* Compiler: XC8 (v1.38, MPLAX X v3.40)
* Program Version: 1.1
**Added additional comments
*
* Program Description: This Library allows you to control the
ds1302
*
* Created on April 18th, 2017, 11:40 PM
*/

#include "ds1302.h"

/****************************************************************
****************
* Function:void DS1302_Reset()
*
* Returns: Nothing
*
* Description: Resets the DS1302
*
****************************************************************
**************/

void DS1302_Reset()
{
SCLK = 0;
```

```
CE = 0;
CE = 1;
}

/****************************************************************
****************

* Function: unsigned char DS1302_WriteByte(unsigned char W_Byte)
*
* Returns: Nothing
*
* Description: Writes a byte of data into the DS1302
*
****************************************************************
**************/

void DS1302_WriteByte(unsigned char W_Byte)
{
unsigned char i;

for(i = 0; i < 8; ++i)
{
IO = 0;

if(W_Byte & 0x01)
{
IO = 1; /* set port pin high to read data */
}

SCLK = 0;
SCLK = 1;
W_Byte >>= 1;
}
}
```

```
/*************************************************************
****************
* Function: unsigned char DS1302_ReadByte()
*
* Returns: Nothing
*
* Description: Reads a byte of data from the DS1302
*
*************************************************************
**************/

unsigned char DS1302_ReadByte()
{
unsigned char i;
unsigned char R_Byte;
unsigned char TmpByte;

R_Byte = 0x00;

Data_Tris = 1;
IO = 1;

for(i=0; i<8; ++i)
{
SCLK = 1;
SCLK = 0;
TmpByte = (unsigned char)IO;
TmpByte <<= 7;
R_Byte >>= 1;
R_Byte |= TmpByte;
}
Data_Tris = 0;
return R_Byte;
}
```

```
/*****************************************************************
****************
* Function: void DS1302_Initialize(byte sec, byte min, byte hr,
byte day, byte date,
byte mth, byte year)
*
* Returns: Nothing
*
* Description: Initializes the DS1302 with time/date specified
by user
*
*****************************************************************
**************/

void DS1302_Initialize(byte sec, byte min, byte hr, byte day,
byte date,
byte mth, byte year)
{

byte sec1 = get_bcd(sec);
byte min1 = get_bcd(min);
byte hr1  = get_bcd(hr);
byte day1 = get_bcd(day);
byte date1 = get_bcd(date);
byte mth1 = get_bcd(mth);
byte year1 = get_bcd(year);

DS1302_Reset();
DS1302_WriteByte(0x8e); /* control register */
DS1302_WriteByte(0); /* disable write protect */
DS1302_Reset();
DS1302_WriteByte(0x90); /* trickle charger register */
DS1302_WriteByte(0xab);/* enable, 2 diodes, 8K resistor */
```

```
DS1302_Reset();
DS1302_WriteByte(0xbe);/* clock burst write (eight registers)
*/
DS1302_WriteByte(sec1);
DS1302_WriteByte(min1);
DS1302_WriteByte(hr1);
DS1302_WriteByte(date1);
DS1302_WriteByte(mth1);
DS1302_WriteByte(day1);
DS1302_WriteByte(year1);
DS1302_WriteByte(0); /* must write control register in burst
mode */
DS1302_Reset();
}

/****************************************************************
****************
* Function: unsigned char get_bcd(unsigned char data)
*
* Returns: number in BCD format for RTCC
*
* Description: Converts decimal time into BCD format
*
****************************************************************
**************/

unsigned char get_bcd(unsigned char data)
{
unsigned char nibh;
unsigned char nibl;

nibh=data/10;
nibl=data-(nibh*10);
```

```
return((nibh<<4)|nibl);
}

unsigned char get_dec(byte var)
{
unsigned char var2;

var2 =  (var >> 4) * 10;
var2 += (var & 15);

return var2;
}
```

We also need to create source files for the touch screen (see Listing 15-7) and the setup headers (see Listing 15-8) we declared earlier.

Listing 15-7. Touch Screen Source

```
/*
 * File: touchscreen.c
 * Author: Armstrong Subero
 * PIC: 16F1717 w/Int OSC @ 16MHz, 5v
 * Program: Library file for Nextion Touchscreen
 * Compiler: XC8 (v1.41, MPLAX X v3.55)
 * Program Version: 1.0
 *
 * Program Description: This Library allows you to send commands
 to the Nextion
 * touchscreen
 *
 * Created on April 21st, 2017, 2:30 PM
 */

#include "touchscreen.h"
#include "EUSART.h"
```

```
/*
Send commands to Touchscreen
*/
void touchscreen_command(char* string)
{
EUSART_Write_Text(string);
EUSART_Write(0xFF);
EUSART_Write(0xFF);
EUSART_Write(0xFF);
__delay_ms(1000);
}

void touchscreen_data(char* cmd, char* string2)
{
EUSART_Write_Text(cmd);
EUSART_Write_Text(string2);
EUSART_Write(0xFF);
EUSART_Write(0xFF);
EUSART_Write(0xFF);

__delay_ms(100);
}
```

Listing 15-8. Setup Source

```
/*
* File: setup.c
* Author: Armstrong Subero
* PIC: 16F1717 w/Int OSC @ 16MHz, 5v
* Program: Library file for Nextion Touchscreen
* Compiler: XC8 (v1.41, MPLAX X v3.55)
* Program Version: 1.0
*
```

```
* Program Description: This Library allows you to setup for the
clock
*
* Created on April 21st, 2017, 2:30 PM
*/

#include "setup.h"
#include "ds1302.h"
#include "oled.h"
#include "EUSART.h"
#include "touchscreen.h"

/****************************************************************
****************
* Function: void initMain()
*
* Returns: Nothing
*
* Description: Contains initializations for main
*
* Usage: initMain()
****************************************************************
**************/

void initMain(){
// Run at 16 MHz
internal_16();

// Setup pins for EUSART
TRISBbits.TRISB2 = 0;
ANSELBbits.ANSB2 = 0;

TRISBbits.TRISB3 = 1;
ANSELBbits.ANSB3 = 0;
```

```
///////////////////
// Setup Serial
///////////////////

// Setup pins for I2C
ANSELCbits.ANSC4 = 0;
ANSELCbits.ANSC5 = 0;

TRISCbits.TRISC4 = 1;
TRISCbits.TRISC5 = 1;

PPSLOCK = 0x55;
PPSLOCK = 0xAA;
PPSLOCKbits.PPSLOCKED = 0x00; // unlock PPS

RC4PPSbits.RC4PPS = 0x0011;    //RC4->MSSP:SDA;
SSPDATPPSbits.SSPDATPPS =0x0014;    //RC4->MSSP:SDA;
SSPCLKPPSbits.SSPCLKPPS =0x0015;    //RC5->MSSP:SCL;
RC5PPSbits.RC5PPS = 0x0010;    //RC5->MSSP:SCL;

RB2PPSbits.RB2PPS = 0x14;    //RB2->EUSART:TX;
RXPPSbits.RXPPS = 0x0B;    //RB3->EUSART:RX;

PPSLOCK = 0x55;
PPSLOCK = 0xAA;
PPSLOCKbits.PPSLOCKED = 0x01; // lock PPS

// Setup RTCC pins
TRISD = 0;
ANSELD = 0;

// Initialize I2C
I2C_Init();

__delay_ms(500);
```

```
// Initialize OLED
OLED_Init();

__delay_ms(500);

// Dim Touchscreen
OLED_YX(0, 0);
OLED_Write_String("Init");

__delay_ms(1000);

// clear OLED
OLED_Clear();

__delay_ms(500);

// Initial time and date
byte sec = 51;
byte min = 59;
byte hr = 23;
byte day = 2;
byte date = 30;
byte month = 4;
byte year = 17;

// Initialize DS1302
DS1302_Initialize(sec, min, hr, day, date, month, year);

//Initialize EUSART module with 9600 baud
EUSART_Initialize(9600);
__delay_ms(2000);

// clear OLED
OLED_Clear();
```

```
/////////////////////
// Configure Timer0
/////////////////////

// Select timer mode
OPTION_REGbits.TMR0CS = 0;

// Assign Prescaler to TIMER0
OPTION_REGbits.PSA = 0;

// Set Prescaler to 256
OPTION_REGbits.PS = 0b111;

// enable Timer0 interrupt
INTCONbits.TMR0IE = 1;

// enable global interrupts
ei();

}
```

Finally, we have the main code in Listing 15-9. The interrupt routine updates the display date and time every five seconds. There is a "green" function that lessens the brightness of the display. The main code is simply a series of checks of the buffer read from UART. If any of the string we want to be sent by the touch screen is detected, then the display is updated accordingly.

Listing 15-9. Main Code

```
/*
* File: Main.c
* Author: Armstrong Subero
* PIC: 16F1717 w/Int OSC @ 16MHz, 5v
* Program: P05_Clock
* Compiler: XC8 (v1.38, MPLAX X v3.40)
```

```
* Program Version: 1.0
*
*
* Program Description: This Program creates a clock using the
PIC17F1717
* microcontroller and the DS1302. The display is
* the intelligent Nextion 2.4 LCD. There are two screens
* the main screen displays. The main screen displays the
* time and date. The second screen allows the user to set
* the current time and date.
*
* Hardware Description: The DS1302 is connected to the
microcontroller as
* follows:
*
* CE    -> RD0
* SCLK -> RD1
* IO    ->  RD2
*
*
* Created April 21st, 2017, 7:11 PM
*/

/****************************************************************
****************
*Includes and defines
****************************************************************
**************/

#include "16F1717_Internal.h"
#include "I2C.h"
#include "oled.h"
#include "ds1302.h"
```

```c
#include "EUSART.h"
#include "setup.h"
#include "touchscreen.h"
#include "bool_support.h"
#include <string.h>

// Variables for date and time
unsigned char yr1, mn1, date1, dy1, hr1, min1, sec1;
unsigned char yr2, mn2, date2, dy2, hr2, hr3,  min2, sec2;

// Arrays for int to ascii conversion
char min_arr[8];
char hr_arr[8];
char dt_arr[5];
char minute_arr[10];
char hour_arr[10];
char date_arr[10];
char mth_arr[10];
char month_arr[10];

// Arrays to hold date, month and time string
char time_string[10];
char date_string[10];
char hour_string[10];
char min_string[10];
char date1_string[10];
char month_string[10];
char mth_string[10];
// String constants for commands
const char screen_time[] = "time.txt=";
const char screen_date[] = "date.txt=";
const char screen_mth[]  = "month.txt=";
const char screen_hour[] = "t0.txt=";
const char screen_mins[] = "t1.txt=";
```

```c
const char screen_date1[] = "t2.txt=";
const char screen_month[] = "t3.txt=";

// Array containing months
const char* months[] = {"MMM", "JAN", "FEB", "MAR", "APR",
"MAY", "JUN",
"JUL", "AUG", "SEP", "OCT", "NOV", "DEC"};

// buffer for UART
char buf[50];

// Variables to store values for min, hour, month and date
unsigned char  x = 1;
unsigned char  y = 0;
unsigned char  m = 1;
unsigned char  d = 1;

// energy efficient function
void green(char* buf);

/****************************************************************
****************
* Function: Main
*
* Returns: Nothing
*
* Description: Program entry point
****************************************************************
***************/

void main(void) {
initMain();

char* hour1;
char* min1;
```

```c
char* date3;
char* month1;
char* set1;

while(1){

// Read EUSART
EUSART_Read_Text(buf, 11);

// Check for if energy save enabled
green(buf);

/////////////////////////
// Check buffer for each
// string from display
/////////////////////////
hour1  = strstr(buf, "hour");
min1 = strstr(buf, "mins");
date3  = strstr(buf, "date");
month1 = strstr(buf, "month");
set1   = strstr(buf,  "set");

///////////////////
// If minute found
///////////////////
if (min1)
{
// Convert date and time to strings
itoa( minute_arr, y, 10 );

strcpy(min_string, "\"");

// If less than 10 pad with a 0
if (y < 10){
```

```
strcat(min_string, "0");
strcat(min_string, minute_arr);
}
// Else show min as is
else
{
strcat(min_string, minute_arr);
}

strcat(min_string, "\"");

if (y < 59){
y++;
}

else {
y = 0;
}

// Write time
touchscreen_data(screen_mins, min_string);
}

/////////////////////
// If hour found
/////////////////////
if (hour1){

// Convert date and time to strings
itoa( hour_arr, x, 10 );

strcpy(hour_string, "\"");
strcat(hour_string, hour_arr);
strcat(hour_string, "\"");
```

```
if (x < 12){
x++;
}

else {
x = 1;
}

// Write time
touchscreen_data(screen_hour, hour_string);
}

////////////////////
// If date found
////////////////////
if(date3)
{
// Convert date and time to strings
itoa( date_arr, d, 10 );
strcpy(date1_string, "\"");
strcat(date1_string, date_arr);

strcat(date1_string, "\"");

if (d < 31){
d++;
}

else {
d = 0;
}

// Write time
touchscreen_data(screen_date1, date1_string);
}
```

```
///////////////////
// If month found
///////////////////

if(month1)
{
// Convert date and time to strings
itoa( month_arr, m, 10 );

strcpy(month_string, "\"");
strcat(month_string, month_arr);
strcat(month_string, "\"");

if (m < 12){
m++;
}

else {
m = 1;
}

// Write time
touchscreen_data(screen_month, month_string);
}

///////////////////////
// If user pressed set
///////////////////////

if (set1){

// Initial time and date
byte sec = 00;
byte min = y-1;
byte hr = x-1;
```

```
byte day = 2;
byte date = d-1;
byte month = m-1;
byte year = 17;

// Re-Initialize DS1302 with new values
DS1302_Initialize(sec, min, hr, day, date, month, year);
touchscreen_command("page 0");
}

}

return;
}
/****************************************************************
****************
* Function: void green (char* buf)
*
 Returns: Nothing
*
* Description: Enables or disables green feature of display
****************************************************************
**************/

void green(char* buf)
{
char* green1;

green1 = strstr(buf, "ener");

if (green1 == NULL)
{
return;
}
```

```
else
{
if (!on){
touchscreen_command("t0.txt=\"ON\"");
__delay_ms(100);
touchscreen_command("dim=30");
__delay_ms(100);

on = true;
}
else {
touchscreen_command("t0.txt=\"OFF\"");
__delay_ms(100);
touchscreen_command("dim=100");
__delay_ms(100);

on = false;
}
}
}

/*****************************************************************
****************
* Function: void interrupt isr(void)
*
* Returns: Nothing
*
* Description: Timer0 interrupt at a rate of approx. 5 seconds
that updates
* the time on the display
*****************************************************************
**************/
```

```
void interrupt isr(void)
{
// Start count at 0
static int count = 0;

// Reset flag after overflow
INTCONbits.TMR0IF = 0;

// Zero timer
TMR0 = 0;

// Increment count
count++;

// Value = fclk / (4 * 256 * 256 * fout)
//|-- Frequency out (in Hz)
//|-- Prescaler value
// Value =  16 000 000 / (262 144)
// Value =  61.04 for 1 s
// Therefore 305 for approx 5 secs
if (count == 305){

/////////////////////////////
// Read DS1302 clock burst
/////////////////////////////

DS1302_Reset();
DS1302_WriteByte(0xBF);

sec1 = DS1302_ReadByte();
min1 = DS1302_ReadByte();
hr1 = DS1302_ReadByte();
date1 = DS1302_ReadByte();
mn1 = DS1302_ReadByte();
dy1 = DS1302_ReadByte();
yr1 = DS1302_ReadByte();
```

```
DS1302_Reset();

/////////////////////////
// Convert all BCD data
// to Decimal time format
/////////////////////////

// Year
yr2 = get_dec(yr1);

// Month
mn2 = get_dec(mn1);

// Date
date2 = get_dec(date1);

// Hour
hr2 = get_dec(hr1);

// Minute
min2 = get_dec(min1);

// Seconds
sec2 = get_dec(sec1);

/////////////////////////
// Convert 24 hr to 12 hr
// format
/////////////////////////

if (hr2 <= 12 && hr2 > 0){
hr3 = hr2;
}

else if (hr2 >= 13 && hr2 < 24)
{
hr3 = (hr2-12);
}
```

```
else {
hr3 = 12;
}

//////////////////////////
// Convert date and time
// to strings
//////////////////////////

itoa( min_arr, min2, 10 );
itoa( hr_arr, hr3,  10 );
itoa( dt_arr, date2, 10);

//////////////////////////
/// Create date string
//////////////////////////

strcpy(date_string, "\"");
strcat(date_string, dt_arr);
strcat(date_string, "\"");

//////////////////////////
// Create month string
//////////////////////////
strcpy(mth_string, "\"");
strcat(mth_string, months[mn2]);
strcat(mth_string, "\"");

//////////////////////////
// Create time string
//////////////////////////

strcpy(time_string, "\"");
strcat(time_string, hr_arr);
strcat(time_string, ":");
```

```
// If less than 10 pad with a 0
if (min2 < 10){
strcat(time_string, "0");
strcat(time_string, min_arr);
}
// Else show min as is
else
{
strcat(time_string, min_arr);
}

strcat(time_string, "\"");

// Write time
touchscreen_data(screen_time, time_string);

// Write month
touchscreen_data(screen_mth, mth_string);

// Write date
touchscreen_data(screen_date, date_string);

// Reset count
count = 0;
}

else {
/ No need to do anything
}

}
```

The final results are shown in Figures 15-7 and 15-8.

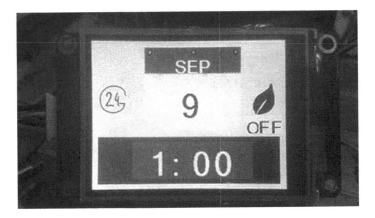

Figure 15-7. Screen 1

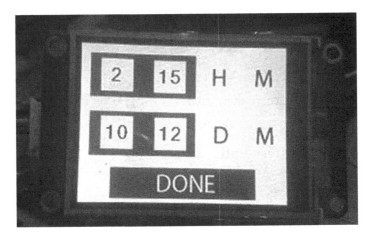

Figure 15-8. Screen 2

Conclusion

At last, the finale. This chapter we looked at building two projects using the PIC® microcontroller. It first covered building a simple temperature controlled fan followed by a touch screen clock.

You have now reached the end of this book. I hope you learned enough that you can successfully build your own projects. Happy tinkering!

APPENDIX A

Resources

This book covered the process of learning to work with PIC® microcontrollers. Once you complete the book, you will be very proficient at programming 8-bit microcontrollers and your skills and understanding will be directly applicable to other families of microcontrollers you will work with. This appendix lists some resources for working with PIC® microcontrollers so that you do not have to reinvent the wheel.

On my GitHub, there are a lot of projects, some presented here and others not, that work with the PIC16F1717 microcontroller:

`https://github.com/ArmstrongSubero/PIC16-Projects`

The MPLAB® Xpress code examples are all modifiable and work with the microcontroller presented in this book:

`https://mplabxpress.microchip.com/mplabcloud/example`

Microchip Technology Inc. also provides embedded code source that has a few noteworthy libraries:

`http://www.embeddedcodesource.com/`

© Armstrong Subero 2018
A. Subero, *Programming PIC Microcontrollers with XC8*,
https://doi.org/10.1007/978-1-4842-3273-6

There is also the developer help resource that provides information about the different microcontrollers made by Microchip Technology Inc.:

`http://microchipdeveloper.com/`

MikroElektronika provides a lot of code examples on their community that you can view here:

`https://libstock.mikroe.com/`

Making Your Own PCBs and Schematics

Once you have built the circuits in this book, you may be wondering how to make your own circuit diagrams and produce PCBs with your designs. The topic of designing PCBs and using schematic diagrams deserves a book itself, and there are books available that detail the process of creating your own. However, this appendix provides links to resources that will get you started making your own diagrams and PCBs.

Fritzing

If you are new to schematic and PCB design, I recommend that you use Fritzing. Fritzing allows beginners to easily get started. Fritzing is free and they also provide a production service. You can learn how to design PCBs with Fritzing here:

`http://fritzing.org/learning/`

Altium Circuit Maker

Let's be realistic, Fritzing is designed for the Arduino ecosystem. For that reason, I recommend, if you want to make your own PCBs and schematics, that you use Circuit Maker. It is designed for makers, after all.

425

© Armstrong Subero 2018
A. Subero, *Programming PIC Microcontrollers with XC8*,
https://doi.org/10.1007/978-1-4842-3273-6

Also, it provides a good path to upgrading to a more professional tool like Altium Designer, one of the best EDA tools on the market. You can find information about Circuit Maker here:

```
http://www.altium.com/circuitmaker/overview
```

Scheme-it

What if you are interested only in drawing schematics? Then I recommend you use Scheme-it from Digi-Key. It is an online tool that allows you to create your own schematics easily and then save them as images. You can use Scheme-it here:

```
https://www.digikey.com/schemeit/project/
```

Index

© Armstrong Subero 2018
A. Subero, *Programming PIC Microcontrollers with XC8*,
https://doi.org/10.1007/978-1-4842-3273-6

Get the eBook for only $5!

Why limit yourself?

With most of our titles available in both PDF and ePUB format, you can access your content wherever and however you wish—on your PC, phone, tablet, or reader.

Since you've purchased this print book, we are happy to offer you the eBook for just $5.

To learn more, go to http://www.apress.com/companion or contact support@apress.com.

Apress®

Printed in the United States
By Bookmasters